The Best

OF

The WORD FOR YOU TODAY

365 Days of Strength and Guidance

The Best of The Word for You Today

International Standard Book Number: 9781931727181

Dedicated

To: _____

From: _____

Date: _____

How To Get the Most
Out of This Devotional

Set aside a definite time each day to read it,
asking God, "What are You saying to me?"

Is someone you know hurting? Give them a copy.
It could change their lives.

Are you in business? Give it to your clients and
customers.

Do you work in a hospital...a prison...
a rehab center...or a retirement home?
This devotional is the perfect tool for
reaching people with God's love.

WHY USE SO MANY TRANSLATIONS?

For two important reasons. First, the Bible was originally written using 11,280 Hebrew, Aramaic, and Greek words, but the typical English translation uses only around 6,000 words. Obviously, nuances and shades of meaning can be missed, so it is always helpful to compare translations.

Second, we often miss the full impact of familiar Bible verses, not because of poor translating, but simply because they have become so familiar! We think we know what a verse says because we have read it or heard it so many times. Then when we find it quoted in a book, we skim over it and miss the full meaning. Therefore we have deliberately used paraphrases in order to help you see God's truth in new, fresh ways.

INDEX OF ABBREVIATIONS

All scripture references are from the King James Version, unless otherwise noted.

AMP	Amplified Bible
CEV	Contemporary English Version
GWT	God's Word Translation
NAS	New American Standard
NCV	New Century Version
NIV	New International Version
NKJV	New King James Version
NLT	New Living Translation
NRS	New Revised Standard Version
PHPS	The New Testament in Modern English
TEV	Today's English Version
TLB	The Living Bible
TM	The Message

Old Testament

Abbreviations

Genesis	Ge	Ecclesiastes	Ecc
Exodus	Ex	Song of Solomon	SS
Leviticus	Lev	Isaiah	Isa
Numbers	Nu	Jeremiah	Jer
Deuteronomy	Dt	Lamentations	La
Joshua	Jos	Ezekiel	Eze
Judges	Jdg	Daniel	Da
Ruth	Ru	Hosea	Hos
1 Samuel	1Sa	Joel	Joel
2 Samuel	2Sa	Amos	Am
1 Kings	1Ki	Obadiah	Ob
2 Kings	2Ki	Jonah	Jnh
1 Chronicles	1Ch	Micah	Mic
2 Chronicles	2Ch	Nahum	Na
Ezra	Ezr	Habakkuk	Hab
Nehemiah	Ne	Zephaniah	Zep
Esther	Est	Haggai	Hag
Job	Job	Zechariah	Zec
Psalms	Ps	Malachi	Mal
Proverbs	Pr		

New Testament

Abbreviations

Matthew	Mt	1 Timothy	1Ti
Mark	Mk	2 Timothy	2Ti
Luke	Lk	Titus	Tit
John	Jn	Philemon	Phm
Acts	Ac	Hebrews	Heb
Romans	Ro	James	Jas
1 Corinthians	1Co	1 Peter	1Pe
2 Corinthians	2Co	2 Peter	2Pe
Galatians	Gal	1 John	1Jn
Ephesians	Eph	2 John	2Jn
Philippians	Php	3 John	3Jn
Colossians	Col	Jude	Jude
1 Thessalonians	1Th	Revelation	Rev
2 Thessalonians	2Th		

YOUR YEAR OF GRACE AND FAVOR

The Lord longs to be gracious to you.
Isaiah 30:18 NIV

On December 31st the clock strikes midnight ushering in another New Year. Three hundred and sixty-five days to fan the flames of your unfilled hopes and dreams. A new beginning. A gift full of promise. But you must accept it, unwrap it and use it. Not everybody does. Maybe you dread what the New Year holds; retirement, the empty nest, chronic illness, unemployment, life without a loved one. Well, God loves to take people at the end of their rope and set them on the road to peace, joy and victory. He's the expert at drying tears, calming fears, injecting courage into anxious hearts and removing the sting of old memories. He "make[s] all things new" (Rev 21:5). But He never leads you back, just forward.

Listen: "The Lord *longs* to be gracious to you." What do you want to see happen this year? Does it include owning your own business? Losing some weight? Reuniting with your family? Only you can complete the question, "What if I could...?" because you alone know what makes your heart leap. Stephen Covey says, "Begin...with the image of the end of your life as your frame of reference...Each day will then contribute to the vision you have of your life as a whole." Seek God. Determine your goals. Write them down, then release the outcome to Him who "longs to be gracious to you." To be gracious means "to show favor." *The desire of God's heart is that you walk in His grace and favor every day of this year.*

BURY THE PAST

Who will rescue me from this body of death?
Romans 7:24 NIV

*I*n New Testament times capital punishment was sometimes carried out by tying a murder victim's body directly onto the perpetrator's back. That way wherever he went he was literally weighed down by his crime, with no way to escape the stench of decomposing flesh. Eventually the bacteria-filled corpse infected him too and he died an agonizing death. Some days Paul felt the weight of his old nature pressing in, reminding him of things from his past that he couldn't change or eradicate. And recognizing how past events can color the present, Paul describes himself as "a wretched man," and asks, "Who will rescue me from this body of death?" "Thanks be to God—through Jesus Christ our Lord" (Ro 7:25 NIV).

The fact is, you can't move ahead with "the old man" still clinging to you; you must bury him. Even death doesn't have the finality that burial does; part of coming to closure involves disposing of the body. Funerals are for the living; they give people an opportunity to accept that their loved one has gone and that the relationship as they knew it is over. So, as you embark on this New Year, isn't it time you stopped carrying the past around on your back—and on your mind? Paul says, "Present yourselves to God as those alive from the dead" (Ro 6:13 NAS). In other words, refuse to let old memories negotiate a deal with you! Bury them, and do it today!

ATTENTION WORRYWARTS!

Give…your worries…to God.
1 Peter 5:7 NLT

A lady whose friend was a chronic worrier said to her one day, "Do you realize that 80% of the things you worry about never happen?" "See," her friend replied, "it works!" Seriously, Jesus said, "Don't get worked up about what may… happen tomorrow. God will help you deal with whatever… come[s] up" (Mt 6:34 TM). Worry doesn't rid tomorrow of its sorrows, it just robs today of its joy. Plus when you make a mountain out of a molehill you end up having to climb it. A salesman who usually drove an old car and wore outdated clothes turned up at his office one day in a designer suit, driving a BMW. "What happened?" his buddy asked. "Remember how I used to worry about everything?" he said, "Well, I hired a team of professional worriers; now I tell them my problems and they do all my worrying while I go out and sell." "How much do they charge?" his friend asked. "$5,000 a week," he replied. "How can you afford that?" his buddy asked. Smiling he replied, "That's *their* worry, not mine!"

Wouldn't you like to have somebody to handle all *your* worries? This year? You do; His name is Jesus, and He said, "If you are tired from carrying heavy burdens…Come to me…I will give you rest" (Mt 11:28 CEV). God promised, "As your day is, so shall your strength…be" (Dt 33:25 AMP). That's because He only gives us *today's* strength for *today's* needs. Remember, it's impossible to wring your hands and roll up your sleeves at the same time. So instead of wasting today worrying about tomorrow, "Give…your worries…to God" (1Pe 5:7 NLT), and get busy living the life He gave you to enjoy!

INVEST WHAT GOD'S GIVEN YOU

To one he gave five talents,
to another two, and to another one.
Matthew 25:15 NKJV

*I*n Jesus' story, the first 2 servants "went and traded." They pondered their options, crunched the numbers, took the plunge, and dared to fail. And their Master said "Well done, good and faithful servant" (v.21). Here Jesus points us to the day when the "earth and all its works [will be] exposed to the scrutiny of judgment" (2Pe 3:10 TM). What's the point? Dare to take great risks for God! Not foolish risks, but prayed-over, well-considered risks in response to faith. The only mistake—is not to risk making a mistake.

And how about the third servant? "I was afraid, and went and hid your talent in the ground" (v.25). The first two invested theirs; he buried his. The first two went out on a limb; he hugged the trunk. He made the most tragic and common mistake of giftedness. He failed to benefit the Master with his talent. Some invest their talents and give God credit. Others misuse them and give God grief. Some honor Him with fruit. Others insult Him with excuses. How did the Master feel about it? "Get rid of this 'play-it-safe' who won't go out on a limb" (Mt 25:29-30 TM).

Fear is the opposite of faith. And, "without faith it is impossible to please [God]" (Heb 11:6). This year, step out in faith; He won't let you down. Take a risk; He won't let you fail. Even if you fail several times on your way to success, God invites you to dream of the day when you'll feel His hand on your shoulder saying, "Well done, good and faithful servant!"

DOING WHATEVER IT TAKES

I have finished my course.
2 Timothy 4:7-8

*B*ob Ireland crossed the finish line on Thursday, November 6, 1986, as the New York City Marathon's 19,413th and final finisher—the first person to run a marathon with his arms instead of his legs! Bob, who was 40 years old, had his legs blown off in Vietnam. He recorded the slowest time in the marathon's history: 4 days, 2 hours, 48 minutes, 17 seconds. When asked why he ran, he gave 3 reasons: (1) to show that being a Christian gives you a plus in life; (2) to test his conditioning; (3) to promote physical fitness and courage in others. "Success is not based on where you start," he said, "it's where you finish—and I finished." Wow! With 2 good legs and all our faculties, most of us won't even get out of bed an hour earlier to discover and pursue our God-given destiny.

Success always comes at a price. Cicero practiced speaking before friends every day for 30 years to perfect his eloquence. Milton rose at 4 o'clock every morning to have enough hours for writing his *Paradise Lost*. Gibbon spent 26 years on his *Decline and Fall of the Roman Empire*. Noah Webster labored 36 years writing his dictionary, crossing the Atlantic twice to gather material. Byron rewrote one of his poetic masterpieces 99 times before publication, and it became a classic. Before Paul wrote: "I have finished my course," he wrote: "I have worked harder, been put in jail oftener, been whipped times without number, and faced death again and again and again" (2Co 11:23 TLB). Go ahead, measure yourself by that standard! Then seize this new year and say, "I'm going to do whatever it takes."

WHEN JESUS COMES

It was noised that he was in the house.
Mark 2:1

*W*hen Christ enters your life: *(1) He'll rearrange things!* Your quiet, well-ordered existence will probably get turned upside down. One thing's for sure, you'll never be the same again. When He showed up at this house in Capernaum "it was noised." As a result the house was packed out with people. Not a square inch left. Four men carrying a paralyzed friend, hoping Christ would heal him, had to break up the roof and lower him to the feet of Jesus. Miracles can cause upheaval. *(2) You'll get two kinds of reaction!* The religious crowd will be threatened. When Jesus claimed to have power not only to heal but also to forgive the man's sins, the Pharisees said, "Who can forgive sins but God only?" (Mk 2:7). The danger of institutional religion is that often its proponents love the institution more than the individuals they're called to serve. So expect some flack, and don't back down! Whatever it takes to get to Jesus, do it; He won't disappoint you. He makes this standing offer, "Him that cometh to me I will in no wise cast out" (Jn 6:37). *(3) All get what they come for!* Those who come to mock, criticize, or defend their religious viewpoint leave more lost than ever, and more convinced that they're right. But those who come for help, get it. Listen: "Blessed are they which do hunger and thirst after righteousness: for they shall be filled" (Mt 5:6). All Christ asks of you today is the humility to acknowledge your need of Him, and the faith to reach for and accept what He offers you.

FILLING BIG SHOES

Direct my footsteps according to your word.
Psalm 119:133 NIV

*H*ave you ever seen a small child trying to walk in the shoes of a big person? It's funny to watch. It's also significant: some day those tiny feet *will* grow up and fill those big shoes—or bigger ones. Do *you* feel like you're trying to fill some big shoes today, like you need to grow up fast because you've no option? Life doesn't wait until we're as mature as we'd like to be before handing us some of our greatest tests of faith. Most of our training is on the job. And like a little one trying to fill big shoes, at first we do it badly, then awkwardly, and never stumble-free. But the only thing that can stop us from growing into those big shoes—is the fear of putting our feet into them! The grace comes with the assignment. Grace is immediate, but growth takes time. Don't be discouraged: "He who began a good work in you *will* carry it on to completion" (Php 1:6 NIV).

Another thing about filling big shoes, it makes us a lot more understanding toward others trying to walk in them too. "How could you do such a thing?" is a question we don't tend to ask because we already know the answer from personal experience. Ever see a parent holding the hand of a child trying to walk in shoes that are too big, beaming with pride and delight simply because they attempted it, steadying them up, encouraging them to keep going, picking them up when they trip and bump their head? That's what our God does with us!

HOW DO YOU HANDLE INTERRUPTIONS?

Laying his hands on each one, he healed them.
Luke 4:40 NIV

*W*hen someone interrupts your task at hand for the sake of conversation, how do you react? If you relax and converse until the chat has natural closure, you're *people oriented*. If you squirm your way out with a bombardment of verbal and nonverbal clues, you're *task oriented*.

Jesus spent more time with people than in any other action. Though He'd only 3-1/2 years to train 12 men to change the world, He spent most of His time meeting needs, helping people amid the unbearable pressure to perform tasks—and that's the model He left us. At the end of one of His busiest days it's recorded that, "When the sun was setting, the people brought to Jesus all who had various kinds of sickness, and laying his hands *on each one,* he healed them." What's ministry all about? People or production? Obviously much of our paperwork and production is aimed at helping people. But often there's precious little time or energy left for the people— because we're exhausted accomplishing all those tasks! Whether we like to admit it or not, paperwork, deadlines and crowded day-timers often preoccupy us and create a barrier between us and the opportunity of connecting with people and meeting their needs. Henry Nouwen writes, "A few years ago I met an old professor at the University of Notre Dame. Looking back on his long life of teaching, he said with a funny twinkle in his eyes: 'I have always been complaining that my work was constantly interrupted, until I slowly discovered that my interruptions *were* my work.'"

LORD...AND SHEPHERD

The Lord is my shepherd.
Psalm 23:1

*W*hen Lloyd Douglas, author of *The Robe,* attended college, he lived in a boarding house. A retired wheelchair-bound music professor resided on the first floor. Each morning Douglas would stick his head in the professor's door and ask, "What's the good news?" The old man would tap his tuning fork on his wheelchair and say, "That's middle C! It was middle C yesterday, it'll be middle C tomorrow, and it'll be middle C a thousand years from now. The tenor upstairs sings flat. The piano across the hall's out of tune, but, my friend, that's middle C." And don't we all need a middle C? Haven't we had enough changes? Relationship changes. Job changes. Health changes. Weather changes—but the One Who ruled the earth last night is the same One Who rules it today. He never changes! David writes, "From everlasting to everlasting you are God" (Ps 90:2 NIV). Counselors may comfort us in the storm, but we need a God Who can still the storm. Friends may hold our hand at our deathbed, but ultimately we need the One Who defeated the grave. Remember the Wizard of Oz? Dorothy followed the Yellow Brick Road only to discover that the Wizard was a wimp! All smoke and mirrors. Is that the kind of God we need? No. We need One Who can place a hundred billion stars in our galaxy, and a hundred billion galaxies in our universe; a God Who, while so mind numbingly mighty, can come and touch us with the gentleness of a mother's hand. We need both Lord and Shepherd. Both strength and tenderness—and that's what we've got!

GOD'S STRANGE CHOICE

God chose the weak things of the world to shame the wise.
1 Corinthians 1:27 NIV

*H*as someone told you you're not qualified? If so, read on:

"Dear Paul the Apostle: We received your application for service under our missions board. Frankly we're amazed you've been able to pass as a missionary. Here's why:

(1)We're told that you're afflicted with eye trouble. We require 20/20 vision. (2) We hear that you have to make tents on the side to support yourself. How come? (3) Is it true that you have a prison record? Think how this would reflect on our organization. (4) It's reported from Ephesus that you made so much trouble for the local business community there, that they refer to you as the man who "turned the world upside down." We deplore sensationalism in ministry. (5) You refer to yourself as "Paul the aged." Our new pension policies don't anticipate a surplus of elderly recipients. (6) Doctor Luke, the physician, reports that you are a frail little man, frequently sick, and always so agitated over your churches that you sleep very poorly. He indicates that you pad around the house praying half the night. Our ideal applicant has a clear mind and a robust body. We believe that a good night's sleep will give you zest and zip so that you will wake up full of zing. So, we regret to inform you, Brother Paul, that in all our experience we've never met a candidate so opposite to the requirements of our board. If we should accept you we would be breaking every principle of current missionary practice. Signed, Most surely, J. Flavius Fluffyhead, Secretary, Foreign Missions Board."

NEW TESTAMENT CHRISTIANITY (1)

The disciples were first called Christians in Antioch.
Acts 11:26 NAS

The disciples were first called "Christians" at Antioch—because they walked and talked like Jesus! Is something getting in the way of your living like Jesus? Figure it out and eliminate it. Is your life so complicated that it's difficult for you to juggle everything, yet still remain Christ-like? Simplify your life. Are you unable to find words that describe how you believe God has called you to know, love and serve Him? Develop a new language. Is society dragging you in the opposite direction from where Jesus calls you? Acknowledge that your life is part of a spiritual war between God and Satan, declare your side and get on with it. Admit that you are better off "fighting the good fight" and suffering on earth for the cause of Christ, than winning the world but losing your soul for the balance of eternity. Get used to the fact that your life is lived in the context of spiritual warfare. Every breath you take is an act of war. To survive and thrive in the midst of this spiritual battle you must seek to be more Christ-like. Your mission demands single-minded commitment and a disregard for the criticisms of those who lack the same dedication to Christ. You answer to only one Commander-in-Chief, and you alone will give an explanation for your choices. Do whatever you have to, to prove that you honor God, you love Him, you serve Him—yes, and that you live only for Him. That's New Testament Christianity. Not just *going* to church—but *being* the church! That's what it means to be called a "Christian."

NEW TESTAMENT CHRISTIANITY (2)

The disciples were first called Christians in Antioch.
Acts 11:26 NAS

The New Testament Christians dedicated themselves to one thing only—making Jesus Lord of their lives and establishing His rule wherever they went. Listen: "All the believers devoted themselves to the apostles' teaching, and to fellowship and to sharing meals (including the Lord's Supper), and to prayer. A deep sense of awe came over them all, and the apostles performed many miraculous signs and wonders. And all the believers met together in one place and shared everything they had. They sold their property and possessions and shared the money with those in need. They worshipped together at the temple each day, met in homes for the Lord's Supper, and shared their meals with great joy and generosity—all the while praising God and enjoying the good will of all the people. And each day the Lord added to their fellowship those who were being saved" (See Ac 2:42-47).

Did it cost them? Yes: "The high priest and his officials …were filled with jealousy. They arrested the apostles and put them in public jail…then they brought the apostles before the high council, where the high priest confronted them…but Peter and the apostles replied, 'We must obey God rather than any human authority'…They [the high council] called in the apostles and had them flogged. Then they ordered them never again to speak in the name of Jesus, and let them go. The apostles left the high council rejoicing that God had counted them worthy to suffer disgrace for the name of Jesus" (See Ac 5:17-18: 21, 29, 40-42). *That's* what it means to be a New Testament Christian.

BIDDY CHAMBERS

I served the Lord with great humility.
Acts 20:19 NIV

My Utmost For His Highest is perhaps the world's best known devotional book. Yet without his wife Gertrude Chambers, the unrecognized driving force behind Oswald Chambers' writings, we wouldn't have this book at all. In the Foreword, she tells how the selections came from his various speaking engagements. Yet she signed only with the initials B.C. Who was this remarkable woman? Her husband affectionately called her "Biddy," a term of endearment. Oswald died as a result of complications following surgery in Egypt where he'd been ministering to the British troops. Thousands mourned his death at 43. So well loved was he by those he ministered to that in spite of the fact that he wasn't part of the military, he was still given a full military burial in the old British cemetery in Cairo.

They were married for just seven years when, at age 34, Biddy became a widow and the single mother of a little girl. Actually, the real story of the man's fame began at his death. Before she met Oswald, Biddy was a stenographer. She could take shorthand faster than many of us could talk. So she began listening to her husband's messages and took shorthand notes—hundreds of them—never thinking that one day they'd be transcribed into books and that she would become the publisher of them. The world owes a debt of gratitude to this humble and generally unknown woman whose efforts are still blessing so many. May God give us more people like her; people who believe that great things can be accomplished when no one cares who gets the credit.

IT'S ABOUT HIM—NOT US!

At the center of all this, Christ rules.
Ephesians 1:22 TM

$\mathcal{U}$ntil Copernicus showed up in 1543, we were able to claim, "The universe revolves around us." And what Copernicus did for the earth, God does for our souls. He points us to His Son and says, "At the center of all this, Christ rules." At a time when the theme of many preachers is "what God will do for *you,*" Paul points out that God doesn't exist to make a big deal out of us; we exist to make a big deal out of Him. Max Lucado writes: "We struggle with this idea because we've been demanding our way since infancy. 'I want a spouse who makes me happy, co-workers who respect me and ask my opinion, weather that suits me, a government that serves me, and a God who gives me everything I want.' It's all about *me!* What if an orchestra followed that approach, each artist clamoring for self-expression? Tubas blasting non-stop; percussionists pounding to get attention, the trumpeter standing on the conductor's stool tooting his horn. Harmony? Hardly. Happiness? Not at all. Who enjoys confusion, or contributing to a cacophony? What would happen if we each took our place, played our part, followed the score He gave us, and made His song our song? What if there was less 'here's what I want' and more 'what do you suppose God wants?' Paul answers, 'Beholding as in a glass the glory of the Lord, [we] are changed into the same image from glory to glory' (2Co 3:18). Getting our eyes off ourselves and onto Christ, makes us more like Him. It changes us—and couldn't we use a change?"

THINKING ABOUT HEAVEN (1)

Set your minds on things above, not on earthly things.
Colossians 3:2 NIV

*G*ary Larson captured a common misconception of heaven in one of his *Far Side* cartoons. In it a man with angel wings and a halo sits on a cloud, doing nothing. A caption reads: "Wish I'd brought a magazine."

How come we talk so little about heaven? Why has it fallen off our radar screens? Listen: "[Satan] opened his mouth to blaspheme God...and his dwelling place and those who live in heaven" (Rev 13:6 NIV). Satan slanders 3 things: (1) God's person; (2) God's people; (3) God's place—heaven. After being evicted from heaven (Isa 14:12-15), it must be maddening to know we're now entitled to the beautiful home he was kicked out of. What better way for him to attack us than to whisper lies about the place Paul tells us to set our minds on? If we believe his lies we'll set our minds on this life, not the next. And we won't be motivated to take others with us when we go. C.S. Lewis writes, "The Christians who did the most for this world, were those who thought most of the next. The apostles, who set on foot the conversion of the Roman Empire, the great men who built up the Middle Ages, the English Evangelicals who abolished the Slave Trade, all left their mark on Earth— precisely because their minds were occupied with Heaven. It is since Christians have largely ceased to think of any other world, that they have become so ineffective in this one. Aim at Heaven and you will get earth 'thrown in,' aim at earth and you will get neither."

THINKING ABOUT HEAVEN (2)

His servants will serve him...and they will reign for ever.
Revelation 22:3-5 NIV

*H*eaven is pictured in the Bible as a garden, a city, and a home. All 3 require skill, work and maintenance. Is that why we're told we'll *serve* God in heaven? Service is active, not passive. Seems like heaven will involve lasting accomplishment, unhindered by decay and fatigue, enhanced by unlimited resources. The Bible says we'll reign with Christ, exercising leadership, making important decisions. (See Lk 19:17-19). That means we'll set goals, devise plans and share ideas. Actually, our best workdays on earth are just a foretaste of the joy our work will bring us in heaven. Indeed, our *service* to Christ now, will determine our *position* then. Jobs that depend on aspects of our fallen world probably won't exist—such as dentists (decay), police officers (crime), funeral directors (death), and many others. But that doesn't mean we'll be unemployed. What's an interest or hobby now, may become our main vocation then. Others however may continue with work similar to what they do now, whether it's gardeners, engineers, builders, artists, animal trainers, teachers, musicians, scientists, crafts people, or hundreds of other vocations. The difference is, we'll work without the hindrances of toil, pain, corruption and sin (Rev 21:4-5).

Author Victor Hugo spoke of anticipating his work in heaven: "I haven't given utterance to the thousandth part of what lies within me. When I go to the grave I can say, 'my day's work is done.' But I cannot say, 'my life is done.' My work will recommence the next morning. The tomb is not a blind alley; it is a thoroughfare. It closes upon the twilight, but it opens upon dawn."

BIG GOALS—SMALL STEPS!

Does anyone dare despise this day of small beginnings?
Zechariah 4:10 TM

*D*o you feel like there's a huge gap between your present job and your ultimate career destination? You say, "Yes, I'd like to be a teacher, but that means I'd have to go back to school and finish my degree. That would take years!" "Sure, I'd love to switch careers, but this job has security; I don't think I could take the risk." "It would be fun to try and market my own product, but I don't know how to get started." The excuses pile up like dirty dishes in a sink; it feels like it would take too long, cost too much, require too many sacrifices to get from point A to point B. Whether it's going back to school, starting your own business or entering the ministry, the temptation is to always put it off until another time. Maybe when my wife gets a job, maybe when the kids are grown, maybe when I retire. Maybe, maybe, maybe!

How do you overcome the fear of starting? *You reach big goals by taking small steps!* While it's tempting to think that the amount of time required is too long, those days and years will pass—whether you're pursuing your goal or not! God wants you to heed His call, to show up for duty and leave the provisions—including the time, money, open doors, favorable relationships and material resources—to Him. If you do your part, He'll do His. The Psalmist writes: "No good thing will he withhold from them that walk uprightly" (Ps 84:11). Just trust God and take the first small step!

"WITH MY TEEEEEEEEEEEETH!"

We were forced to trust God totally.
2 Corinthians 1:9 TM

*F*our guys decided to go mountain climbing. In the middle of the climb one fellow slipped over a cliff, dropped about sixty feet and landed with a thud on the ledge below. The other three, hoping to rescue him, yelled, "Joe, are you okay?" He replied, "I'm alive, but I think I broke both my arms." The three said, "We'll toss a rope down to you and pull you up." "Fine," answered Joe. After dropping one end of the rope they started tugging, working feverishly to pull their wounded friend to safety. When they had him about three-fourths of the way up, they suddenly remembered that he said he'd broken *both* his arms. "Joe! If you broke both of your arms, how in the world are you hanging on?" Jaw taut, Joe responded, "With my teeeeeeeeeeeeeth." Some days the best we can do is just hang on by the skin of our teeth. Even the strongest and wisest amongst us have times when we don't have the answers and can't see the way forward; all we can do is look up and trust God to pull us through—and He does. If you're in a tight spot today, don't let go of the rope. If you have to, hang on by your teeth. Some things are just a job for God. Be still. Trust Him and let Him work.

That's where Paul was when he wrote, "Instead of trusting in our own strength or wits to get us out of it, we were forced to trust God totally—not a bad idea since he's the God who raises the dead!" (2Co 1:9-10 TM).

YOU MUST LEARN TO DELEGATE

Two are better than one, because they have
a good return for their work.
Ecclesiastes 4:9 NIV

*S*noopy is lying on top of his famous doghouse, complaining that there's too much to do. In the final frame of the cartoon, he sighs, "I hate being head beagle!" If you like the privileges of being head beagle but not the responsibilities, you probably haven't learned the scriptural art of delegation (Ac 6:1-6). D.L. Moody said, "You can do the work of ten men, or get ten men to do the work." So why are we unable (or unwilling) to delegate?

(1) Fear of losing authority. Some of us would rather look for compliant people to implement our wishes. *(2) Fear of work being done poorly.* In some cases you're right! But often our hang-up is not being willing to allow others to do the work their way. *(3) Fear of work being done better.* That's pride! You should surround yourself with people who have the potential to do an even better job, then your work will outlive you. *(4) Unwillingness to take the necessary time.* Task-oriented people just want to get the job done. They've little patience when it comes to waiting for others to learn through trial and error and become capable. *(5) Lack of training and positive experience.* Nobody ever believed enough in us to delegate stuff to us, so we learned to work as independents. That can be fatal. Theodore Roosevelt said, "The best leader is the one who has sense to pick good people to do what he or she wants done, and enough self-restraint to keep from meddling with them while they do it."

BEWARE OF LEGALISM

By His doing you are in Christ Jesus.
1 Corinthians 1:30 NAS

A food company released the perfect cake mix. It required no additives. Just mix some water with the powder, pop into the oven and prepare yourself for a treat. Only one problem: nobody bought it! Puzzled, the manufacturer conducted surveys, identified the problem and reissued the cake with a slight alteration—add one egg. Sales skyrocketed.

Why are we like that? What makes us want to add to what's already complete? Paul asked the same question. Legalists angered him by adding their work to Christ's finished work. Not much, just one small rule "you must be circumcised to be saved." How does Paul respond? With a verbal blowtorch! "Watch out for those [dogs] who do evil…who demand to cut the body" (Php 3:2 NCV). "Evil," "dogs." We dismiss legalists as harmless; after all, they promote morality. They don't dismiss Christ, they trust in Him a lot. But—they don't trust in Him *alone!* They look at the cross and say, "Great work, Jesus. Sorry You couldn't finish it, but I'll take up the slack." So Paul writes, "How is it that you are turning back to those weak and miserable principles? Do you wish to be enslaved by them all over again?" (Gal 4:9 NIV). Legalism is miserable because legalism is endless. It leaves you with the anxiety that having done everything you know, you might not have done enough. Can our efforts make us more worthy of salvation? If so, we get a little of the credit, and deep down that's what our proud heart wants. No, salvation is not about what *you* do, it's about trusting only in what *He's* already done!

ENCOURAGE YOUR PASTOR!

Give a bonus to leaders who do a good job,
especially…at preaching and teaching.
1 Timothy 5:17 TM

A mother watched her son begin to drain of energy as the week went on. By the end of the week he'd lost his desire to get out of bed. She heard the alarm go off through his bedroom door. Apparently he just kept punching the little snooze button on the top. Finally, after 3 or 4 extra rings she walked in and said, "Son, it's time to get up." He peeked out from under the covers, "Can you give me a good reason to get up?" She said, "Yes. First, it's Sunday—time for church. Second, you're 43 years old and you know better. Third, you're the pastor and they expect you to be there." Your pastor is always on call. He gets drained; he needs encouragement. Give him some!

Richard DeHann writes, "Here are some creative ways a church can get rid of their pastor. First, you could look him straight in the eye while he's preaching and say 'Amen,' and he'll preach himself to death in a few weeks. Or you could acknowledge his good points, and he'll probably work himself into the grave by the end of the year. Or you could dedicate your life to Christ and ask him to give you a job, such as winning others to Christ, and there's a good chance he'll die immediately of heart failure. Or you could get the whole church to unite in prayer behind him, and soon he'll become so effective that some larger church will take him off your hands and you won't have to worry about it anymore."

GLORIFYING GOD

Before all the people I must be glorified.
Leviticus 10:3 NKJV

$\mathcal{A}$t the end of His life, Jesus declared His mission a success by saying "I have brought you glory on earth by completing the work you gave me to do" (Jn 17:4 NIV). David writes, "Not to us, O Lord, not to us, but to Your name give glory" (Ps 115:1 AMP). The breath you took as you read that last sentence was given to you for one reason, that you might "reflect the Lord's glory" (2Co 3:18 NIV). Before Moses was qualified to lead Israel he first had to pray, "show me your glory" (Ex 33:18 NCV). We cross a line when we make such a request. When our deepest desire is not the *things* of God, or the *favor* of God, but *God Himself,* we cross a threshold. Less self-focus, more God-focus. Less about us—more about Him. This calls for the death of ego. It rubs us the wrong way. It's a truth we must constantly remind ourselves of. "God made all things, and everything continues through him and *for* him. To him be glory forever" (Ro 11:36 NCV). And if you still haven't got the message: "There is only one God, the Father, who created everything, *and we exist for him"* (1Co 8:6 NLT). Why does the earth spin? For Him. Why do you have talents and abilities? For Him. Whose Word matters? His. Whose will must be done? His, not ours. God's to-do list consists of one item: "Reveal My glory." Heaven's framed and mounted statement of purpose reads: "Declare God's glory." Everything and everyone exists to reveal His glory—including you! Try to remember that.

WHY BE HONEST?

*Far better to be right and poor
than to be wrong and rich.*
Proverbs 16:8 TM

*A*fter a week of special meetings, the guest preacher approached the airline desk to purchase a flight for home. Ticket in hand, he took a seat in the waiting area. Checking his credit card receipt, he realized the attendant had undercharged him almost fifty percent. "It's wonderful how God provides," he rationalized. The church hadn't paid him too well and the bills were piling up at home. For the next half hour he wrestled with himself, although, deep down he knew what he had to do. Finally he returned to the desk and said to the attendant, "I think you made a mistake." "No," she replied, "you see, I was in church last night when you spoke on honesty, and I thought I'd put you to the test." Why be honest? Because people are watching. Your actions and attitudes, in even the smallest of details, are forming the opinions of those who hear you claim to be a follower of Christ.

There's a golden moment in the life of Samuel the prophet. It's his retirement. Standing before the nation he'd led for 40 years, he asks, "Have I ever taken advantage of you or exploited you? Have I ever taken a bribe or played fast and loose with the law? Bring your complaint and I'll make it right. 'Oh no,' they said, 'never have you done any of that'" (1Sa 12:3 TM). When those who've known you best for 4 decades can say that about you, you did it right. And that's as good as it gets!

DO YOU PRACTICE COMPASSION?

Greater love has no one than this,
that one lay down his life for his friends.
John 15:13 NAS

*T*he phone rang in a high society Boston home. A son who'd just returned from Vietnam was calling from California. His folks were the cocktail-circuit, party kind. The boy said, "I just called to tell you that I want to bring a buddy home with me." His mother said, "Sure, bring him along for a few days." "But mother, there's something you need to know about him. One leg's gone, one arm's gone, one eye's gone, and his face is disfigured." His mother said, "It's okay, bring him home for a few days anyway." The son said, "You don't understand, I want to bring him home to live with us." After a long pause the mother began to make excuses, "What would people think? How could we take care of him, given our busy lives?" And the phone clicked. A few hours later the California Police Department called. Again the mother picked up the phone; a voice said, "We have found a boy with one arm, one leg, one eye and a mangled face. He just committed suicide. His identification papers say he's your son."

Showing compassion demands dying to self-interest. It disrupts our well-ordered lives. It costs us money we planned to use for other things. It calls for time, often years of care giving, when we feel like we've hardly enough time for ourselves. What is compassion? Laying down your life for others! That's why Jesus said, "Greater love has no man than this, that one lay down his life for his friends." Do *you* practice compassion?

SERVANT LEADERSHIP (1)

Neither...being lords over God's heritage.
1 Peter 5:3

 re you called to be a leader in the home, the workplace or the church? Do you aspire to leadership? Understand this: today's generation is unwilling to submit to, or follow those who practice the old "top down" style of leadership that says, "I'm in charge, and the sooner you figure that out the better." You don't demand leadership; you earn it—every day. How? By being a servant! By putting others first and yourself last. That's what Jesus taught and practiced. You're not called to be at the *top* of the pyramid. The New Testament model for leadership is an inverted pyramid with you at the *bottom,* supporting the others, holding them up, bringing out the best in them, laying aside your own comfort and desires to serve those you're called to lead so that the job can get done, and done better. This means gently correcting mistakes and tying up loose ends while people learn. It also calls for breaking a sweat and getting dirt under your fingernails.

A.W. Tozer wrote: "A true and safe leader is likely to be one who has no desire to lead, but is forced into a position of leadership by the inward pressure of the Holy Spirit, and the press of the external situation. A person who is ambitious to lead is disqualified as a leader. The true leader will have no desire to lord it over God's heritage, but will be humble, gentle, self-sacrificing and altogether as ready to follow as to lead, when the Spirit makes it clear that a wiser and more talented man than himself has appeared."

SERVANT LEADERSHIP (2)

Christ…made himself of no reputation.
Philippians 2:5-7

If He Who is called "Lord of Lords" became a servant of all, how can *you,* in your right mind, think you should be served by those you lead? Paul writes: "Christ…made himself of no reputation" (Php 2:5-7). Reputation is so important to us. We want to be seen with the right people, remembered in the right light, live in the right neighborhood and drive the right car. Not Christ. He made Himself of no reputation. If you're obsessed with the size of your congregation (or business), the famous people you can reach on speed-dial, the trappings of your lifestyle or the image you've carefully cultivated, read John, Chapter 13. Jesus stooped low enough to wash the feet of crude Galilean fishermen, then said, "I have given you an example, that ye should do as I have done" (Jn 13:15). Whose feet did He wash? The feet of common people. Surely those people walked away changed, humbled by a lesson they'd never forget—one we all need to learn!

Peter writes, "I have a special concern for you church leaders…Here's my concern: that you care for God's flock with all the diligence of a shepherd. Not because you have to, but because you want to please God. Not calculating what you can get out of it, but acting spontaneously. Not 'bossily' telling others what to do, but tenderly showing them the way… God has had it with the proud, but takes delight in just plain people. So be content with who you are, and don't put on airs. God's strong hand is on you; he'll promote you at the right time" (1Pe 5:1-6 TM).

BE A TITUS—ENCOURAGE SOMEONE!

How delightful is a timely word.
Proverbs 15:23 NAS

*S*ome of the people around you, even successful ones, are dying on the vine for lack of encouragement. Solomon writes, "How delightful is a timely word." Isn't that true? It's delightful to receive a timely word. *The Message* says, "The right word at the right time—beautiful!" Encouragement brings emotional healing, restores hope by putting the problem into perspective, and makes the day more bearable. Is there someone you know who needs encouragement? A prisoner trying to stay strong in a hostile environment while repaying his debt to society? A divorcee trying to rebuild their life? A bread-winner who's out of work, worried about their family? A widow who needs companionship? A servant of God laboring in an obscure and difficult ministry? Everyone is struggling with something—so everyone needs encouragement.

William Barclay writes, "One of the highest of human duties is the duty of encouragement…it is easy to laugh at men's ideals; it is easy to pour cold water on their enthusiasm; it is easy to discourage others. The world is full of such dis-couragers. But we have a duty to encourage one another. Many a time a word of praise or thanks or appreciation or cheer, has kept a man on his feet. Blessed is the man who speaks such a word." Paul writes: "Outside, trouble was on every hand… within us, our hearts were full of dread and fear. Then God who cheers those who are discouraged refreshed us by the arrival of Titus. Not only was his presence a joy, but also the news that he brought" (2Co 7:5-7 TLB). So, be a Titus—encourage someone today.

PUT YOUR FAMILY FIRST

There are those who curse their fathers and
do not bless their mothers.
Proverbs 30:11 NIV

$\mathcal{D}$r. Christiaan Barnard, the world-renowned heart transplant surgeon, tells of leaving Minneapolis to return to his wife and children in Cape Town after being gone for months. "I was unprepared for her greeting. 'Why did you come back?' There was no longer a smile in her eyes. *Oh God,* I thought, *I've made the most horrible mistake of my life.* 'Don't look so surprised' she said. 'We gave up on you.' I responded, 'It was only a little delay. I wrote you about it.' 'No, you wrote once to say you weren't coming home.' He answered, 'But we were building aortic valves to save lives.' 'No, you were building a family. That is, until you dumped it into my lap,' she said bitterly. 'We have ceased to exist for you.' I wanted to say I'd come home because I love my children and I loved her. I wanted to because I felt it, but what could I say now that would not sound meaningless."

Dr. James Dobson writes, "A sixth grade teacher in an upper-middle-class neighborhood was shocked to see the results of a creative writing task about their family, assigned to her students. A few of their actual sentences read: I wish my mother didn't have a boyfriend…I wish I could get straight "A's" so my father would love me…I wish I had one mom and one dad so that kids wouldn't make fun of me. I have three moms and three dads and they botch up my life." Parent, wise up. Put your family first or you'll live to regret it!

EXPERIENCING THE MIRACULOUS

Do whatever he tells you.
John 2:5 NAS

$\mathcal{D}$o you need a miracle? Reread the story of Jesus turning water into wine. Notice what Mary said to the attendants at the wedding reception: "Do whatever [Jesus] tells you." Do it, even though:

(1) You're not in the right place. They were at a wedding, not a church, when Jesus performed this miracle. Some of our greatest blessings will be at "other places" if we'll just be sensitive and obedient to God. *(2) You've got a lot of problems.* They'd run out of wine for their guests. How embarrassing. Too often our problems drive us away from Jesus instead of to Him. Miracles begin when we focus on God's power instead of our problems. *(3) You're not being encouraged.* When Mary turned to Jesus for help He tested her faith saying, "Dear woman, why do you involve me…My time has not yet come" (Jn 2:4 NIV). But she passed the test. Instead of being discouraged Mary laid hold of the possibility of a miracle, believed God and received one. *(4) You haven't walked with Christ very long.* The attendants who obeyed Jesus had just met Him. And His disciples had just started following Him. Yet they were all expected to obey Him. So are you. *(5) You haven't yet seen Him work miracles in your life.* This was Jesus' first miracle. They had to obey Him without the faith that comes from a previous track record. That's always challenging! *(6) You don't understand the process.* Why pour water into empty containers? Answer: give Jesus what you've got and He'll give you back what you need. *That's* how to experience the miraculous!

"OLDER BROTHER" ATTITUDES!

The older brother became angry and refused to go in.
Luke 15:28 NIV

*T*here were *two* prodigals! The younger brother was guilty of the sins of the flesh; the older was guilty of the sins of the spirit (attitude). When Jesus' parable closes it's the older brother, the second prodigal, standing outside the father's house. When we focus only on our own interests we become like the older brother. We nurture attitudes of jealousy and selfishness. Understand this: Christians who possess no greater cause than themselves, are usually not as happy or fulfilled as those who don't know Christ yet have a purpose greater than themselves. This older brother attitude has 3 possible results:

(1) It's possible to be a son yet refuse to act like a brother. Outwardly the older brother was correct, but look at his resentful attitude. A wrong relationship with your brother and sister in Christ always results in a strained relationship with your Heavenly Father. *(2) It's possible to serve God faithfully yet not be in sync with His will.* The elder brother had no idea why their father would rejoice over a disobedient son's return. Self-centered, judgmental people never "get it." *(3) It's possible to be an heir to all your father possesses yet have less joy and liberty than one who possesses nothing.* The hired servants were happier than the older brother. They ate, laughed and celebrated while he stood outside demanding his rights. The older brother attitude robbed him of the blessings of his father, the love of his brother, and the joy of the servants. And an older brother attitude will block the flow of God's blessing in *your* life too.

HAVE YOU FOUND YOUR CALLING? (1)

I have filled him with…skill, ability and
knowledge in all kinds of crafts.
Exodus 31:3 NIV

*H*ave you read about two builders named Bezalel and Oholiab? God speaks about them: "I have chosen Bezalel …and…filled him with the Spirit of God, with skill, ability and knowledge in all kinds of crafts…Moreover, I have appointed Oholiab…to help him" (Ex 31:2-6 NIV). And there are other examples where God's call was not "religious" in a formal sense, like Nehemiah the wall builder, Daniel the government man in Babylon, Luke the first century physician. So consider this: your job could be your calling! When you demonstrate Christian character there, and use your income to fulfill God's purposes on earth, you are as called as any minister.

And your past doesn't disqualify you. Paul wrote, "I was …a blasphemer…and a violent man" (1Ti 1:13 NIV). Happily, God doesn't consult our past to determine our future. Furthermore, God will call you to a job that looks too big for you. Why? So you'll never forget where your strength and success come from. Calls are not classified ads; you don't volunteer, you respond! God speaks, He persistently nudges you. In *Chariots of Fire,* Eric Liddell says, "When I run, I feel God's pleasure." All your human accolades and accomplishments will eventually leave you empty. Lasting pleasure, the kind only God provides, comes from knowing you are doing what *He's* told you to do. Eventually Eric Liddell became a missionary; so your call can begin one place then take you to another. Whenever you know you're doing what God has called you to do—you experience a lasting pleasure that simply can't be found anywhere else!

HAVE YOU FOUND YOUR CALLING? (2)

We are God's workmanship,
created in Christ Jesus to do good works,
which God prepared in advance for us to do.
Ephesians 2: 10 NIV

*W*hen God calls you to do something, His call comes in several ways: *(1) You feel "moved."* There's a moment of certainty when God puts His hand upon you, nudging you toward a particular need, usually an unmet one. You know it in your "knower." *(2) It's confirmed by others.* People will discern that God's at work in your life. People who know you well, watch; they volunteer comments such as, "You're at your best when you…" "You shine when you're doing that." *(3) You'll be gifted to do it.* There are times when a person starts off with seemingly no specific capacities at all, but this is rare. With a call comes giftedness—that special empowerment God gives to the "callee." When you're in your calling you soar in spite of obstacles. And people tend to stand back in amazement. Ever seen Joni Eareckson Tada speaking to an auditorium full of people in wheelchairs? The whole place comes alive when she rolls up to the microphone in her wheelchair. *(4) You'll see results!* You'll change things, touch lives and glorify God. St. Patrick had a dream in which the Irish people were saying, "We appeal to you, Holy Servant Boy, to come and walk among us." And Patrick responded. He combed the Irish countryside preaching to chiefs and kings. An entire nation began its journey toward Christianity. Now, you may not be called to do that, but you're called to do *something* for God. So, find your calling and fulfill it!

DAD, BE MORE OPEN AND AFFECTIONATE!

Tear down your father's altar...
build a proper kind of altar.
Judges 6:25-26 NIV

*D*uring a leadership seminar on attitudes, a man told Dr. John Maxwell the following story: "From my earliest recollections I do not remember a compliment from my father. His father also thought it unmanly to express affection or even appreciation. My grandfather was a perfectionist who worked hard and expected everyone else to do the same, without any encouragement. And since he was neither positive nor relational, he had a constant turnover in his employees. Because of my background it has been very difficult for me to nurture or encourage my family. This critical and negative attitude has hindered me in life. I've raised five children and tried to live as a Christian before them. Sadly, it's easier for them to recognize my love for God, than my love for *them*. They're starved for affection and approval. The tragedy is, they've received my bad attitude trait and now I see them passing it down to my precious grandchildren. Never before have I been so aware of 'catching an attitude.' Obviously, this wrong attitude has been passed along for five generations. So, it's time to stop it! Today I make a conscious decision to change. This will not be done overnight, but it will be done. It will not be accomplished easily, but by God's grace it will be accomplished!"

God told Gideon to tear down his father's altar and build a proper kind of altar [attitude]. Dad, it's time to tear down your old attitudes and ways of relating, and start building attitudes that bless your children and honor God.

DAVID'S FIVE "I WILLS"

I will sing of mercy and judgment.
Psalm 101:1

$\mathcal{N}$otice the five "I wills" of David in Psalm 101: *(1) "I will sing of mercy and judgment"* (v.1). When dealing with others, some of us are all mercy and no justice; others are all justice and no mercy. God requires both. *(2) "I will behave myself wisely"* (v.2). People are more impacted by your behavior than by your beliefs. Your children may not always follow your advice, but count on it, they'll follow your footsteps. Those not persuaded by your theology, can still be won by your love and lifestyle. *(3) "I will walk within my house with a perfect heart"* (v.2). Charity begins at home. If your family thinks you're joyless and judgmental, you'll never attract them to Christ. David prayed, "How I need your help, especially in my own home, where I long to act as I should" (Ps 101:2 TLB). *(4) "I will set no wicked thing before mine eyes"* (v.3). Get real. Television is on 7 hours a day in most homes. So ask yourself: "What am I exposing myself and my family to?" What you tolerate, you've no right to complain about! You say you've no time to read God's Word and pray. No, the truth is, you don't have a strong enough desire to. *(5) "I will early destroy all the wicked"* (v.8). The Living Bible states, "I will not tolerate anyone who secretly slanders his neighbors; I will not permit conceit and pride. I will make the godly of the land my heroes, and invite them to my home" (Ps 101:5-6 TLB). Those are 5 "I wills" you should live by.

THE NEED FOR APPRECIATION

Encourage one another and build each other up.
1 Thessalonians 5:11 NIV

*A*fter 30 years of marriage his wife was ready to throw in the towel. "I have had it, living with you. You never tell me you love me anymore." The husband replied, "I told you I loved you when we got married—if I change my mind I'll let you know." Too many leaders expect their followers to run on autopilot, like the hard-hearted husband. They don't understand that people thrive on appreciation. They need it. Sometimes Christian organizations are the worst: "You're working for the Lord and He'll reward you." Yes, we're all working for that final pat on the back in the sky, but God expects us to pat others on the back along the way. Paul writes: "Encourage one another and build each other up."

Some people don't need encouragement. They're so strong and so busy that attempts at praising them would be nothing more to them than a pesky gnat flying around their face. They'd brush it off with a look of confusion. There are also people who view praise with suspicion because others have taken advantage of them. With them, all you need to do is cultivate kindness. But most of us do need encouragement—and lots of it. Phillis Theroux writes, "One of the commodities in life that most people can't get enough of is compliments. The ego is never so intact that one can't find a hole in which to plug a little praise. Compliments by their very nature are highly bio-degradable and tend to dissolve hours or days after we receive them—which is why we can always use another."

NO UNITY, NO BLESSING

The new wine is found in the cluster.
Isaiah 65:8

$\mathcal{G}$od told Isaiah, "The new wine is found in the cluster...Destroy it not; for a blessing is in it." You can't get wine from just one grape, you need a cluster. You can't win a football game with just one player, you need a team. Notice some things about teamwork: *(1) The team members must care for one another.* Uncaring people on a team remind us of two guys in a sinking boat, sitting together at one end doing nothing. As the people at the other end are bailing furiously, one says, "Thank God that hole isn't in our end of the boat." *(2) The team members must communicate.* In Hurricane Katrina, people died while those who could have rescued them stood by. Why? Communication broke down. *(3) "Your rights" must take second place.* The team's success must always be of greater value than your own individual interests. Your "I'll do it myself, that way I know it'll get done right" attitude, robs others of the opportunity to participate, learn and grow, and leaves the job undone or poorly done. A farmer noticed a highway department truck pulling over on to the shoulder of the road. A man got out and dug a hole, then got back into the truck. Then the other occupant got out, filled up the hole and got back in the truck. Every fifty yards this amazing process was repeated. "What are you doing?" the farmer asked. The driver replied, "We're on a highway beautification project, and the guy who plants the trees is home sick today." What's the bottom line? God blesses those who work together in unity.

GOD KNOWS YOUR NAME

He calleth his own sheep by name, and leadeth them.
John 10:3

*W*hen we see a flock of sheep, we see exactly that —a flock. All alike. Not so with a shepherd; to him every sheep has a story and every face a name. When we see a crowd, we see exactly that—a crowd, filling a stadium or flooding a mall. Not so with Jesus; to Him each of us has a story and every face a name. "I have written your name on my hand" (Isa 49:16 NLT). That's awesome! Your name—written on God's hand where He sees it constantly. Your name is on His lips. Maybe you've seen your name on some impressive things—like an award or diploma, or the walnut door of the executive suite. But on *God's* hand and on *God's* lips—quite a thought, isn't it?

That means what matters to you, matters to God. You probably think that's true when it comes to big stuff like death, disease, sin and disaster. But what about smaller things like financial pressures that make us insecure, arguments with loved ones that leave us drained, bodies that do less while demanding more? Understand this: you are God's child. John writes: "We really are his children" (1Jn 3:1 NCV). It's as if John knew some of us would shake our heads and say, "No, not me. Mother Teresa, maybe. Billy Graham, alright. But not me." If those are your feelings, John adds this phrase just for you: "We really are his children." That means if something is important to you, it's important to God! Try to hold on to that truth!

DEVELOPING SPIRITUAL DISCIPLINE

Watch your life and doctrine closely.
1 Timothy 4:15 NIV

*J*ust talking about spiritual discipline won't get you very far. Nor is there any value in talking about how badly others need it. Describing some friends he'd known for a lifetime, Scott Turow writes, "Many years ago I learned their dirtiest, most crabbed secret. That their passion to change the world derived from the fact that they could not change themselves." Hello! Do you talk a lot about things you haven't personally experienced, as a kind of smokescreen for your own shallowness? Understand this: developing spiritual discipline is demanding, mostly done in secret, usually humbling, and not always fun. Let's break that down.

Demanding? Absolutely. It means being harder on yourself than you want to be. It calls for regularly examining your speech, relationships and life choices, then correcting them if necessary. *Done in secret?* Yes. When you're striving to develop spiritual discipline it's wise not to talk too much about what you're in to. Talk is cheap. "Just do it," goes the well-known slogan. *Humbling?* No question about it. Some days it will feel like one step forward and two back. Spiritual discipline calls for "staying the course," while others walk away in denial or excuse making. *Not always fun?* Developing a life of spiritual discipline is a satisfying experience, but it's not always a fun experience. Listen to Paul: "I'm running hard for the finish line. I'm giving it everything I've got. No sloppy living for me! I'm staying alert and in top condition. I'm not going to get caught napping, telling everyone else all about it and then missing out myself" (1Co 9:26-27 TM).

KNOWING GOD INTIMATELY!

That I may know him.
Philippians 3:10

*L*uke gives us a fascinating description of a lady called Anna, who recognized the Christ-child when His parents first brought Him to the temple: "Anna the prophetess was also there...by now a very old woman. She had been married seven years and a widow for eighty-four. She never left the Temple area, worshipping night and day...At the very time Simeon was praying, she showed up, broke into an anthem of praise to God, and talked about the [Christ] child to all" (Lk 2:36-37 TM). *Anna never stopped searching for God!* What a challenge to those whose spiritual life has never evolved and deepened with age. They slowly empty their tank of yesterday's zeal, and now go through the motions of a faith that makes no sense and has no appeal on the streets of the real world.

Oswald Chambers once made an entry in his journal that reads, "A great fear has been at work in my mind, and God has used it to arouse me to prayer. I came across a man I knew years ago, a mighty man of God. Now ten years have gone by and I met him again—garrulous and unenlivened. How many of us seem to become like that after forty years of age?" *Garrulous?* It describes someone who talks a lot but says little. *Unenlivened?* It describes a person whose spirit is unexercised, undeepened, and starved almost to the point of death. But it doesn't have to be that way for you; the *rest* of your life can be the *best* of your life, if you dedicate it to one purpose—knowing God intimately.

WHEN IT'S TIME TO BOW OUT

Moses…laid his hands on him.
Deuteronomy 34:9 NIV

*S*ome subjects are hard to talk about. Bowing out and passing the torch to someone else, is one of the most difficult. But it's not about *you*—it's about God's kingdom! Stepping down calls for humility. The future of any work depends on it. For 40 years Moses dreamed of leading his people into the Promised Land—but it was not to be. Joshua, his successor, would be the man to fulfill that dream. How did Moses handle it? With grace and dignity: "Joshua…was filled with the spirit of wisdom because Moses had laid his hands on him. So the Israelites listened to him and did what the Lord had commanded Moses" (Dt 34:9 NIV). The plan worked, the transition was smooth and the followers immediately transferred their allegiance to Joshua. Why? Because Moses had placed his hands on Joshua and prayed for God's blessing on his leadership. That's leadership in its finest form and final hour—when it counts *most!* Is this hard to do? Yes, for 7 reasons: (1) Job security—"What am I going to do next?" (2) Fear of retirement—"Me, retire?" (3) Resistance to change—"The saddle is so comfortable." (4) Self worth —"This job is my life." (5) Lack of confidence—"Who else can do this job like I do it?" (6) Love for the job—"I really love my job and the people I work with." (7) Loss of investment—"I've put too much into this to let it go." What's the answer? Rejoice in your God-given accomplishments, bow out graciously, bless and assist your successor, then ask God "What's next?"

UNTIL THE LAST SPIKE IS DRIVEN

I press on toward the goal to win the prize.
Philippians 3:14 NIV

*S*tephen Ambrose's book, *Nothing Like It in the World,* tells the story of the building of the Transcontinental Railroad in America. He describes the moment when construction was to begin and certain people decided that there ought to be a great ceremony. A host of dignitaries were invited to gather at the place where the first rail was to be laid. One of those invited was Collis Huntington, perhaps the railroad's most important West Coast backer in California. But he declined, saying, *"Anybody can drive the first spike, but there are months of labor and unrest between the first and the last spike."* When construction of the railroad was finally completed in May, 1869, the last spike, a golden one at that, was pounded into place and a telegram sent to President Ulysses S. Grant: "Sir, we have the honor to report that the last rail is laid, the last spike is driven, the Pacific Railroad is finished." Now Collis Huntington had something to celebrate!

Paul felt that way too: "Forgetting what is behind…I press on toward the goal to win the prize" (Php 3:13-14 NIV). Almost fifty years ago Thomas Merton wrote, "If you want to identify me, ask me not where I live, or what I like to eat, or how I comb my hair. But ask me what I think I am living for, in detail, and ask me what I think is keeping me from living fully for the thing I want to live for—Christ!" *That's a question we each need to ask ourselves—daily!*

GENEROUS WITH...WHAT?

May the Lord make your love increase
and overflow for each other.
1 Thessalonians 3:12 NIV

*S*o, what does it mean to be generous? And generous with...what? *(1) Your time.* Listen: "May the Lord show mercy to...Onesiphorus, because he often refreshed me and was not ashamed of my chains...when he was in Rome, he searched hard for me until he found me" (2Ti 1:16-18 NIV). Wouldn't you love to know more about Onesiphorus? He's the kind who'll stand by you when you're under attack—he'll even visit you in prison. Ever visit a prisoner? Jesus said you should! (See Mt 25:35-40). *(2) Your encouragement.* Paul had a friend named Barnabas ("son of encouragement"). It was Barnabas we have to thank (in part) for the incredible success of Paul. When the early church doubted Paul's conversion, Barnabas welcomed him into fellowship. The last we hear of Barnabas is defending John Mark, a failed young man who needed a second chance. Are you willing to do that for others? God did that for you! *(3) Your money.* Jesus watched folks giving to attract attention. Interestingly, none of them are named in Scripture. Who was? A poor widow. Suddenly Jesus called His disciples and said, "Hey, I want you to watch this." People with little to give, tend to be avoided. Who notices them? Jesus! Listen: "This poor widow has put more into the treasury than all the others. They all gave out of their wealth; but she, out of her poverty, put in everything—all she had to live on" (Mk 12:43-44 NIV). We tend to seek out glamour and power, but the eyes of Jesus seek out true generosity. So you say you're generous? Generous with...*what?*

REPAIRING THE PAST

If I have cheated anybody out of anything,
I will pay back four times the amount.
Luke 19:8 NIV

*Z*acchaeus discovered that you can't be right with God until you're first right with those you've hurt. Joseph discovered that being Prime Minister doesn't mean much if your family relationships are strained. Relationships are like a house. If you don't maintain it your task won't be to repair it—it'll be to rebuild it. We each carry within us the experience of our yesterdays. They influence our relationships, our choices, our view of ourselves, even our understanding of God. You can't live in a spiritually healthy fashion if you've an unrepaired past.

For a long time Jacob lived that way. He took advantage of his brother Esau, manipulating him out of his inheritance. Then when things got bad between them he fled the country. When he returned home, he did so fearing the face of his brother. In his case the relationship was healed, but it doesn't always end that way. Repairing the past is best done immediately. Patching up wounded relationships, dealing with festering regrets, letting go of feelings toward someone who's betrayed you; these issues lie deep within us as if asleep. Then suddenly they're awakened by some "trigger." It could be an anniversary, an old face in the crowd or a particular song on the radio, but they don't go away until we *deal* with them. How? By forgiving, and when possible making restitution. You see, forgiveness isn't just for the other person's benefit—it's for yours. So, is there a relationship you need to repair today? If so, take care of it!

THE POWER AND REACH OF MEMORY

Forget the former things; do not dwell on the past.
See, I am doing a new thing!
Isaiah 43:18-19 NIV

$\mathcal{G}$ordon MacDonald writes, "When I asked a ninety-three-year-old man if he and his ninety-year-old wife ever have conflict, he assured me they do. I asked him how they treat each other in such moments, and he told me how important it is that he *speaks tenderly* to her. When I asked why, he told me that when his wife was a girl her father always spoke to her in a harsh and hurtful tone of voice. 'Now whenever she hears any man speak in an angry manner, the feelings of hurt and fear return.' 'But that was eighty-five years ago,' MacDonald replied, 'are you telling me that she *still* remembers?' 'More than ever!' he responded emphatically." In our earliest years we watch those who are largest in our lives and note how and when they express anger, joy, sadness or fear. And we take our cues from what we see. So, "What do I do with those painful memories?" you ask. The Bible gives us at least 4 answers: (1) Practice repentance; acknowledge your own mistakes. (2) Demonstrate grace; forgive others—and yourself. (3) Show gratitude; focus on what's good, not what's bad. (4) Find wisdom; turn your pain into a learning experience.

When Israel crossed the River Jordan, God commanded Joshua to erect a memorial of 12 stones saying: "In the future, when your children ask you, 'What do these stones mean?' tell them...These stones are to be a memorial" (Jos 4:6-7 NIV). In other words, remember with repentance, with grace, with gratitude, and with wisdom.

WAYS TO ENRICH YOUR MARRIAGE

Live in…harmony…each with the attitude
of Christ toward the other.
Romans 15:5 TLB

*S*omebody said the difference between courtship and marriage is like the difference between the pictures in a seed catalog and what actually comes up in your garden. But it doesn't have to be that way. Author Steve Stephens offers this advice:

"Start each day with a kiss…always wear your wedding ring [it was placed there to cut off your circulation!)…go on regular 'dates' with your spouse…accept your differences…be polite…be gentle…give little gifts…smile often…touch…talk about your dreams…adopt a song as 'your song'…give back rubs…laugh together…send cards for no reason…do what your partner wants *before* they ask…and learn to listen for what *isn't* being said…encourage one another…do it his or her way …compliment one another daily…call during the day…slow down…hold hands…cuddle…ask for your mate's opinion… be respectful…always welcome your spouse when he or she comes home at the end of the day…make an effort to always look your best…wink at each other…celebrate special events …learn to apologize…forgive quickly…set up regular romantic getaways…ask, 'What can I do to make you happier?'…be positive…be kind…be vulnerable…respond quickly to your spouse's requests…talk about your love…reminisce about favorite times together…treat each other's friends and relatives with courtesy…send flowers on Valentine's Day and anniversaries…when you're wrong, admit it…be sensitive to your spouse's sexual needs…watch sunsets together…say 'I love you' often…never go to sleep angry…end every day with a hug…get professional help when you need it…and above all, pray daily for (and with) each other."

HAVING A GRATEFUL HEART

Where are the other nine?
Luke 17:17 NIV

*O*ne day 10 men with leprosy came to Jesus saying, "Have pity on us!" *Pity*—it was an admission that they were desperate for whatever charity another person might provide. "Go, show yourselves to the priests" was Jesus' response. "As they went," the Bible says, "they were cleansed" (Lk 17:14). But the story doesn't end there. "One of them, when he saw he was healed, came back, praising God in a loud voice. He threw himself at Jesus' feet and thanked him—and he was a Samaritan" (Lk 17:15-16 NIV). What takes place next is very interesting. Jesus asks, "Where are the other nine?" (Lk 17:17 NIV). Jesus is making a point: gratitude is important to Him. This story is there to underscore the importance of having a grateful heart. Two statements are worth underlining: "He came back," and "Where are the other nine?" Gratitude is "coming back" to say thanks to the One Who made it all possible. Gratitude isn't a natural or instinctive thing for most of us, it's a learned discipline, one that comes with a realization that we neither deserve nor are entitled to God's blessings. At best, we're graced recipients of all we have and are. The old cowboy doffs his hat and says, "Much obliged." The words imply *humility:* that I cannot get along by myself. They imply *reliance:* that I need people around me, and that I need God. They imply *value:* that I recognize the cost involved in giving. They imply *gladness:* that my life has been filled with a joy that only comes when I reach out to, and receive from others with grace.

LOVING THE UNLOVABLE

*Inasmuch as you did it to one of the least
of these...you did it to Me.*
Matthew 25:40 NKJV

*H*er parents didn't want her so at birth they placed her in foster care. Shuffled from place to place, she dreamed of the day they'd return. It never happened. So she lashed out at the world by attempting suicide. Then through a series of events she found her parents again. She lived with them but things were strained. When they told her they wanted to adopt a baby and "start over," she longed to be included. But when she said, "I don't want to be a burden, so maybe I should go," her dad helped her pack. Cramming her possessions in a grocery bag, he pressed $10 into her hand and said goodbye. Today she lives on the streets, sleeps in doorways and eats from garbage cans. Sadly, her story's not unique. It's been multiplied into infinity. In fact, there's probably somebody just like her in *your* neighborhood—forgotten, unloved and isolated. They're usually the hardest to reach because they *feel* unwanted and useless. They wrestle with inferiority, poor self-image and lack of self-respect.

What do we do? Instead of loving them we label them. Instead of caring, we criticize. *What should we do?* Open our hearts. Love is much more than shaking hands in church. It takes time to develop and grow. So be gracious. Remember, that tough exterior is just a cover-up. Look for new ways to reach out, encourage, and show hurting people you care. *Why?* Because Jesus said, "Inasmuch as you did it to one of the least of these ...you did it to Me." And that's reason enough!

BEFORE YOU OPT FOR DIVORCE

Don't begin until you count the cost.
Luke 14:28 NLT

A counselor who had a friend contemplating divorce writes: "She didn't want to hear anything from us... she'd made up her mind. So in frustration my friends and I compiled a list: *what we wish we'd known before we got divorced.* We'd each experienced the upheaval of divorce and watched our friends' second marriages end." *(1) Life will change more than you realize:* Dividing assets isn't always equitable. Instead of 2 people parenting your kids, if you have custody, you become breadwinner, spiritual advisor and disciplinarian. Stress levels become staggering. You ache watching your children doling out their time in an effort not to alienate either parent. And the hassles don't end when your kids grow up and marry, they continue with your grandkids. *(2) Life won't be more carefree:* Every birthday, holiday, wedding or funeral is a potential nightmare. Emotional wounds pop open when you least expect. One woman says, "Every Christmas I become depressed. After 20 years it still hits me; I was married in December and my childhood sweetheart left me for another woman 15 Decembers later." You're seldom free from the effects of that broken first marriage. *(3) It affects more than just you.* Friends who don't want to pick sides, distance themselves. Relationships with those who remain loyal—change. Family members who loved and cared for your ex, are forced to "divorce" as well. Blending children from previous marriages brings problems...Life's more complicated than ever. Like children, we let our desire for momentary pleasure pull us from God's best, rather than doing the hard work it takes to turn short-term pain into long-term gain.

GO TO THE RIGHT PERSON

We are his people, the sheep he tends.
Psalm 100:3 NCV

*L*ike sheep, most of our wounds come from living in the pasture. Thorns prick. Rocks cut. Heads butt. Mosquitoes bite. So our Shepherd regularly inspects His sheep searching for wounds. That's because He doesn't want today's wound to become tomorrow's infection. Hence, David writes, "We are his people, the sheep he tends." Others may guide us to God, but no one does the work of God for only God can heal. He "heals the brokenhearted" (Ps 147:3 NIV).

So, your first step is to go to the right *person*—go to God. Your second step is to assume the right *posture*—bow before God. To be anointed with the oil that heals and protects, the sheep must stand still, lower its head and let the shepherd do his work. Peter writes, "Be humble under God's powerful hand so he will lift you up when the right time comes" (1Pe 5:6 NCV). When we come to God we make requests, not demands. We state what we want, but we pray for what's right. Like Paul, if God gives us the prison in Rome instead of the mission in Spain, we accept it because we know God will always give what is right to His people (See Lk 18:7 NCV). Now, the sheep don't understand how the oil repels mosquitoes or heals wounds. In fact, all the sheep know is that something happens in the presence of their shepherd that doesn't happen anywhere else. And that's all we need to know as well. Hence David writes, "Lord, I give myself to you; my God, I trust you" (Ps 25:1-2 NCV).

STANDING IN THE GAP

I sought for a man among them who would...
stand in the gap... but I found no one.
Ezekiel 22:30 NKJV

*W*hen Chris Milbrath went to work with *Co-Mission* in the Ukraine, the last thing he envisioned was being hospitalized. He experienced a persistent stomach-ache and his doctor diagnosed a ruptured appendix and told him that without surgery he'd die. Things didn't go well and infection set in. Halfway across the world a lady who was one of Chris's supporters woke suddenly during the night. She didn't know why, but she knew she *had* to pray for him. Later, comparing notes and making adjustments for the different time zones, they discovered that her prayer-burden "just happened to coincide" with the time he was clinging to life. Within 24 hours a missions group in Moscow heard about the situation. A small jet "just happened to be available" to airlift Chris to Geneva where one of Switzerland's best surgeons "just happened to be available" to perform additional surgery that saved his life. Chris later said, "I can't help wondering what would've happened to me if that woman had just rolled over and said, 'I'll pray for Chris tomorrow.'"

God says, "I sought for a man among them who would...stand in the gap...but I found no one." Interceding is a lonely business. You don't volunteer—God calls you. True intercessors realize what's at stake and stay on their knees until they sense they've broken through and God's heard them. James writes, "When a believing person prays, great things happen" (Jas 5:16 NCV). So when God prompts you to pray for somebody, don't wait—do it! Your prayers may be the *only* thing standing between that person and catastrophe.

STAY IN TOUCH (1)

Pray all the time.
1 Thessalonians 5:17 TM

*P*aul says, "Pray all the time." Why? Because whether you're exercising, driving, shopping, or just sitting at your desk, God *loves* to hear from you—He really does. Author Cheri Fuller writes: "I used to think if I didn't pray at a certain time each day, my prayers didn't count. Then I discovered that Paul's command to 'Pray all the time,' means more than just spending a lot of time on your knees; it means having *constant* communication with God, and an increasing awareness of His presence. This didn't really sink in until my son left for college. Busy with his studies, he didn't call home often. But when he did I'd drop everything just to hear his voice! Now I realize that God feels the same way about me, only 100 times more! I also noticed throughout the Bible God used short prayers to accomplish great things—like raising the dead and parting the Red Sea. Then it dawned on me that thoughts such as, 'If I can't pray for an hour, why bother?' are foolish. It's wonderful to have longer prayer sessions when I can, but knowing short prayers have a big impact, encourages me to pray throughout the day."

Here's a remarkable thing: John writes, "There was silence in heaven for about half an hour" (Rev 8:1 NRS). Why? What were they listening to? John explains, "The prayers of the saints went up before God" (See Rev 8:4). Heaven stops to listen each time you pray. Think about that! Your thoughts, struggles, concerns and goals may not mean much to others, but they register with God and He responds to them.

STAY IN TOUCH (2)

Pray all the time.
1 Thessalonians 5:17 TM

*F*inding time to pray every day will always be a challenge for you. That's because prayer is a learned behavior; nobody ever "masters" it. So:

(1)Start your day right. When you first wake up say, "Lord, thanks for giving me this day. Help me to rejoice and be glad in it." (See Ps 118:24). Then before other demands creep in, spend time in God's Word. Let it lead you into meditation, then praise. One woman says she prays while she walks on her treadmill. She says, "I *know* those treadmill-prayers work because I've experienced the answers first-hand!" *(2) Tune in to visual clues.* Use your daily activities as springboards to prayer. For example, whenever you meet somebody, silently ask God to bless them. When you're showering, pray, "Lord, give me a clean heart and a right attitude" (See Ps 51:10). When your fellow workers act badly, pray, "Lord, make me an instrument of grace, a light where it's dark." Are these rituals? No! It's how you "pray all the time." *(3) Devise ways to stay focused.* Ever notice how your mind wanders the minute you start praying? If that's a problem try taking a note pad and jotting down the things that are distracting you. Once your mind is clear, say, "I'll get to that later," then talk to God. And remember, God wants to talk to you too, so sit still and listen. What He tells you will be more important than anything else you'll hear that day. With a little planning and some commitment, you can "pray all the time." But you have to *want* to—do you?

MONEY MATTERS

Fools spend whatever they get.
Proverbs 21:20 NLT

$\mathscr{R}$ather than exercising financial discipline, the Bible says, "Fools spend whatever they get." Here are some of their excuses: (1) "I'm okay, I'm making ends meet." That's like saying you feel great carrying too much weight. Debt is putting a strain on you, whether you notice it or not. God says, "Pay all your debts" (Ro 13:8 NLT), because when you're over-committed one financial slip can spell disaster. (2) "Interest rates are low, why worry?" Why? Because when rates increase—and they do—property values can decrease, and a hefty mortgage may mean owing more than your property is worth. Plus, when your debt-to-income ratio is too high it stops you from obtaining future credit. (3) "I plan to work till I drop." What'll happen if you can't work? Instead of just working to pay off debt, put your money to work for you. The sooner you develop a wise investment strategy, the better. "A good man leaves an inheritance for his children's children" (Pr 13:22 NIV). (4) "It's my partner's fault." Money can fuel your best dreams or your worst nightmares. It's the main reason couples argue, and the leading cause of divorce. Solomon says, "There is treasure…in the dwelling of the wise." Freedom from financial pressure means that instead of always arguing about money, you can plan how to allocate it. So get on the same page, create a financial plan you can both live with—and involve God by honoring Him with a tithe of your income (See Mal 3:10). Having God's input on your investments and His blessing on your finances, is the only way to go!

WORKPLACE CONTAMINATION

Be prepared.
Ephesians 6:13 TM

*T*he "toxins" in our work environment can invade our attitudes, thoughts and behaviors. So, stay focused on the spiritual battle that awaits you. Prepare for it each morning by putting on your armor. What armor? Listen: "Be prepared. You're up against far more than you can handle on your own. Take…every weapon God has issued, so that when it's all over but the shouting you'll still be on your feet. Truth, righteousness, peace, faith, and salvation are more than words. Learn how to apply them. You'll need them…God's Word is an indispensable weapon…prayer is essential in this ongoing warfare…Keep your eyes open. Keep each other's spirits up so that no one falls behind" (Eph 6:13-18 TM). Perhaps you'd like to pray the following prayer to get you started: "Father, thank You for the blessings of my present job. As I suit up for work today, protect me, strengthen me, use me and bless me. Let me remain focused on You, allowing Your Word and Your presence to shield me from all contaminants such as pride, insensitivity, being short-tempered, and failure to show love. My worth comes from You, not my job, so I rest in the knowledge that You see all I do and that my labor will not go unrewarded. Amen."

Ships sail on water, but if water gets in even a battleship will sink. So go through the waters of your work environment without allowing them to contaminate you. And be realistic in expecting what the job will deliver. Keep your focus on why you're there, Who sent you, Who sees you, and Who's preparing you for greater things.

CALLED TO A HIGHER STANDARD

From the one who has been entrusted with much,
much more will be asked.
Luke 12:48 NIV

*C*hristians can be some of the most sour and selective people on earth. Many times we feel obligated to show our faith by criticizing people with whom we work rather than loving them and seeking a chance to say something encouraging. We ruin our testimony because others know that while we talk about Christ, we don't act Christ-like. Often our testimony suffers because of our poor work ethic, long breaks, reading the Bible on company time, talking on the phone for hours with our friends, etc. But the worst thing is, we alienate ourselves as an elite group and leave others feeling "less than." Not Jesus! He rubbed elbows with everybody. He was adept at reaching out to those society looked down upon—the prostitutes, the tax collectors, the lepers. We like to put people into two boxes: the ones we like and the ones we don't. Jesus said, "From the one who has been entrusted with much, much more will be asked." Hey, you've been called to a higher standard; one that requires exercising wisdom, humility, and grace in the midst of tension. When King Saul threw javelins at David, he ducked and kept on serving. While he was innocent of any wrongdoing, David handled the situation without becoming "defensive." If your fellow workers don't go to church the only chance they have of seeing the fruits of the Spirit in operation, is in *your* life. By responding with patience, love and professionalism you'll make a lasting impact on them—one that could attract them to the Christ you claim to serve.

LEARN TO PACE YOURSELF!

The vision is yet for an appointed time...
Though it tarry, wait for it...it will surely come.
Habakkuk 2:3

We're multi-tasking today to the point of never focusing clearly on any one thing. If you don't take time to see the big picture, you'll get lost in the details. Ask yourself, "What is it that only I can do?" Then give yourself to that, and delegate the rest or drop it! Multi-tasking is good, but you must learn to focus without distraction on your God-ordained priorities. When we're anxious about our goals we're not being fueled by them—we're being stressed by them! You can be a great visionary, yet be out of balance and end up neglecting what's important. You can only pick what's ripe. Don't let what God's given you spoil on the vine while you chase what tomorrow may bring. Start to manage your time better. In order to be ready for the future you must learn to pace yourself so you're able to reap the harvest God has promised you. Failure to do this will cause you to ruin great opportunities because you underestimated what it would take to get you to your destination.

Don't overlook the basics like food, sleep, exercise and time with God. Some of us take better care of our dogs and cats than we do of ourselves. Too often we view sleep and exercise as luxuries and not necessities. Yes, there's a time to work late or pull an all-nighter, but this must not be a lifestyle. If you want to reach your destiny you must plan accordingly and learn to pace yourself.

DEALING WITH OUR GUILT

Repent, then, and turn to God,
so that your sins may be wiped out.
Acts 3:19 NIV

*W*hether by thought, word or deed, we all sin more than we care to admit. And there are 3 ways of dealing with it: *(1) Blow it off.* Don't think about it; don't ask what damage lies back there; don't ask if there is mopping up to do. Bury yesterday in a flood of distracting experiences. Just keep on running. Perhaps the past won't have time to catch up with us. *(2) Accept the burden and get used to it.* This means living with an increasing weight of guilt, recognizing that life will get slower and slower as the burden gets greater and greater. That's a recipe for depression. *(3) Deal with it.* A lot of us spend our lives apologizing and feeling bad about our habits and hang-ups—but we never do anything about them! Repentance literally means "a change of direction." Jesus told the story of the Prodigal Son who squandered half of his father's wealth before making a total mess of his life. When he reached a point at which the pigs he tended were eating better than he was, he finally acknowledged that he was lost: "How many of my father's hired men have food to spare, and here I am starving to death! I will…go back to my father and say to him: 'Father, I have sinned against heaven and against you'" (Lk 15:17-18 NIV). The moment he uttered those words his father opened his heart and his arms and welcomed him back home. *And God will do that for you too, if you'll just repent.*

INVEST IN YOUR RELATIONSHIPS

Love the Lord…Love your neighbor.
Matthew 22:37-39 NIV

$\mathcal{T}$hink back to your best moments: your highest highs, your greatest victories, your most daunting obstacles overcome. How many happened to you alone? Very few, right? When you understand that being connected to others is one of life's greatest joys, you realize that life's best comes when we invest in solid relationships. Of the people you know, who seems to enjoy life more—the negative, suspicious and antisocial? Hardly! The Scrooges of life don't enjoy much of anything. Jesus summed life up like this: "Love the Lord …with all your heart…Love your neighbor as yourself" (See Mt 22:37-39 NIV). On the other hand, people who love God and love people, live joyfully. If you love God and people you'll find friends wherever you go. And you'll get further in life too! John Luther says, "Natural talent, intelligence, a wonderful education—none of these guarantees success. Something else is needed: the sensitivity to understand what other people want, and a willingness to give it to them. You don't win fame, recognition or advancement just because you think you deserve it. Someone else has to think so too."

There's no substitute for a loving attitude when it comes to getting ahead. People who alienate others have a hard time. Here's why: (a) When others don't like you they'll try to hurt you. (b) If they can't hurt you they won't help you. (c) If they're forced to help you, they'll hope you don't succeed. (d) When they hope you don't succeed, life's victories are empty. So if you want more out of life, start investing in solid relationships!

BECOME A BETTER LISTENER

Be quick to listen, slow to speak.
James 1:19 NIV

*W*ant to become a good leader? Become a good listener! Here are two stories of what happens when we don't take time to listen. The first is from a young woman hurt by a manager who constantly cut her off: "We expected he would wait and give us answers to serious questions about our work. Many times he walked off when we were in mid-sentence, having heard nothing." The next is from a church youth director who was fired: "After serving the Lord there for two years, I was called into an elders' meeting. They took out a list of all the things I'd done wrong in the past two years. Most of what they said was true, for I was brand new in this work. Then they called for my resignation. What did I learn? (a) Not once did anyone care enough to coach or shepherd me. (b) I'd no idea or warning that I was doing anything wrong. (c) The church leaders never built a relationship with their staff."

Why is it so hard for leaders to listen? Because leaders love to *talk,* and as they gain more authority they think they have less reason to *listen.* Leaders by their very nature tend to be removed from the frontlines of battle. To win, they must constantly *listen* to those who are in the trenches and rely on that information to make wise decisions. Before Ezekiel was qualified to prophesy or lead God's people, he wrote: "I sat among them for seven days—overwhelmed. At the end of seven days the word of the Lord came to me" (Ez 3:15-16 NIV).

WHEN THE WALL GIVES WAY

Woe to him who builds his palace by unrighteousness.
Jeremiah 22:13

You can only hide your lack of integrity for so long. Eventually you'll experience failure, and whatever influence you've temporarily gained will be swept away. Hurricane Katrina taught us that. When the storm came the levee walls in New Orleans broke and the city went under. You see, integrity is like a wall—erected one brick at a time. That's why it's crucial to take care of the little things. A lot of us don't understand that. We think we can do whatever we want when it comes to small things; we believe so long as we don't have any major lapses we're doing well. But that's not the way it works. Webster's New International Unabridged Dictionary describes integrity as *adherence to moral and ethical principles, soundness of character, honesty.* Ethical principles are not flexible. A little white lie is still a lie. Theft is still theft, whether it's one dollar or one million. The truth is, if you can't be trusted at all points you probably can't be trusted at any point. Each time you break a moral principle you create a crack in the wall of your character, and when times get tough it becomes harder to act with integrity—not easier. You see, character isn't created in a crisis; it just comes to light. Everything you've done in the past, including the things you've neglected to do, come to a head when you're under pressure. One Christian leader writes, "Integrity commits itself to character over personal gain, people over things, service over power, discipline over impulse, commitment over convenience, and the long view over the immediate."

IN THE EYE OF THE STORM

*He that dwelleth in the secret place of the most High
shall abide under the shadow of the Almighty.*
Psalm 91:1

*T*he eye of the storm is the most peaceful place on earth. While wind and rain wreak havoc all around, pilots who fly storm-tracker planes say that all is perfectly still in that special place. In Psalm 91, David speaks about...terror... plagues...ten thousand falling at your right hand "but it will not come near you." Why? Listen: "He that dwelleth in the secret place of the most High shall abide under the shadow of the Almighty. I will say of the Lord, He is my refuge and my fortress: my God; in him will I trust. Surely he shall deliver [me]" (Ps 91:1-3).

There are two ways to go through a storm: in panic or in peace. When a storm suddenly threatened their boat the disciples cried, "Carest thou not that we perish?" (Mk 4:38). And where was Jesus? Sleeping peacefully in the back of the boat. That's because He understood: (a) to get to where God wants to take you, you must go through certain storms. It's not optional; (b) when you're in the center of God's will the storm can't take you under; it's in the storm, not the calm that you discover this; (c) when it's over you come out knowing God better and more equipped to help others! "So trust in the Lord (commit yourself to Him, lean on Him, hope confidently in Him) forever; for the Lord God is an everlasting Rock [the rock of ages]" (Isa 26:4 AMP). *That's* what it means to live in the eye of the storm!

KODAK CHRISTIANS

You will receive power…and you will be my witnesses
in Jerusalem, and in all Judea and Samaria,
and to the ends of the earth.
Acts 1:8 NIV

*I*t's possible to be so committed to preserving what's good from the past and enjoying what's good in the present—that we're blind to, or resistant to what God has for us next. Jerusalem was an exciting place to be: "All the believers met together constantly and shared everything with each other, selling their possessions and dividing with those in need. They worshiped together regularly…met in small groups in homes for Communion, and shared their meals with great joy…The whole city was favorable to them" (Ac 2:44-47 TLB). Now there's just one problem: nobody wants to leave Jerusalem and carry the message to Judea, Samaria, and the ends of the earth. Life's too good. So how does God get us out of our comfort zone to fulfill His purposes? Clearly, just *telling* us won't do it. The answer is *persecution!* And it's an idea we don't like because we tend to be *Kodak Christians*. Remember the famous Kodak Camera ad? "Freeze the moment!" Here's how God deals with Kodak Christians: "There was a great persecution against the church which was at Jerusalem; and they were all scattered abroad throughout the regions of Judea and Samaria…Those who had been scattered preached the word wherever they went" (See Ac 8:1&4). Here's a thought: God could be permitting the tough time you're going through to: (a) dig you out of your rut; (b) get you out of neutral and moving toward what He has for you next. Bottom line: staying in Jerusalem too long is bad for you.

SAVED TO SERVE

Only as you accept your part of that body
does your 'part' mean anything.
1 Corinthians 12:27 TM

*W*hen it comes to finding and fulfilling your role in God's kingdom, notice 3 things: *(1) Every believer has a ministry.* Less than 10 percent of Christians are involved in any form of service. They go to church "for what they can get out of it." Service in Christ's body isn't optional. In God's army there are no volunteers—He's drafted us all into service. *(2) Every ministry is important.* There are no insignificant ministries. Listen: "God has arranged the parts in the body, every one of them, just as he wanted them to be…The eye cannot say to the hand, 'I don't need you!'" (1Co 12:18-21 NIV). *(3) We are dependent on each other.* No single ministry can accomplish all we've been called to do. Like a jigsaw puzzle, each piece is required to complete the picture. You always notice the missing piece first, right? When one part of your body malfunctions, the other parts don't work as well. Our preoccupation with individualism must be replaced with the biblical truth that we *need* each other, that we've been *called* to work together. That doesn't mean you should try to be like somebody else; what God made you to *be,* determines what He intends for you to *do.* Your ministry is determined by your make up. When your gifts don't match the role you play, you feel like a square peg in a round hole. Not only does this produce poor results, it's also a waste of your talents, time and energy. So find your place, then make up your mind to excel in it.

SIMPLE FAITH

You must be born again.
John 3:7 TLB

*W*hen Jesus told Nicodemus, "You must be born again," Nicodemus didn't get it: "Can a man...enter into his mother's womb a second time and be born?" (Jn 3:4 NKJV). Sometimes bright people can be their own worst enemy. They think, "Unless I can explain it I can't accept it." Jesus told Nicodemus, "Look at the wind. You can't see it or control it. So is everyone who is reborn through God's Spirit" (See Jn 3:8). In other words, "You didn't have anything to do with your first birth, so you've nothing to do with your second one. God prepared your heart by sending the right people, the right circumstances, and the right word at just the right time to show you your need of Him."

In the belly of the fish Jonah prayed: "Salvation is of the Lord" (Jnh 2:9). Jonah realized, "If I'm to get out of this mess it'll have to be God's doing. I can't work my way out or reason my way out." So he prayed: "Out of the belly of hell cried I" (Jnh 2:2). Sometimes we have to go to hell and back before we're willing to do it God's way. "Without faith [trust without analysis or preconditions] it is impossible to please God" (Heb11:6 NIV). The things of God cannot be explained, only revealed. Anything less would be unfair for then the sharp folks would get it and the slow ones wouldn't. Jesus said unless we become as little children we won't even be aware of His kingdom. Our biggest struggles come from wanting a reason for everything. All God asks is that we trust Him. *When we do, life works the way it's supposed to.*

NEEDED: A SPIRITUAL MINDSET

Be ye transformed by the renewing of your mind.
Romans 12:2

*P*aul gives us two important Scriptures. First: "Be ye transformed by the renewing of your mind." Second: "Though our outward man perish, yet the inward man is renewed day by day" (2Co 4:16). Your mind is like a computer; it responds to what's programmed into it. Having a spiritual mindset means pulling out the old disk and putting in the new one. And this must be done "day by day." A Christian with a carnal mind is someone who's still receiving signals from the flesh, not the Spirit. They're frustrated because one moment they're talking out of a Spirit renewed mindset, the next moment they're talking out of a carnal one. They're being fed from both sides. Again Paul writes: "The natural man receiveth not the things of the Spirit of God: for they are...spiritually discerned" (1Co 2:14). It's important that you understand this because:

(1) A Spirit controlled mindset gives you God's input. What an advantage! God can reveal to you the motives of others, the enemy's strategy, and the pitfalls waiting down the road. He can tell you when to buy and when to sell, when to come to the table and when to walk away. Stop confining God to church!

(2) A Spirit controlled mindset gives you victory where you've known only defeat. This is especially important for those who come from addictive backgrounds and are vulnerable to "seducing spirits." The old mindset has proven it can't cope with the driving compulsions of the flesh. Without God's help we'll go back to the chaos we came from. *That's* why we need to work each day on developing a spiritual mindset!

IT'S THE MESSAGE, NOT THE MESSENGER!

He that receiveth whomsoever I send receiveth me.
John 13:20

*I*f you're wise you'll focus on the message, not the messenger. "But shouldn't leaders set a good example; shouldn't they be called to a higher standard?" Yes, those entrusted with great responsibility experience greater correction. But God does that—not you. Though King Saul repeatedly tried to kill David, David realized God had chosen Saul. When he'd a golden opportunity to take Saul's life, David said, "The Lord forbid that I should stretch forth mine hand against the Lord's anointed" (1Sa 26:11). This may come as a shock—God has no perfect messengers. So He uses what He's got. And many of them are still struggling in certain areas. They're being developed even while they're delivering the message God wants you to hear.

A perfect word from imperfect lips—that's how God does it. Samuel led Israel for 40 years. He even anointed David to be King, yet his own sons went astray. David, whom God called a man after His own heart, committed adultery and covered his tracks with murder. Yet the Bible says, "He...served the purpose of God in his own generation" (See Ac 13:36 NAS). Peter's dark chapter of denial didn't prevent him from winning multitudes to Christ. So, when a leader proves to be imperfect what should you do? (a) Learn from his or her mistakes. (b) Pray for them. After all, if you can't find mercy in the House of God where are you going to find it? (c) Keep listening to their message, for Jesus said, "He that receiveth whomsoever I send receiveth me" (Jn 13:20).

TROPHIES OF GRACE

He must…go through Samaria.
John 4:4

*I*n spite of His overwhelming schedule Jesus *walked* miles out of His way to speak to a lonely woman at a well. He did what a lot of ministers today are unwilling to do. And you have to ask why. Didn't Jesus have a secretary who said, "He's busy, I'll try and fit you in next month." Pastor, could your schedule be getting in the way of God's? Maybe you're a tiger in the pulpit but a wimp on the street. You can script it for the crowd but you haven't learned to share it one-on-one. Come on, pastor; do you personally win souls or do you just talk about it?

Jesus not only walked to that well, He *waited* until she showed up. Who did He wait for? Some famous personality with all the right connections? A big donor with a big checkbook capable of underwriting His ministry? Most preachers would fly halfway around the world for that. But no, she was a no-name, five times divorced, promiscuous woman with a bad reputation and a live-in boyfriend. Please understand: when others are looking at your past, Jesus has His eye on your future. With Him every weed is a potential rose! Whatever you've done, God's not holding it against you. Jesus didn't see this woman as *bad*—He saw her as *lost*. Big difference! Once she was "found" she was the kind of person who'd be as strong for God as she'd been for the devil. This woman was destined to shake up the entire city of Samaria: "Many of the Samaritans from that town believed in him because of the woman's testimony" (Jn 4:39 NIV).

BE CAREFUL WHO YOU PICK

Don't appoint people to
church leadership positions too hastily.
1 Timothy 5:22 TM

*I*t's dangerous to promote someone to church leadership simply because they're successful in the secular arena. We must allow time for their character to be seen. If someone is unwilling to wait, or serve in a lower spot, they probably don't have the maturity to handle a higher one. Leaders who follow in the footsteps of the One who "made himself of no reputation" (Php 2:7), nail their ego to the cross and humbly serve where there's a need. We are in a constant battle with "the spiritual forces of evil" (Eph 6:12 NIV). And how do they come in? Often on two feet, complete with resumes and talent. Paul warned Timothy, "Don't appoint people to church leadership positions too hastily." It's a lot easier to get someone on to the board than off it. Meanwhile God's work can get hurt.

When Philip went to Samaria to preach the whole city came to Christ. If ever a church needed leadership in a hurry, they did. And that's when Simon the Sorcerer showed up. Talk about a successful career! "All the people, both high and low, gave him their attention" (Ac 8:10 NIV). And that's not all: "Simon himself believed and was baptized. And he followed Philip everywhere, astonished by the...miracles he saw" (Ac 8:13 NIV). But then the mask comes off and he offers Peter money saying, "Give me this power" (Ac 8:19 NKJV). Wow! The old power play! Peter replied, "May your money perish with you...your heart is not right before God. Repent" (Ac 8:20-22 NIV). And Simon did. Be careful who you pick!

THE POWER OF CRYING OUT (1)

In my distress, I…cried unto my God.
Psalm 18:6

*I*n his book, *The Power Of Crying Out,* Bill Gothard writes: "The most significant difference between the prayers of God's people in Scripture (so powerfully effective) and our prayers today (so seemingly ineffective) is this: *there was a fervency in the prayers of biblical saints—a fervency that is inherent in crying out.* When we grasp this fact, the pages of Scripture come alive with sound!"

David said: "In my distress, I…cried unto my God: he heard my voice" (Ps 18:6). The Hebrew word that describes David's outcry is *shava,* a higher pitched cry for help. Again the Psalmist says: "I called to you for help and you healed me" (Ps 30:2 NIV). We know from our own families that a true father's heart hears his children's cries, and that his children naturally cry to him. In the same way, crying out to God is our child-to-father impulse, planted within us by the Holy Spirit. "[Because we are His children]," Paul says, "[We] have received the Spirit of adoption, whereby we cry, 'Abba, Father!'" (Ro 8:15). The Greek verb here for crying out is a strong word usually translated as "shouting." Away with dignity and decorum! Desperate situations call for desperate measures. We must allow the Holy Spirit to cry out from within us. Why? Because God *hears* and *answers* the cry He Himself inspires. Ever found yourself deliberately suppressing an urge to cry out to God? Could you be quenching the Spirit of God? If so, it's time to make a change—to respond to Him in humility and obedience by "crying out."

THE POWER OF CRYING OUT (2)

In the day when I cried out, You answered me.
Psalm 138:3 NKJV

*M*ost of us find it humbling and difficult to cry out to God in times of trouble. Especially men! They prefer to be known as the strong, rugged, self-sufficient types. They'd rather endure tenaciously and conclude with pride, "I did it."

Bill Gothard tells of several thousand men kneeling in a convention center in Knoxville, Tennessee, crying out in a loud voice, "Abba, Father, in the name of Jesus deliver me from anger and lust!" Some months later a man who had battled pornography for many years wrote to him saying: "I have long been held captive by lust. In the third grade I picked up what looked like a comic book. It was my first exposure to pornography. My young heart was captured. Lust nearly ruined my marriage on numerous occasions. I wanted to be free from it and confessed it many times to God. I even sought help from Christian counselors. In May 2001 your message on crying out was given at our men's meeting. For two more weeks I struggled with lust. Finally, on the way to work I stopped the car and cried out to God for deliverance. God was faithful, and the bondage has been broken."

David said, "In the day when I cried out, you answered me, and made me bold with strength in my soul." If you've tried every way you know without success, why not try God's way? Do what men and women have done throughout the Scriptures —get alone with God and cry out to Him. He'll give you the strength to say "no" to your old ways.

LOOKING FOR JESUS

Sir, we would see Jesus.
John 12:21

*O*ne day some Greeks came to Philip saying, "Sir, we would see Jesus." And if you listen—that's what people around you are still saying today. You say, "Tell them to go to church and they'll see Jesus." Maybe, maybe not. Get close to some folks who fill a church pew every Sunday and you just might see the devil at work. One of America's finest ministers was sitting on a plane one day reading his Bible. The lady in the next seat turned to him and asked, "Are you a preacher?" He said, "Yes, Ma'am." Then she asked, "Do you believe in a real literal devil?" With a chuckle he replied, "Lady, have you ever been to an annual church business meeting?" You may smile, but if you've been in church a while you know he's telling the truth.

Board member, people are looking for more than just a good budget, they want to see Jesus—in you. *Choir member,* you may sing like an angel and bring the house down, but when your song ends people want to see Jesus—in you. *Pastor,* you may be a skilled expositor and a gifted orator, but when the sermon's over people want to see Jesus—in you. *Sir, lady,* when you get through telling the folks at work what you stand for, they want to see Jesus—in you. You don't have to defend Him, just display Him through your attitudes and actions each day. Jesus said, "If I be lifted up...[I] will draw all men unto me" (Jn 12:32). We do the lifting; Jesus does the drawing—that's how it works!

DON'T GET HOOKED

Ye know not what manner of spirit ye are of.
Luke 9:55

*F*ace it; some people are unwilling to take responsibility for their lot in life, so they plough through each day complaining about everything. And because they're incapable of loving themselves they can't extend love to others. Often their negative edge just masks their real struggle. Deep down they're afraid of being rejected, so they don't get too close to anyone—except kindred spirits.

So how should you respond to such people? Don't get hooked! If you can't lift them up, make sure they don't drag you down. When Nehemiah's enemies criticized the wall he was building he replied, "I am doing a great work! Why should I stop it to come and visit with you?" (Ne 6:3 TLB). And what was the result? "The wall was finally finished...just fifty-two days after we had begun! When our enemies...heard about it, they were...humiliated, and they realized that the work had been done with the help of our God" (Ne 6:15 TLB). Was it easy working around people like that? No. How did Nehemiah do it? When he started getting discouraged he prayed, "Lord God, please strengthen me!" (Ne 6:8 TLB). Notice, he didn't say, "Lord, zap them." Or, "Lord, make them nice to me." No, he asked for strength, maintained a good attitude and prayed that God would take care of his critics. And God did. Many of the people who aggravate you have no idea why—it's just their nature. When Christ's own disciples wanted to call down fire on the heads of those who wouldn't accept their message, Jesus said, "Ye know not what manner of spirit ye are of."

JUST GLOVES

The Holy Spirit…will produce this kind of fruit in us.
Galatians 5:22 TLB

*W*e are just the glove. The Holy Spirit is the hand that fills it, empowers it and makes it function. Without Him, we're sunk! The Christian life isn't hard, it's impossible—without God's indwelling Spirit. "What will the Holy Spirit do for me?" you ask.

(1) Move you forward. "The earth was without form, and void…the spirit of God moved…and God said, Let there be light: and there was light" (Ge 1:2-3). The first thing God's Spirit will do for you is move you out of darkness and into light [understanding]. You can't be filled with God's Spirit and stay where you are; He'll always move you forward. *(2) Comfort you.* Jesus referred to the Holy Spirit as the "comforter" who would never leave us (See Jn 14:16). When you wake up anxious about your day He whispers, "Don't worry, I've got everything under control." When you feel like you can't go on, He holds your hand, stays by your side, strengthens you and says "I'm right here with you." The Greek word for comforter is *paraklete,* which means, "one who comes alongside to help." What a promise! You're not in this fight alone—you've got God's help. Use it! *(3) Protect you.* "When the enemy shall come in like a flood, the spirit of the Lord shall lift up a standard against him" (Isa 59:19). When the enemy moves against you all you have to do is pray, "Holy Spirit, be my standard bearer and my defender." Go ahead; try it. Those who did it in Bible days saw their foes scattered, took home the spoils of battle and enjoyed God's richest blessings—and you will too!

BUY A TENT!

Anyone inquiring of the Lord would go to the tent.
Exodus 33:7 NIV

$\mathcal{M}$oses did something we need to do: "Moses used to take a tent and pitch it outside the camp some distance away, calling it the 'tent of meeting.' Anyone inquiring of the Lord would go to the tent" (Ex 33:7 NIV). And what would happen in that tent? "The Lord would speak to Moses face to face, as a man speaks with his friend" (Ex 33:11 NIV). Face time with God! *That's* what you need. Turn off your mobile phone. Sell your TV and buy a tent. God has your answer.

And what did they talk about in that tent? Moses prayed: (a) "Let me know whom you will send with me" (Ex 33:12 NIV). Some of the problems you're experiencing are because of the people who are influencing you. (b) "Teach me your ways" (Ex 33:13 NIV). You say your way of doing things doesn't seem to be working too well. Get God's input! (c) "So I may know you" (Ex 33:13 NIV). This word "know" is not a casual acquaintance; it's intimacy between two people. How well do you know God? (d) "So I may…continue to find favor with you" (Ex 33:13 NIV). God's favor—you've got to have it! It opens doors, gives you the advantage, and influences people before you speak a word. And what did God say back to Moses in that tent? "I will do the very thing you have asked, because I am pleased with you and I know you by name" (Ex 33:17 NIV). How would you like to be on a first name basis with God? Buy a tent!

WHERE GOD GUIDES, HE PROVIDES!

A great door…has opened to me.
1 Corinthians 16:9 NIV

*D*r. David T. Demola says, "Where God guides, He provides." If you're doing all you know yet nothing's happening, it could be that: (a) it's your season for sowing, not reaping. So be patient; (b) you're in a time of training and preparation. So learn each lesson well; (c) you could be off course, doing something God didn't call you to do. So go back and check with Him. Moses told God: "If your Presence does not go with us, do not send us" (Ex 33:15 NIV). If God's not behind it, you don't want to be involved in it. Humility demands that sometimes we stop and say—"Oops, that was me, not God."

Does this mean it's always smooth sailing in God's will? No. Even when God is in something you'll still deal with delays, discouragement and setbacks. Paul wrote, "A great door for effective work has opened to me, and there are many who oppose me" (1Co 16:9 NIV). Opportunities and obstacles, they go together. What you *don't* want to do, however, is allow it to become a self-esteem issue: "Does God love me? Has He really called me? Am I in His will?" Jesus took His disciples on a trip that involved going through the worst storm of their lives. All you need to know is that *He's* on board. Why? Because He's promised to bless *His* plans, not yours. If God's guiding, providing and blessing you in spite of the storm, rejoice. If He's not, seek fresh direction. Ask Him what He wants you to do. God will bless you every time—when you're doing what He's told you to do.

SEVEN LESSONS FROM THE CROSS (1)

Father, forgive them; they don't know what they're doing.
Luke 23:34 TM

Lesson 1: Forgive those who hurt you. Two kids were playing when one accidentally hit the other with a stick. That night the injured boy's Mom said, "Son, you must forgive Harry before you go to sleep." Grudgingly he replied, "Okay, but unless I die before I wake up, he'd better watch out tomorrow morning!" Hello! When people hurt us it's hard to believe it could've been unintentional or done in ignorance. Yet amazingly, after being flogged, humiliated and nailed to the cross, Jesus said, "Father, forgive them; they don't know what they're doing." Forgiving means refusing to remain a victim. By not holding grudges or retaliating you free yourself from the control of those who offend you. Jesus said, "Pray for anyone who mistreats you" (Mt 5:44 CEV). Dietrich Bonhoeffer, who was persecuted by the Nazis, said, "God doesn't promise that when we bless our enemies they'll not despitefully use us. They will. But that can't hurt or overcome us, so long as we pray for them. By praying for them, we are doing for them what they can't do for themselves."

Professor Tony Campolo routinely asks his secular college students what they know about the teachings of Jesus. The response is always the same: "Love your enemies." More than anything else this command stands out as the thing that differentiates Christians from non-Christians. Jesus said, "Give as freely as you have received!" (Mt 10:8 NLT). Practicing forgiveness stems from a deep gratitude to God for wiping out a debt so great, we could *never* have repaid it.

SEVEN LESSONS FROM THE CROSS (2)

Assuredly...today you will be with Me in Paradise.
Luke 23:43 NKJV

Lesson 2: Reach out to others. When Jesus was hanging on the cross the Bible says, "One of the criminals hanging alongside cursed him...But the other...made him shut up: 'Have you no fear of God...We deserve this...he did nothing.' Then he said, 'Jesus, remember me when you enter your kingdom.' [Jesus] said...'Today you will join me in paradise'" (Lk 23:39-43 TM). While one man mocked, the other acknowledged his sins and received mercy. The truth is, as much as it galls judgmental people, God said, "If you confess and reject [your sin], you *will* receive mercy" (Pr 28:13 NCV). And that promise is for the lost, the least, and the lowest among us.

Jesus could have been so focused on His own pain that He failed to see the suffering of those around Him. But instead He reached out in love as a fellow-sufferer. In the depth of His own agony He not only promised the thief on the cross eternal life, He comforted him with these amazing words; "Today you will be with Me in Paradise!" There's a lesson here for you—one that Job the patriarch learned. Job lost all his children and his fortune in a single day; how did he stay sane? Yet he found healing and went on to greater things. How? *"After Job had prayed for his friends,* the Lord made him prosperous again and gave him twice as much as he had before...After this, Job... saw his children and their children to the fourth generation" (Job 42:10 &16 NIV). It's in reaching out to others that we ourselves are restored again.

SEVEN LESSONS FROM THE CROSS (3)

Woman, here is your son.
John 19:26-27 TM

*L*esson 3: *Take care of the people who depend on you.* In addition to losing her son, Mary was also losing His protective "covering" in a society where women were often treated as second-class citizens after the family males died. So as well as coping with her grief as a mother, Mary may have been wondering what the future held for her. Jesus recognized that. In the midst of the chaos, when He saw her and "the disciple he loved standing near…He said to his mother, 'Woman, here is your son.' Then to the disciple, 'Here is your mother.'" When the other disciples fled in fear, John followed Jesus all the way to Calvary. Then he went even further. The Bible tells us (and history confirms it) that once Jesus committed Mary to his care, John fulfilled that charge, and "From that moment… accepted her as his own mother" (Jn 19:26-27 TM).

Here's what we learn from this. *Never let your own suffering blind you to the needs of those who depend on you.* When you're enmeshed in your own problems it's easy to assume that your loved ones automatically understand where you're coming from. Not necessarily. While it's okay to let them help, never "dump your stuff" on them, or expect them to suffer because you're suffering. The Bible says, "Do not let selfishness …be your guide…give more honor to others than to yourselves. Do not be interested only in your own life, but…in the lives of others" (Php 2:3-4 NCV). Jesus was *always* more concerned with other people's needs than His own—and we should take our cue from Him.

SEVEN LESSONS FROM THE CROSS (4)

God, why have You forsaken Me?
Matthew 27:46 NKJV

Lesson 4: Direct the hard questions to God. At Calvary Jesus asks one of the most heart-wrenching questions ever recorded, "God, why have You forsaken Me?" These words are also found in Psalm 22:1-3 (TM), where David poured out his soul in despair, asking God, "Why did you dump me... Are you indifferent?" Ever felt like that? The Bible says that at Calvary God made Jesus "who knew no sin to be sin...so ...we might become the righteousness of God in Him" (2Co 5:21 NAS). In order to break sin's hold on us and make salvation possible, Jesus underwent a temporary separation from His Father. At that moment He felt "Godforsaken." If you've ever felt overwhelmed and abandoned, you know from experience that there's not another living soul who has a satisfactory answer to your "Why?" With the best of intentions our loved ones can only go so far. God alone can pour His healing balm into your breaking heart and help you make sense of (or at least accept) what's happening. That's why you need to go to *Him* for your answers.

But here's the flip side to directing the tough questions to God—you must be willing to *accept* His answer and do what He says. The Bible says, "God has given us...his promise and his oath" (Heb 6:18 NLT), so even if you don't get the answer you want, you can rest assured He hears you. You can also be certain of something else: the One Who makes "everything... work together for...good" (Ro 8:28 NLT) always sends the answer that's in your best interests. So you can trust Him!

SEVEN LESSONS FROM THE CROSS (5)

I'm thirsty!
John 19:28 TM

Lesson 5: Acknowledge your humanity. Combine the torment of being crucified in the intense Judean heat, with the loss of bodily fluids, and you can understand why Jesus was thirsty. However, the Bible says that when they offered Him water containing "a mild painkiller…he wouldn't take it" (Mk 15:23 TM). Why? Because it would have dulled His senses and He wanted to stay alert. Make no mistake, Jesus could have summoned a host of angels to deliver Him. But instead He chose to die for our sins. He said, "No one takes my life…I give it up willingly!" (Jn 10:18 CEV). This also explains why John wrote: "Jesus, seeing…everything had been completed" (He deliberately fulfilled every Old Testament prophecy concerning His crucifixion) said "I'm thirsty!" His next statement would be so history changing that He wanted His voice to be loud and clear: "It is finished!"

When you're in a dark valley like Jesus was that day it can cloud your thinking and make you lose perspective—unless you voice your needs to those around you. By acknowledging His physical thirst, Jesus reminded each of us that there are times when we're not self-sufficient, when we need help from others. Why else would Paul write: "Bear one another's burdens, and… fulfill the law of Christ" (Gal 6:2 NAS)?

David writes: "As a father has compassion on his children …the Lord…remembers that we are dust" (Ps 103:13-14 NIV). *God* remembers we are just human—*we* are the ones who forget! The bottom line is, Jesus was humble enough to acknowledge His humanity, and we need to learn to do the same.

SEVEN LESSONS FROM THE CROSS (6)

It is finished.
John 19:30 NKJV

Lesson 6: You can add nothing to it. In the Old Testament tabernacle there were different items of furniture such as the table of showbread representing our need for fellowship, the lamp stand representing our need for light and understanding, etc. But there were no chairs. Why? Because the priest's work was never finished! He couldn't sit down. But after Jesus cried, "It is finished" He returned to heaven and sat down at the right hand of His Father—the work of redemption was complete! The Greek words for "It is finished" literally mean "paid in full." It's what folks in those days wrote across a receipt when the bill was paid. Christ's death covers your every sin—from the cradle to the grave. And to offer your good works as partial payment, insults God. You can't add to a finished work! Imagine seeing a finely crafted coffee table sitting in a carpentry shop ready for delivery. You reach for a wood plane and say, "It's good, but not good enough, let me show you." The master carpenter immediately steps in and says, "No, you'll ruin it!" Or imagine receiving a very expensive gift from a loved one. Immediately you pull out a $5 bill and say, "Here, let me help you with the cost." No, the smaller the gift the greater the offense. You're robbing the giver of his joy and the sacrifice of its worth. Listen: "This is not from yourselves, it is the gift of God—not by works, so that no one can boast" (Eph 2:8-9 NIV). Saving faith requires —trusting only in a finished work of Christ!

SEVEN LESSONS FROM THE CROSS (7)

Into Your hands I commit My spirit.
Luke 23:46 NKJV

Lesson 7: Release it to God. Some of the issues we struggle with seem to be never-ending, like money worries, family problems and health concerns. Even when we get a break and should be resting, we sit up anticipating the worst, wondering, "How long, Lord?" The only way to have *real* peace is to commit the outcome to God. When Jesus cried, "Father, into your hands I commit my spirit," it wasn't a cry of defeat or resignation. No, it was an act of trust that meant surrendering control to the Father. His atoning blood had been shed, salvation's work was finally complete. But before Jesus could pray that prayer He first had to pray, "Not my will, but yours be done" (Lk 22:42 NIV). And that's a prayer we must each learn to pray.

In Philippians 3:10 Paul wrote, "I want…to know Christ and the power that raised him to life…to suffer and die as he did…that…I…may be raised to life" (CEV). We all want to rule and reign with Christ *some day,* we just don't want to submit our will to His *today.* But it doesn't work like that. Jack Hayford writes: "The charted course…always has been… 'the way of the cross.' The cross not only calls us to *Jesus,* it also calls us to a *life,* to the wisdom of God's ways in all our relationships and pursuits…to the pattern of Jesus…in the face of our deepest struggles." So whatever you're wrestling with today, release it to God once and for all. When you do you'll experience His peace, *and* you won't be disappointed with the outcome.

IN SPITE OF EVERYTHING—HE LOVES YOU!

His unfailing love…
is as great as the height of the heavens above.
Psalm 103:11 NLT

*N*o matter what the other disciples told him about the resurrection, Thomas wanted to see for himself—so for 7 days he sat on his hands. He needed firsthand evidence. And Jesus gave it to him. "Put your finger here and see my hands. Put your hand into the wound in my side. Don't be faithless any longer. Believe!" (Jn 20:27 NLT). And Thomas did—"My Lord and my God!" (Jn 20:28 NLT). Only God could come back from the dead. And only a God of love would come back for a doubter.

Know what? Our doubts don't separate us from God's love! Listen: "For his unfailing love toward those who fear him is as great as the height of the heavens above" (Ps 103:11 NLT). The big news of the Bible is not that you love God—but that He loves you! He says your name is engraved on the palm of His hand. His thoughts of you outnumber the grains of sand on the beach. He sees the worst in you yet still believes the best. Your sins of yesterday and your failings in the future don't surprise Him; He knows them all. Every day and every deed of your life has passed before His eyes and been calculated in His decision. He knows you better than you know yourself. And He's reached His verdict: "I love you!" No discovery will disillusion Him, no rebellion dissuade Him. He loves you with an unfailing love, and that knowledge can lift you, restore you and put you back on your feet.

WHAT FOLLOWERS SHOULD EXPECT

Honor one another above yourselves.
Romans 12:10 NIV

If God's called you to lead, more is required of you. Those you're called to lead have the right to expect 8 things:

(1) To know your character. If I follow you will I know who you really are? Will you deal with me with integrity? (2) That you'll take the time to explain your vision. What's the future and where do I fit? Is there a place for me or will you simply use me? (3) To never be left in isolation. Will you 'be there' for me? Will you love me? Will you care about my needs? (4) To be heard. To whom will you listen? When you're busy and overloaded will I still be heard, taken seriously and appreciated? (5) To be trusted. Can I take initiative without fear? Will my ideas be rewarded and encouraged or will I be regarded with suspicion and distanced? (6) To be given an opportunity to grow. Will I be encouraged to be a lifelong learner? Will my gifts be increasingly identified and expressed? Will I be developed? (7) To be held accountable. Will I be fairly evaluated for my performance? Will I be lovingly held to the highest standards and to God's best for my life? Will you show me how to do it better and be patient while I learn and self-correct? (8) To be the object of grace. Will I be forgiven even in the face of shortcomings, inadequacies and failure? Will I have the freedom to be who God made me to be? Will I be led with kindness? *That's* what followers have the right to expect of you—so don't let them down!

UNDERSTANDING THE LORD'S PRAYER (1)

Lord, teach us to pray.
Luke 11:1

One day Jesus' disciples watched and listened as He prayed. When He got through they said: "Lord, teach us to pray." As a result He gave them what's become known as "The Lord's Prayer." Can you remember when you last prayed it? If not, how come? Maybe you learned it by rote and you don't understand its significance or power. Or perhaps it was repeated like a meaningless ritual at the end of a church service as people put on their coats and headed for the parking lot. That tells you more about the hearts of the people than the power of the prayer. "Well, I think we need more contemporary prayers geared toward fast-trackers." Really? Have you listened to some of the stuff they've replaced the Lord's Prayer with? Jesus warned us about prayers that are just "babbling" (See Mt 6:7 NIV). There are lots of prayers in the Bible: prayers for deliverance, for guidance, for forgiveness, for unity, etc. Here's the score: when you pray it should be (a) passionate; (b) scriptural; (c) intimate; (d) unhurried; (e) faith-filled. Take a moment and meditate on each of those 5 things. They're your keys to answered prayer.

We only tend to keep doing what rewards us, so when prayer becomes an unrewarding experience we quit. If that's why you no longer pray The Lord's Prayer, don't feel condemned—feel challenged. For the next few days let's go back to the *only* prayer Jesus Himself gave us to pray. After all, who knows more about prayer? Can you imagine Jesus giving us a prayer that didn't move God, get a hearing and bring the needed answers?

UNDERSTANDING THE LORD'S PRAYER (2)

Our Father.
Matthew 6:9

*J*esus taught His disciples to pray: "After this manner therefore pray ye: Our Father" (Mt 6:9). Don't miss this: the relationship you have with someone determines the level of comfort and confidence with which you approach them. So Jesus begins by emphasizing:

The person. "Our Father." Now, if you had an absentee father who was never there for you, or an abusive father who hurt you, or an emotionally unavailable father who never showed you much love or acceptance, then you need a new concept of God—a Scriptural one; otherwise your past will sabotage you. Before you can trust someone you have to know they really care about you. Once that happens you'll open up to them. Only then can your wounded areas be made whole. "Our Father"—that puts an address on the envelope! You need to understand Who you're talking to and the relationship you have with Him. You approach God on the basis of who you are to Him, and Who He is to you. Your Heavenly Father is a covenant making, covenant keeping God. When two people in Bible days made a covenant it wasn't a casual "call me sometime" with no commitment. No, they sealed it with blood, meaning, "I'll give my life for you if necessary."

You can actually call God "Papa" without a trace of irreverence: "This resurrection life you received from God is… adventurously expectant, greeting God with a childlike 'What's next, Papa?'…We know who he is, and we know who we are: Father and children" (Ro 8:15-17 TM). So, to pray the Lord's Prayer effectively we must recognize and rejoice in who He is to us—"our Father."

UNDERSTANDING THE LORD'S PRAYER (3)

Which art in heaven.
Matthew 6:9

*W*hen we pray to the God Who is in heaven, we recognize:

His position. Daniel said, "The Most High rules in the kingdom of men" (Da 4:17 NKJV). That's God's answer to frightening headlines and fear-filled hearts. A late-night TV comedian recently quipped: "Tsunamis, earthquakes, hurricanes, tornadoes, floods, and now the Avian Flu. Maybe this isn't such a good time to be trying to take God out of the Pledge of Allegiance." If God is not in control—who is? The President? The Prime Minister? Nice folks, and no doubt well intentioned, but not good enough if you enjoy the idea of sleeping peacefully in your bed at night. The Psalmist said, "My help cometh from the Lord" (Ps 121:2). Think: if He's Lord over every circumstance, and if He's promised to help us when we call on Him, what do we have to worry about?

You say, "What about terrorism? The Middle East?" No problem. God had it all on the drawing board before a shot was fired. God moves men and nations like we move pawns in a chess game. Look at modern day Israel. God promised 3,000 years ago: "I will bring back my exiled people Israel; they will rebuild the ruined cities and live in them…never again to be uprooted from the land I have given them, says the Lord your God" (Am 9:14-15 NIV). Still think God's not running the show? He's God, and He's in charge. And one more thing you need to know: "At the Name of Jesus every knee should bow… and…every tongue should confess that Jesus Christ is Lord, to the glory of God the Father" (Php 2:10-11).

UNDERSTANDING THE LORD'S PRAYER (4)

Hallowed be thy name.
Matthew 6:9

*I*f you ever get invited to Buckingham Palace and have the privilege of meeting the Queen, don't show up in cut-off blue jeans and a raggedy T-shirt. They won't let you in. You're not coming to a pizza parlor, you're entering a palace, you're addressing royalty. Keep that in mind. When Jesus told us to pray, "Hallowed be thy name," He was teaching us:

His protocol. There's only one way to enter God's presence. And it's not with a shopping list of all the things you want. If the only time someone comes to visit you is when they need something, you'll soon stop answering the door. David tells us how to approach God: "Know ye that the Lord he is God: it is he that hath made us, and not we ourselves...Enter into his gates with thanksgiving, and into his courts with praise: be thankful unto him, and bless his name" (Ps 100:3-4). Did you get that? We should enter His gates with thanksgiving for all He's *done*. Then walk across His courtyard with praise for Who He *is:* "My Savior, my deliverer, my defender, my provider, my source of strength, my way-maker, the center of my joy, the lover of my soul, the author and finisher of my faith." You say, "But I'm not the emotional type." Come on, you've no trouble expressing yourself when your team's winning. Whether you're a *morning* person or a *night* person, the Bible says, "From the rising of the sun unto the going down of the same the Lord's name is to be praised" (Ps 113:3). The way to enter, to enjoy, and to live in God's presence—is through praise.

UNDERSTANDING THE LORD'S PRAYER (5)

Thy kingdom come. Thy will be done.
Matthew 6:10

*I*n the kingdom of self, you rule. By the way, how are things going in *your* kingdom these days? Not too well? That's because the wrong person's in charge! In the Kingdom of God, Christ rules. His Word settles all issues. No, "Yeah, buts." When Jesus taught us to pray "Thy kingdom come. Thy will be done," He was teaching us:

His priorities. The fastest route to success in any job is to find out what the boss wants, and get it done with excellence. Bosses notice people like that. Jesus said, "Seek ye first the kingdom of God [His agenda, His priorities]" (Mt 6:33). The rules are different in God's kingdom: (1) The way up, is down. "Humble yourselves...that he may exalt you in due time" (1Pe 5:6). Note the words, "due time." Your blessing is already scheduled on God's calendar. Just keep your head down. (2) By forgiving others you free yourself. At the point of forgiveness, all the energy lost to self-pity and resentment is reclaimed and redirected—and you get your peace back. What a deal! One of the last songs Elvis ever sang was, "I Did It My Way." In the Kingdom of God we do it *His* way. Each time God's will is done, a little more of His Kingdom comes. "But why do we have to pray, 'Thy kingdom come. Thy will be done in earth, as it is in heaven?'" Because *we* can't make it happen! The needed energy must come from another source. So, our prayers are more than just an invitation for God to show up—they're the conduit through which His Kingdom power flows into our circumstances.

UNDERSTANDING THE LORD'S PRAYER (6)

Give us this day our daily bread.
Matthew 6:11

*T*here are 2 reasons for praying, "Give us this day our daily bread" and they have to do with:

His provision. First, while we may have so much food that our prayer is, "Lord, help me to lose some weight," multitudes go to bed hungry. They pray this prayer because without an answer they won't make it. And we dare not turn away from them because: "God blesses those who are kind to the poor. He helps them out of their troubles. He protects them...he publicly honors them and destroys the power of their enemies" (Ps 41:1-2 TLB). Second, Jesus said, "Man shall not live by bread alone, but by every word that proceedeth out of the mouth of God" (Mt 4:4). Note the phrase "every word." Some of the bread He feeds us is pleasant; some is painful. And we need both. "Ice cream Christians" pick Scriptures that make them *feel* good. As a result they don't develop the spiritual muscle required to stand strong in the hard times. God's promise to you is, "No weapon that is formed against thee shall prosper" (Isa 54:17). Quit praying that the weapon won't be formed. It will. Just eat right and it won't prosper. It's easy to tell when you're not eating right. People get on your nerves, you go through mood swings, you cave into fear. If that describes you, it's time to pray: "Lord, I'm nervous, give me the bread. Lord, I'm moody, give me the bread. Lord, I'm going through too many temptations and messing up, give me the bread." The truth is, without your daily bread you won't make it!

UNDERSTANDING THE LORD'S PRAYER (7)

Forgive us our debts, as we forgive our debtors.
Matthew 6:12

*T*his is a risky part of the Lord's Prayer. It takes away our right to exact revenge, harbor resentment, or even talk about the situation to others. Here Jesus points us to:

His pardon. Have you been overlooked? Betrayed? Misunderstood? Do you keep giving to others but it never seems to come back? Jesus said, "Offenses will come." So where are you going to go? To the cross. Christ forgave His enemies when He had the power to destroy them. Think, if God: (a) were as selective in forgiving as you are; (b) took His time so you could suffer; (c) told everybody who'd listen what you've done to Him; (d) forgave, but refused to give you another chance; (e) made up His mind to distance and avoid you; (f) next time you were in trouble, refused to help you saying, "Huh, it couldn't have happened to a nicer person," could you live with that? No? Then extend to others the same forgiveness God extends to you. When you pray "Forgive us our debts, as we forgive our debtors" you're asking for a change of heart! Nehemiah writes, "Thou art a God ready to pardon" (Ne 9:17). Aren't you glad he didn't write, "Thou art a God ready to put us on probation." No, pardon is God's fixed attitude toward us. The pardon was in place before the offense was committed. Wow! That unburdens us and sets us free. The only place bitterness can live is in our memory. The only power it can have over us, is the power we give it. Remember that, next time you pray The Lord's Prayer.

UNDERSTANDING THE LORD'S PRAYER (8)

Lead us not into temptation, but deliver us from evil.
Matthew 6:13

*W*hen Jesus taught us to pray "Lead us not into temptation, but deliver us from evil," He was teaching us to pray for:

His protection. Protection from what? "The evil one." Does Satan have power? Look back. Haven't you played into his hands more than once? His agenda is still to "kill, steal and destroy" (Jn 10:10). Satan would rather you never hear these words: "God's Spirit, who is in you, is greater than the devil, who is in the world" (1Jn 4:4 NCV). God told the first century church in Smyrna, "Do not be afraid of what you are about to suffer. I tell you, the devil will put some of you in prison to test you, and you will suffer for ten days. But be faithful, even if you have to die, and I will give you the crown of life" (Rev 2:10 NCV). Notice, God tells them how *long* the attack will last ("ten days"), the *reason* for the attack ("to test you"), and the *outcome* of the attack ("a crown of life"). Every time Satan tries to score—we win! When Satan knocks us down, God picks us up. David, who'd experienced more than his fair share of slips, writes, "The steps of the godly are directed by the Lord...Though they stumble, they will not fall [stay down], for the Lord holds them by the hand" (Ps 37:23-24 NLT). The Lord's Prayer teaches us to pray for protection because the walk is too treacherous to make alone. So we place our small hand into God's big hand and say, "Father, keep me from evil."

UNDERSTANDING THE LORD'S PRAYER (9)

Thine is the kingdom, and the power,
and the glory, for ever, Amen.
Matthew 6:13

*W*hen Christ taught us to pray, "Thine is the Kingdom, and the power, and the glory" He was pointing us to:

His pre-eminence. As we come to the close of The Lord's Prayer the danger is that we'll skim the surface, miss the truth, think it's a nice ending and dismiss it. "Thine is the Kingdom," reminds us that if Jesus is not Lord over all, He's not Lord at all. When you wake up in the morning you should pray: "Father, help me to paint a compelling picture to everyone I meet this day, of how much better life works when it's lived according to the rules of Your Kingdom." "Thine is...the power" reminds us that the purpose of God for our lives can only be fulfilled through God's power at work within us. Self-help is no help! Paul says, "They that are in the flesh cannot please God" (Ro 8:8). Then he adds, "They that are Christ's have crucified the flesh with the affections and lusts. If we live in the Spirit, let us also walk in the Spirit" (Gal 5:24-25). "Thine is...the glory," reminds us that the credit for *all* our achievements must be passed on to the One Who deserves it. Queen Victoria once said that her greatest joy was not to live in a palace or be loved by devoted subjects, but to one day lay down her crown at the feet of Jesus. Do you feel that way? These words simply mean "Lord, You are in charge, not me; You have the power, I don't. And You alone will receive all the glory."

DO YOU KEEP YOUR WORD?

Keep your word even when it costs you.
Psalm 15:5 TM

*I*n 1942 as war threatened the Pacific, Douglas MacArthur told the people of the Philippines, "I shall return." In a speech in Australia 9 days later, the 62-year-old statesman reaffirmed his promise saying, "I shall return." Two and a half years later when he went back to the Philippines he announced, "This is...General MacArthur...I have returned!" Despite overwhelming odds the old soldier kept his promise. That kind of integrity is hard to find these days. In fact the Bible tells us, "In the last days...men...shall be...trucebreakers" (2Ti 3:1-3). Nowadays we question the promises of politicians, business can no longer be conducted on a handshake, parents have good reason to doubt their kids, and even Christians don't do what they say. Solomon says it's "better not to vow than to... not fulfill it" (Ecc 5:5 NIV). And Paul adds: "Whatever you do in word or deed, do...in the name of the Lord Jesus" (Col 3:17 NAS). In Psalms David asks: "Lord, who may...find refuge...on your holy hill?" Here's the answer: "Anyone who leads a blameless life...is truly sincere...and keeps a promise even if it ruins him" (Ps 15:2 TLB). So how about it, do you keep your word even when it costs you? For example, when you promise to pray for somebody—do you? When you say you'll be somewhere on time—are you? When you tell people they can depend on you—can they? When you agree to repay your financial obligations on time—do you? Granted, nobody's perfect. But when you fail, do you admit your mistake without making excuses? As Christ's disciple you should.

STEWARDS—NOT OWNERS!

He must increase, but I must decrease.
John 3:30

*W*hen the crowds left John the Baptist to follow Jesus, he said: "This is the assigned moment for him to move into the center, while I slip off to the sidelines" (Jn 3:30 TM). John thought like a steward. A steward simply manages something for the owner until he comes to take it back. John knew that the crowd leaving him for Christ was never his to begin with. God had simply placed them under his care for a period of time to accomplish certain purposes. With John this was apparently just fine.

John's view of stewardship presents us with an important principle. For his crowds may be our careers, our assets, our natural and spiritual gifts, etc. Are these things owned or merely managed in the name of the One Who entrusted them to us? Your answer depends on whether you're *called* or *driven*. Driven people consider them owned; called people don't. When driven people lose things it's a major crisis; when called people lose them, nothing's changed. Why? Because their calling is not to a position, it's to a person—the person of Christ. Knowing who he was *not,* was the beginning of John knowing who he *was*. And who was he? A steward! And he didn't aspire to anything beyond that.

What is success, as God counts success? It's when others hear you, but follow Jesus. It's when others see some quality in *you* that causes them to fall more in love with *Him*. Only when that happens and you feel like you've lost nothing in the process, can you truly say, "Father, I've done what You called me to do."

OVERCOMING THE
GRASSHOPPER MENTALITY (1)

We were in our own sight as grasshoppers.
Numbers 13:33

You'll never know what you're made of spiritually until you come against something too big to handle alone. That's when you discover what you *really* believe. When Moses sent twelve scouts to check out Israel's new homeland, they all saw the same thing: a land rich in honey, milk—and giants! Yes, Joshua and Caleb saw them too. Faith isn't ignoring the obvious, that's denial. Acknowledging a problem isn't an expression of doubt. And it's not a sin. Paul said, "We would have come unto you…but Satan hindered us" (1Th 2:18). You can't control what you won't confront. The difference between the scouts was in *how* they saw the problem. Ten said, "We saw the giants…and we were in our own eyes as grasshoppers," but Joshua and Caleb said, "Do not fear the people of the land. For they are but bread for us to eat! The Lord is with us" (Nu 14:9 TLB). Real faith feeds off the stuff the enemy throws at you. It says, "Bring it on! The Lord is with me. He has robbed the enemy of his power to hurt me."

The negative report of the ten spies caused 3 reactions in the people. *(1) Fear.* Fear is irrational. It can make you forget every good thing God's promised or done for you. *(2) Retreat.* Some wanted to go back to Egypt—back to how things used to be. Hello! *(3) Settling.* Others wanted to settle in the wilderness. But you can't. You've got to move with the cloud, otherwise today's manna is the last you'll see. So, is the God you serve bigger than the giant you see? He says He is.

OVERCOMING THE
GRASSHOPPER MENTALITY (2)

We were in our own sight as grasshoppers.
Numbers 13:33

*W*hen you come up against a giant, either your faith will cause you to soar or your fear will cause you to sink. The Israelites died 21 miles from the Promised Land, going in circles. Why? "We saw the giants…and we were in our own sight as grasshoppers." If you're to see (and seize) what God's promised you, you'll have to conquer your giants. Now you have the *power* to, but do you have the *will* to? Joshua and Caleb stood alone. Faith will place you in the minority! "The whole congregation…said…would to God that we had died… in the land of Egypt" (Ex 16:2-3). In order to go where God wants to take you, you'll have to rise above the opinions of others. So, who are these good folks with grasshopper mentalities? (1) They constantly talk about life's injustices, about how they've been mistreated and misunderstood. To them Paul answers, "Endure hardness, as a good soldier of Jesus Christ" (2Ti 2:3). (2) They make excuses for not conquering in life. Sometimes they even put others down because they're walking in victory. To them Paul writes, "In all these things we are more than conquerors through him who loved us" (Ro 8:37 NIV). (3) They complain about what they don't have instead of focusing on what they do. To them Peter writes, "His divine power has given us everything we need for life and godliness through our knowledge of him who called us" (2Pe 1:3 NIV). Translation? Get to know God better. Relationships thrive on quality time together. *That's* how to move from a grasshopper mentality to a giant killer mentality!

USE YOUR TIME WISELY!

*I have brought you glory on earth
by completing the work you gave me to do.*
John 17: 4 NIV

*C*ommenting upon the undisciplined life of Samuel Taylor Coleridge, William Barclay writes: "Never did so great a mind produce so little. He left Cambridge University to join the army; he left the army because he could not rub down a horse; he returned to Oxford and left without a degree. He began a newspaper called *The Watchman,* which lived for ten editions then died. It could be said of him 'He lost himself in visions of work to be done, that always remained to be done.'"

Jesus understood His mission and He never deviated from it. He refused to be the victim of peer pressure or the expecta-tions of others. He sought the approval of one person only—His Father! Just before He assumed public ministry He spent 40 days in the wilderness consulting with His Father. And don't forget the night He spent in prayer before choosing His 12 disciples. Finally, there was Gethsemane. Because Jesus was spiritually sharpened by moments alone with the Father, it was never difficult for Him to say "no" to invitations and demands which might have looked good or acceptable to us. Here's a life-changing insight: you *always* have the time to do what God wants done. And you don't burn out in the process. You may not get done what *you* want done, or what *others* think needs done. But so what? Your goal should be to reach the end of life and say like Jesus, "I have brought You glory on earth by com-pleting the work *You* gave me to do."

REFUSE TO SETTLE

You will be made rich in every way
so that you can be generous on every occasion.
2 Corinthians 9:11 NIV

*Y*our enemies can't stop God from blessing you. "Thou preparest a table before me in the presence of mine enemies" (Ps 23:5). God will honor you while your critics look on in amazement. Not everybody is going to celebrate your success. Success breeds contempt. People who hate success are often people who don't believe they're going to have any themselves. Keep your spirit free of competitiveness and resentment. The acid test of character is our reaction to another man or woman's blessing.

Before you criticize someone's level of blessing, examine their seed. How much did they sow in terms of giving, preparing, serving and loving? You're looking at their harvest today, but you don't know the whole story until you know about the seed they sowed yesterday. Where does seed come from? Paul answers: "[God] supplies seed to the sower" (2Co 9:10 NIV). Seed comes from God and He only gives it to sowers. So, are you a sower or a hoarder? The answer may be in your checkbook. If you're a sower God says He'll "increase your store of seed" (2Co 9:10 NIV). When you sow into God's kingdom He promises, "You will be made rich in every way so that you can be generous on every occasion" (2Co 9:11). Rich? Yes, rich in relationships, rich in wisdom, rich in health, rich in finances. Why does God prosper us? For one reason, and only one: so that we may become His instruments to bless others. Jim Elliott said: "He is no fool who gives what he cannot keep, to gain what he cannot lose."

SAVE THE CHILDREN (1)

And its new shoots will not fail.
Job 14:7 NIV

*J*n divorce, children often become weapons used by brokenhearted people who have nothing left that the other person wants, except a visit from a child. Sadly, this visit is withheld because the warring parties are interested in causing as much pain to their now-estranged lovers as they have felt themselves. What they don't realize is, whenever a weapon is fired the ammunition doesn't just destroy its target; the ammunition itself gets destroyed too. Job writes, "There is hope for a tree: If it is cut down, it will sprout again, and its new shoots will not fail. Its roots may grow old in the ground and its stump die in the soil, yet at the scent of water it will bud and put forth shoots like a plant" (Job 14:7-9 NIV).

Job says that a new shoot can grow out of a dead stump. Please don't destroy the shoot because you've lost the stump! Your destiny is in your seed. If you lose your children you cut off your future. God has entrusted them to you. You are rich and you are blessed because you have them. Perhaps you cannot save the relationship, but if you cannot or will not, at least save the children. They don't deserve to become casualties of your war. In the midst of your pain stop and realize that you have a child who needs you, a child entrusted to your care. Providing food and shelter is very good—but don't forget love, and stability, and spiritual guidance. Without these things your pain can become their life-long pain. Don't let that happen—save the children!

SAVE THE CHILDREN (2)

*Arise, lift up the lad...hold him in thine hand...
for I will make him...great.*
Genesis 21:18

*I*n a jealous rage Sarah told Abraham: "Cast out this bondwoman and her son" (Ge 21:10). That's when God intervened. He met Hagar at her lowest point and gave her 4 steps every single parent should take:

(1) "Arise"—raise your own self-esteem. You can't lift others while you yourself are down. Get God's opinion of you. Allow His Word to pull you out of every slump you've fallen into. *(2) "Lift up the lad"—give your children positive reinforcement.* Regardless of your regrets, your pain or your personal state, God will empower you to lift your children. Many people are mere fragments of what they might have been if someone had lifted them up. This is so important. No one can come from the outside and tear down your child if you've truly lifted them up. *(3) "Hold him in thine hand"—initiate personal contact.* A warm hug, a touch, it seems simple but it's powerful. Your hand scents them like sheep are scented by the shepherd. They know his scent. They recognize his voice. They respond to his touch. If the only time your child hears your voice is in criticism they will shy away from you. Psychologists call it "bonding." If our children don't get it they become dwarfed in their personal, spiritual and mental well-being. It's amazing what a touch will do. *(4) "I will make him...great." Never think that you're not raising great children just because you're raising them alone.* God is with you. Your mistakes needn't prevent your children from being great in God's kingdom!

SAVE THE CHILDREN (3)

Teach what you've seen and heard to your children.
Deuteronomy 4:9 TM

$\mathcal{G}$od's grace is amazing! "By an act of faith, Rahab, the Jericho harlot…escaped the destruction that came on those who refused to trust God" (Heb 11:31 TM). Rahab didn't just save herself, she saved her entire household. Single parent, don't let what you've done, or what was done to you, keep God from blessing you and your children. Refuse to carry the unresolved issues of your past into your future. Draw a line in the sand! God's promise is: "All your sons [and daughters] will be taught by the Lord, and great will be your children's peace" (Isa 54:13 NIV). Go ahead, claim that promise. Walk with God and take your children with you: "Teach what you've seen and heard to your children" (Dt 4:9 TM). Your children need to hear you say Who brought you through the dark places. Why? So that when *they* encounter them they'll have confidence in God. What better testimony can there be than a testimony derived from the lips of parents whose scars became stars as they overcame trauma by God's grace. Your wisdom will last them a lifetime. Don't lose faith in yourself because of your past failings. You have an opportunity to bring right out of wrong by pouring strength and wisdom into your child. This is your chance—don't miss it by clinging to guilt, bitterness, pain or hopelessness. Let go of your past and seize your tomorrow. That child is your tomorrow. They are destiny being shaped in your palm. Your fingerprint will be left on his or her soul. So mark them well, and mark them for God!

DEAL WITH IT!

When I refused to confess my sin, I was…miserable.
Psalm 32:3 NLT

*A*re you harboring sin? Are you refusing to deal with your unresolved issues? David did, and he slipped into hell-deep depression. After committing adultery with Bathsheba he arranged to have her husband killed, then he married her—and his world caved in! "I was…miserable." What stops good people from cleaning up their act? Spiritual misconceptions! Damaging beliefs! See if you recognize any. (1) "Negative consequences are just the result of fate; they're not connected to my choices. (2) God's much too forgiving to permit escalating consequences or allow me to experience pain just to get me to stop sinning. (3) The enjoyment I get from my so-called sin outweighs the benefit of stopping. Anyway, my sin isn't really hurting anyone. (4) I can't help myself. The problem goes back to my childhood, so why wouldn't God extend grace rather than impose discipline? (5) Just because I sin doesn't mean I can't do something for God. Hey, God uses crooked sticks—we can't all be the Apostle Paul, you know. (6) Anyway it's not a sin, it's just a part of my personality that I struggle with."

Do you see what you're really saying? "My sin doesn't have consequences. God won't pursue this. I like my sin too much to give it up. I've convinced myself that I can't quit. My sin won't diminish my effectiveness. My problem isn't even a sin." If this describes you, embrace the truth, disregard the lies that have kept you stuck in unnecessary pain and repent. Yes, repent and renounce it! The moment you do you'll receive God's forgiveness—and the heaviness you're living under will lift!

WRING IT OUT

*But Mary treasured up all these things
and pondered them in her heart.*
Luke 2:19 NIV

*A*fter thoroughly washing their clothes, the old timers would wring as much water out of them as possible so they would dry quickly. There's a lesson there: growing in character and maturity calls for more than just "letting life happen." No, it calls for "wringing the wisdom" out of each experience by asking, "What's to be learned here? How could it have been done differently?" Great chess players win because they think several moves ahead. Wisdom asks, "Where does this lead? What are the possible unintended consequences?" Wise people realize that what they do today will affect tomorrow. They're aware that most things are interconnected. Wisdom comes from figuring out where things are going. Talk to people whose lives are lived purely on the surface and ask, "Have you thought about...?" No, they haven't. "Well, what do you think this will do to...?" They have no idea. "Have you ever asked yourself what God...?" Never thought of that.

"But Mary treasured up all these things and pondered them in her heart." This is a picture of someone who takes the time to wring out events and tests them for insight and understanding. Sooner or later Mary may have something to say, but when she says it her words will have substance. In days to come her family will have to flee from Herod's thugs and spend years living in exile in Egypt. All of this will demand courage, depth of spirit, and trust in the purposes of God. And that's what comes to a person like Mary, who takes time to "wring" the wisdom out of the event.

LIVING THE DISCIPLINED LIFE

You…know all about my teaching, my way of life,
my purpose, faith, patience, love, endurance.
2 Timothy 3:10 NIV

*L*iving the disciplined life does 3 things for you:
(1) It strengthens your will! Discipline doesn't make you rigid, it makes you resilient. It provides you with shock absorbers for the potholes of life. And there will be lots of them. It enlarges your capacity to summon up courage when life gets tough. Look at Shadrach, Meshach and Abednego who refused to bow to a pagan king's idol even when threatened with a fiery furnace: "The God we serve is able to save us from it…But even if he does not…we will not serve your gods" (Da 3:17-18 NIV). All of their lives these guys had toughened themselves through discipline in order to face such a supreme moment of testing. And you'll face that moment too! *(2) It brings your gifts to their highest level of effectiveness.* "How do you get to Carnegie Hall?" asks the tourist of a New Yorker. Answer: "You practice, man, you practice." David's first victory wasn't over Goliath. His years of practice as a shepherd defending his sheep against wolves, a lion and a bear, had prepared him for this moment. It had given him the spirit and the skill needed to take on the Philistine champion. *(3) It inspires others.* Paul writes to Timothy, "You…know all about my teaching, my way of life [living it is harder than teaching it], my purpose, faith, patience, love, endurance, persecutions, sufferings" (2Ti 3:10 NIV). Paul's greatest gift to Timothy was the example of a disciplined life. Now Timothy had something to copy—a straightedge of excellent living. And there's no better gift!

WHY NOT?

Be zealous…and be so always.
Galatians 4:18 NIV

$\mathcal{A}$dmiral Hyman Rickover, who was once head of the United States Nuclear Navy, personally interviewed every officer on board his nuclear submarines. Among them was former President Jimmy Carter. This is Carter's account of the interview: "He looked straight into my eyes. He never smiled. I was saturated with cold sweat. Finally he asked a question and I thought I could redeem myself. 'How did you stand in your class at the Naval Academy?' I had done very well so I swelled my chest with pride and answered, 'Sir, I stood fifty-ninth out of a class of eight hundred and twenty!' I sat back waiting for congratulations—which never came. Instead, the question: 'Did you do your best?' I started to say, 'Yes, sir,' but I remembered who this was and recalled several times at the Academy when I could have learned more about our allies, our enemies, weapons, strategy, and so forth. I was just human. I finally gulped and said, 'No, sir, I didn't always do my best.' He looked at me for a long time, then turned his chair around to end the interview. He asked one final question, which I have never been able to forget—or to answer. He said, 'Why not?' I sat there for a while, shaken, then slowly left the room."

That's a question we need to ask ourselves at the end of each day: "Did I do my best?" You can be certain it's a question you'll face when you stand at the Judgment Seat of Christ to be evaluated and rewarded. If you can't answer yes, the question then will be, *"Why not?"*

A SOUND MIND (1)

God hath…given us…a sound mind.
2 Timothy 1:7

In Victor Hugo's *Les Misérables,* there's a line regarding the priest Myriel, who "was fated to undergo the lot of every newcomer to a little town where there were many mouths that speak, but few heads that think." The undisciplined mind becomes a lazy mind. And that's dangerous because it easily succumbs to the culture and influences around it. Little of value is ever learned through one-way monologue, be it a sermon or a lecture. There are many eloquent speakers today who are relentless in offering their opinions on just about every issue, who weave a spell of thought that relieves the individual of exploring things for themselves.

In the Book of Acts we read that the Bereans "examined the Scriptures every day to see if what Paul said was true" (Ac 17:11 NIV). Asking, "Why? How? Who says so?" is not an act of rebellion, it's godly wisdom! One walks around today knowing full well that an inappropriate response to a political comment, a doctrinal issue or a matter of social policy can lose you friends, a reputation, or even a job. The godly mind, however, resists this cookie-cutter approach to thought. It weighs every question and asks if Scripture speaks directly or indirectly to the matter. It examines it in the light of history; how have God's people faced this before? It measures the matter in terms of its ability to reflect the redeeming love of Christ. It enquires, "Will this bring credibility or shame to the Kingdom of God which I represent?"

A SOUND MIND (2)

God hath…given us…a sound mind.
2 Timothy 1:7

$\mathcal{G}$.K. Chesterton once said of Abraham Lincoln: "This great man had one secret vice that was far more unpopular among his followers than the habit of drinking. He had the habit of thinking." Cultivate the company of good thinkers: Solomon says, "He that walketh with wise men shall be wise" (Pr 13:20). When we submit ourselves to Christ He doesn't tell us to abandon our minds, He tells us to "renew" them (See Ro 12:1-2). How do we win someone to Christ? By attacking what they think? No, that alienates them. We must do 3 things: (1) Convince them that we truly care about them. (2) Convince them that God truly cares about them. (3) Find their wounded area and apply the healing balm of God's Word to it. When it comes to sharing our faith a lot of us are only comfortable talking to "down-and-outers." Hey, who's going to reach the "up-and-outers?" Paul said, "I continue…witnessing both to small and great" (Ac 26:22). When Paul visited Athens he ended up on Mars Hill where he addressed some of the city's better minds. His words are a brilliant display of a spirit sharpened mind at work. Paul was not a small parochial man, but a man in touch with his world. He was comfortable in a backwater town like Derbe, a business community like Ephesus, a political capital like Rome, and an intellectual center like Athens. "I am made all things to all men, that I might by all means save some" (1Co 9:22). So discipline your mind, dedicate it to Christ's purposes and use it to attract others to Him.

WON BY LOVE

The kindness of God leads...to repentance.
Romans 2:4 NAS

*E*ver notice that most organizations insist that you earn your way? For example, airlines compensate frequent fliers with free miles, sports franchises reward players who score goals and win games. Some corporations even grade their employees on a scale where they can earn a private office or their own parking space. But God's not like that; you can't earn salvation. Paul says, "The kindness of God leads...to repentance." Notice, he didn't say the scare tactics of a preacher or the legalistic requirements of some church that you keep their standards before God will accept you. No, genuine repentance is our response to the unconditional love of a perfect God. A God who delights in reaching down and restoring the cracked pots and damaged vessels society wants to throw on the garbage heap. When you encounter a Savior like that, you *want* to please Him. It's impossible to experience the unfailing love of a God who stands by you when others fail you, and keep on abusing His love.

The very idea that God's love comes with no strings attached goes against every human instinct. "God so loved the world, that he gave his only begotten Son, that whosoever believeth in him should not perish but have everlasting life" (Jn 3:16). *Love* is the force that draws us to Him. To know Him is to love Him. And to walk with Him is to experience "joy unspeakable." To the hopeless and hurting our God says, "Come. Your past doesn't disqualify you; your problems are not too big for Me—I've handled bigger. Maybe you're not welcome anywhere else, but today you're "accepted in the beloved" (Eph 1:6).

LEARN TO REST IN GOD!

My presence shall go with thee, and I will give thee rest.
Exodus 33:14

*H*as success brought pressures you can't cope with? Has the thing you celebrated yesterday got you all stressed out today? We think we know what we want, because we see it in somebody else's life. But God knows what we need —what we can live with and not fall apart. When God says, "No" it's because He sees down the road. Children don't know what they don't know. Their favorite word is "gimme." When we're tiny and don't get it, we stomp our feet and throw a fit. When we're in our teens and don't get it, we rebel and think, "You're ruining my life." When we're older and wiser we say, "Thank God Mom and Dad said no." Be careful what you pray for, you just might get it.

Here are some sobering words for fast trackers: "Then believed they his words; they sang his praise [but] they soon [forgot] his works; they waited not for his counsel: but lusted exceedingly in the wilderness…and he gave them their request; but sent leanness into their soul" (Ps 106:12-15). Wow! Materially enriched, but spiritually impoverished. That's a battle you'll fight too! Are you experiencing *lean* times in your soul? If you are and you know it, you're blessed. You can still do something about it. It's when you *don't* know it that you're in trouble. You say, "Is God asking me to leave my job or sell my big house?" No, He's telling you you're out of balance. "Where do I find the answer?" God whispers, "My Presence shall go with thee and I will give thee rest." Learn to rest in God!

CHECK YOUR EGO

*Moses was...more humble than anyone else
on the face of the earth.*
Numbers 12:3 NIV

*I*t took 40 years of living like a shepherd (and oh, how the Egyptians despised shepherds!) to discipline Moses' ego. Only then, at age 80, was he ready to live life on God's terms. The man who emerged from the desert was decidedly different from the man who entered it. It's our "desert experiences" that keep our egos in check. Without them, we start believing our own press and get into trouble. God told King Saul, "When you were little in your own eyes I was able to use you" (See 1Sa 15:17). When Colonel Samuel Logan Brengle of The Salvation Army was once introduced as "the great Colonel Brengle," he wrote in his journal: "If I appear great in their eyes, the Lord is most gracious in helping me to see how absolutely nothing I am without him. He does use me. But I'm so conscious that *he* uses me, and that it's not of me that the work is done. The axe cannot boast of the trees it has cut down. It could do nothing without the woodsman. He made it, he sharpened it, he used it, and the moment he throws it aside it becomes only old used iron. Oh, that I may never lose sight of this."

A young English man once came to live in the community led by Gandhi. When assigned to clean latrines, he protested, "Don't you know who I am? I have great things to do." Gandhi replied, "I know you can do great things; what I don't know is if you can do little things." Check your ego!

THE NEED FOR GOD-GIVEN GOALS

We should make plans—counting on God to direct us.
Proverbs 16:9 TLB

*T*here are several reasons why we fail to set goals for our lives: (1) We haven't been taught the blessing or joy of such an action. (2) We don't know how to go about it. (3) We are afraid of failing. If we don't have a goal there's no guilt or embarrassment over not reaching it. (4) We feel intimidated by previous failures. Solomon wrote: "We should make plans—counting on God to direct us." Jesus said: "Suppose one of you wants to build a tower. Will he not first sit down and estimate the cost to see if he has enough money to complete it?" (Lk 14:28 NIV). Goal setting takes time, discipline, courage and perseverance. Between you and your goal there'll be roadblocks, enemy attacks and temptations designed to derail you. "So, what should I do?" (a) Talk to God. Get into agreement with His will for you. (b) Write your goals down. The shortest pencil is better than the longest memory. God told the prophet, "Write the vision, and make it plain" (Hab 2:2). Without written goals you have no compass and you can get swept off course. (c) Focus on your top goals. If you attempt everything you'll accomplish nothing. Remember, a big success is simply several little successes strung together. (d) Be alert to those God sends into your life to help you fulfill His purposes. Draw on the wisdom of experienced people; stand on their shoulders. Even your critics can sharpen you. God has a plan for your life—seek Him and He'll reveal it to you!

DO IT "AS UNTO THE LORD!"

Whatever you do, do it heartily,
as to the Lord and not to men.
Colossians 3:23 NKJV

*W*hen Nicholas Herman entered the Carmelite monastery in Paris in 1666, he expected to live a life of penance because of his wild and sinful past. But instead Herman, who was given the name *Brother Lawrence,* found God's forgiveness and peace, plus a joy he could never have imagined. But his faith was sorely tried in the process. Clumsy by nature, he was very upset at being assigned to the monastery kitchen. Then something happened. There in his kitchen he found that even the humblest, most mundane tasks become significant— when they're done out of love for God! In his classic little book, *The Practice of the Presence of God,* he wrote: "The time of business does not with me differ from the time of prayer...in the noise and clatter of my kitchen while several persons are at the same time calling for different things, I possess God in as great tranquility as if I were upon my knees...We ought not to be weary of doing little things, for God regards not the greatness of the work but the love with which it is performed." Talk about adding dignity to your job!

So, what's the job *you* hate most? Cutting the grass? Doing laundry? Putting out the garbage? Walking the dog? Coming home from work tired and having to cook dinner? Care-giving? Paul said, "Whatever you do, do it heartily, as to the Lord and not to men" (Col 3:23 NKJV). The truth is, there's no difference between the secular and the sacred when it's done "as unto the Lord and not men."

THE POWER OF THE BLOOD

His blood…makes our consciences clear.
Hebrews 9:14 CEV

$\mathcal{G}$od designed blood to deliver oxygen and nutrition to your cells; without it your limbs and organs die. Your white cells are uniquely qualified to act as a "militia" attacking harmful bacteria that could otherwise kill you. And your physical body illustrates the function of Jesus' blood in the church, which is His body. Paul says, "A body is made up of many parts, and each…has its own use. That's how it is with us…we are…part of the body of Christ, as well as…of one another" (Ro 12:4-5 CEV). Regardless of morality, maturity or rank, we *all* need the sin-cleansing, life-giving power of the blood. Without it we've no proof of our son-ship. Just as a doctor draws blood to verify who your earthly father is, the blood of Jesus makes us "[sons and] heir[s], with complete access to [our spiritual] inheritance" (Gal 4:7 TM). Strength and nourishment, plus every promise and blessing, flow to us today through the blood of Jesus. And Satan hates it because not only does it redeem us, it "makes our consciences clear…we can serve…God and no longer do things that lead to death" (Heb 9:14 CEV). One Christian teacher writes: "We've toned down our teaching of the blood…We've learned about the Spirit…but failed to teach about the blood. Consequently we've produced a generation of believers who are empowered by the Spirit but don't feel forgiven…They're exercising spiritual gifts, but living in guilt…The blood must be preached. Without it we've no life." So let's emphasize the power of the blood. Why? "Without the…blood, there is no forgiveness of sin" (Heb 9:22 NLT).

GETTING OUT OF DEBT

Pay…your debts.
Romans 13:8 NLT

$\mathcal{G}$od promised to "supply all your needs" (Php 4:19). But sometimes our definition of needs differs from His! Shelly Smith, whose family accumulated $40,000 in credit card debt, says, "We worried constantly…we just couldn't live that way any more." So they: *Repaid high interest credit cards first.* It's encouraging to see your debt decreasing. Paul said, "Pay…your debts," because when you can't meet your financial obligations you "put yourself under [the lender's] power" (Pr 22:7 TM). *Went cash-only.* They averaged out their weekly expenses and set cash aside to cover them. When it was gone the spending stopped. They refused to write checks for unnecessary expenses. They also cut back elsewhere. This kept them on track and made them think twice about their spending habits. *Got rid of "stuff."* Unlike Paul who learned to be happy and get by on "much or little" (Php 4:11 NLT), the Smiths had lots of stuff. Impulse buys, unwanted gifts, things from relatives. So they sold it all, gave God a tithe and applied the rest towards their debt. *Negotiated with creditors.* It's not easy, but by mustering the courage to call your creditors you can often work out terms. For example, Shelly says, "The months when we couldn't send $100, they agreed to take $50." The Bible says: (a) "Restrain yourself! Riches disappear in the blink of an eye" (Pr 23:4-5 TM). (b) "Honor God with everything…give him the first and…best" (Pr 3:9 TM). (c) "Don't be obsessed with getting more…things" (Heb 13:5 TM). Becoming debt free means changing the habits that got you into trouble. Is it easy? No, but with discipline and God's help you can do it.

TESTING...TESTING

Don't be surprised...that you are going through testing.
1 Peter 4:12 CEV

*H*ave you ever had a teacher tell you at the beginning of a school term that there would be tests without any warning? Sometimes they're called a "pop quiz." Maybe you didn't like it, but at least you knew to be prepared by doing your homework and completing your assignments on time. You understood the tests were coming so you couldn't say you hadn't been warned. God operates on the same principle. His Word says, "Don't be surprised...that you are going through testing." Now, God's tests aren't necessarily ones you'd have chosen for yourself because they never seem to come at the right time and always test you in your weakest areas. That's because they're not for the teacher's benefit, they're for *yours!* The tests of life are designed to sharpen us mentally and strengthen us spiritually. When tests come, and they will, you've got two choices. One: act like a victim and complain that you've been singled out and unfairly treated. Two: let them teach you more about yourself—and the God you serve. Have you ever worked out in a gym? You can use tests as resistance, the kind you push against to grow stronger. Or you can walk around feeling sorry for yourself—and stay spiritually unfit and flabby.

Here's a comforting thought: God will never give you more than you can handle, or a test you can't pass. His Word says He'll "never let you down...let you be pushed past your limit; he'll always be there to help you" (1Co 10:13 TM). So the Word for Today is—be prepared! The test could come at anytime.

SOWING AND REAPING

He has scattered abroad his gifts to the poor.
2 Corinthians 9:9 NIV

It's one thing to give because it puts God on your side financially, but there's an even greater reason: "He has scattered abroad his gifts to the poor; his righteousness endures forever." At first glance you may think, "What's that got to do with anything?" A lot! God's committed to healing the hurts of our world; that's why He speaks of "gifts to the poor." When we get involved with God through this kind of giving, we're taking our place in a plan that's bigger than our own interests—or our tiny bag of seed. We're participating in His plan to reach the world. God's concerned about the poor, and about sharing with every person on earth the good news of the Gospel. Those are *His* objectives and He's committed to them. And they're going to cost money. A lot of it! Now the truth is, God will get the money from somewhere, but He'd like to partner with *you* to accomplish it.

You say, "But I'm afraid if I give more I won't have enough to meet my own needs!" Think about what you just said. *Why* would God drain you of your resources, then not replenish them to accomplish through you what He's committed to doing? That doesn't make sense. If you're a partner with God why would He hinder your ability to give toward the things that matter most to Him: the needy, and winning a lost world? The truth is, God's going to do it with or without you. He's just giving you an opportunity to get involved with Him. Don't miss out on it!

LEARN TO BE CONTENT (1)

I have learned to be content.
Philippians 4:11 NAS

$\mathcal{T}$he average person is bombarded with about 300 advertisements a day, promising everything from whiter teeth to faster cars. It's a mega-billion-dollar industry designed to make us want what they're selling. But there's a subtle message being conveyed. In a word, it's *discontent,* and it eats away at us by creating a desire for bigger, better, more. The Bible says, "We...brought nothing into the world, so we cannot take anything out...If we have food and covering...be content" (1Ti 6:7-8 NAS). Sounds simple enough: food to eat, clothes to wear, a place to sleep. But how we live doesn't bear it out. When Rockefeller was asked, "How much does it take to satisfy a man?" with rare insight he replied, "A little more than he has now."

So does contentment mean not setting goals or aiming higher? Does it mean not enjoying nice things? No, it just means not letting all those nice things "own" you. Learning to be satisfied is a process. That's why Paul said, *"I have learned to be content in whatever circumstances I am...to get along with humble means...to live in prosperity...I have learned* the secret of being filled and going hungry...of having abundance and suffering need." Paul mastered the art of enjoying whatever came along by learning to say, "That's not essential. I can live without it." Paul, who told Timothy to follow his example, was the kind of man who could enjoy hot dogs or filet mignon, a vacation on the Riviera or a bed under a bridge, a gold-covered, diamond-studded, velvet-cushioned chariot, or a dirty burro with a limp. His focus was right on target. He held every earthly 'thing' loosely. So should you!

LEARN TO BE CONTENT (2)

The abundance of a rich man permits him no sleep.
Ecclesiastes 5:12 NIV

*I*n a recent magazine article Jane Hammerslough tells how her family moved into a sparsely furnished rental house while their home was being renovated. Instead of missing what they'd left behind, surprisingly, they were *liberated!* Upon returning home they were overwhelmed by the utter excess of stuff, and gave much of it away. She concludes, "When enough's always just a little more…you don't have room for the truly great things in life." The message isn't new; Solomon said, "The abundance of a rich man permits him no sleep."

But freedom from anxiety is more than just uncluttered closets. It's a firm conviction that what you *do* have is a gift from God (See Ecc 5:19), and that it's meant to be shared with others. Contentment simply frees you to enjoy what He's provided. So with that in mind keep the following principles before you: buy things for their usefulness, not their status. Beware of anything that produces an addiction in you. Make a habit of giving things away. Don't be lured by advertising and glitz. Learn to enjoy things without having to own them, or be owned by them. Be wary of "Buy now, pay later" schemes. Steer clear of anything that prevents you from putting God first in your life. He says He'll "give you all you need…if you live for him and make the Kingdom of God your primary concern" (Mt 6:33 NLT). When your contentment is based on status or possessions, it can be taken away in an instant. But when it's based on your relationship with Jesus, nothing, absolutely nothing can rob you of it!

"SPINNING" THE TRUTH

Love should always make us tell the truth.
Ephesians 4:15 CEV

*H*ow do you think Paul, "the apostle of grace," would have handled the following inquiry: "Dear Paul: We're thinking about hiring Alexander the coppersmith to manage our company, and because you know him well we'd appreciate your opinion?" Knowing the problems Alexander had caused him in the past (1Ti 1:18-20; 2Ti 4:14-15), how would Paul respond? Or how about this one: "Dear Abraham: Lot has applied for a loan to expand his cattle ranch on the land he inherited from you in the Jordan Valley near Sodom. So we're writing to ask you for a character reference?" Would Abraham, who was well aware of his nephew's shady business practices (Ge 13:11-13), be evasive and "fudge" the facts to keep peace in the family? It's doubtful. Or what about this one: "Dear John: We need a mature Christian to fill a slot on our church board. Based on your dealings with Diotrephes, do you think he's the right person?" John knew the trouble Diotrephes had already caused and his need for power and control (See 3Jn 9-10). But would he hedge and take the path of least resistance? Probably not; knowing John he'd be honest and let the chips fall where they may.

So, what would you do? Remember, the Bible says that love should always make us tell the truth. Following Christ means being honest when it would be easier to prevaricate and spin. Hopefully you'd find the courage to be straightforward— and gracious. Yes, gracious! Why? Because being asked for your input doesn't give you a right to resurrect another's mistakes and publicly embarrass them. The Bible says, "Let your conversation be gracious and effective" (Col 4:6 NLT).

OVERCOMING (1)

Despite all these things.
Romans 8:37 NLT

Composer Gian Carlo Menotti said, "Hell begins the day God grants us a vision of…the gifts we've wasted, of all we might have done but we didn't do." Wilma Rudolph, who won 3 gold medals at the 1960 Olympics would agree. What she accomplished isn't as impressive as what she overcame. As a child "Willie" contracted polio and couldn't walk without braces. Then at age 13 she regained the use of her legs and went on to become the fastest woman alive. But her challenges weren't just physical. One of 22 children born to a poor black family, she inspired us by transcending poverty and racial animosity. She said, *"'I can't'* has never been in my vocabulary." At age 2, Scott Hamilton, another famous Olympian skater, stopped growing because of a childhood illness that almost killed him. But his parents encouraged his rehabilitation by teaching him to skate—and the rest is history! In 1976 when Brad Parks was injured in an accident that left him in a wheelchair, he strengthened his arm by whacking tennis balls against his garage door. Three years later he formed the National Foundation of Wheelchair Tennis. Paul said, "Despite all these things…victory is ours through Christ." Rick Warren writes: "Why does God use our weaknesses? Because when he does, he gets all the glory. If God only used your strengths, others would look at you and be jealous…or discouraged. But when God uses you in spite of your weaknesses…they realize 'God could use me too!' Your weaknesses aren't an accident. God…allowed them for the purpose of demonstrating his power through you."

OVERCOMING (2)

My power works best in your weakness.
2 Corinthians 12:9 NLT

At 19 months, Helen Keller contracted the illness that eventually left her without hearing and sight. Back then those labeled "deaf and dumb," were classified as idiots. But Helen's parents didn't agree. They hired teacher Anne Sullivan to work with her and eventually she learned to read and write using Braille. Amazingly, in 1904 she graduated with honors from Radcliffe College, then devoted her life to helping others. Philanthropist Andrew Carnegie paid her an annual income; writers Mark Twain and Robert Louis Stevenson praised her, and almost every President of her day invited her to The White House. Even though Helen died in 1968 her legacy of courage lives on. When asked if there was anything worse than being blind, Helen replied, "Yes, having sight but no vision." At 12 Thomas Edison developed such severe hearing loss that his teachers recommended he be taken out of school. Instead Edison used his handicap to drown out distractions and focus on his work. As a result the boy who was labeled "a slow learner" gave the world over 1,000 inventions, including the light bulb, the phonograph and the motion camera.

Who gets to define "normal" anyway? Is it being short versus tall, or rich versus poor? The truth is, God's given *all* of us unique abilities that He expects us to explore. And interestingly, the *real* handicaps don't belong to those who are born with physical and mental challenges. No, they belong to the so-called *normal* people who've accepted lethargy and limitation as part of life. God said, "My power works best in your weakness," so you can let your difficulties impede or inspire you. Which will it be?

KNOWING YOUR SPEED LIMIT!

It is not good to have zeal without knowledge,
nor be hasty and miss the way.
Proverbs 19:2 NIV

A lot of us drive like the speed limits are just *suggestions!* No, they're there for a reason—our protection. Ignore them and you crash! The same is true about your life. Do you take work home, stay up late after the kids go to bed and your mate's asleep? Are you skipping meals to catch up on paperwork that keeps replenishing itself like weeds along a hillside? Do you drive to meetings checking your Blackberry, drinking coffee and talking on your cell phone? Isn't it crazy to run a portable office while driving at 65 m.p.h. down the highway? Some seasons are busier than others. Occasionally opportunities come along that require extra time and attention —but you can't expect yourself to always travel at warp speed. You're mortal and fragile with physical, emotional and spiritual needs. You aren't a robot, a computer or an engine that can be operated at the flip of a switch. Even these mechanical devices, if you don't keep them fueled and maintained eventually fail.

So, how do you discover and maintain your speed limit? By *knowing* yourself inside out. Pay attention to your body's signals—to your responses to the demands that you (and others) place on you. When your body is tired to the point of distraction, rest. That's what God did! And don't forget your soul—you'll gain more strength, wisdom and perspective by spending time each day with God than by all your blowin' and goin'. The Bible says: "They that wait upon the Lord shall renew their strength" (Isa 40:31). Try it; it works!

"BE THERE!"

*We can comfort those in any trouble with the comfort
we ourselves have received from God.*
2 Corinthians 1:4 NIV

$\mathcal{T}$he most loving thing we can do when someone is in pain is to share the pain—to "be there," even when we've nothing to offer except our presence, even when being there is painful to ourselves.

Paul says that God "comforts us in all our troubles, so that we can comfort those in any trouble with the comfort we ourselves have received from God." One of the fastest and surest routes to spiritual health, is taking the focus off ourselves and helping others. In fact we were born with a natural empathy for those who are hurting. Ever notice that babies in a nursery start crying when other infants cry? Compassion, which literally means, "to suffer with" is the ability to be moved by the troubles of others. When we reach out from our own pain to help others it comes back to us in healing, fulfillment and a sense of worth. Jack Canfield says, "You take it all in. You let the pain touch your heart and you turn it into compassion. What a splendid way to go through life, bringing blessing to all we touch."

One cancer patient said, "What helps me most is just to have somebody try and understand what I'm feeling." Another said, "Just sit here and let me hold your hand. It helps when someone's close." Today ask God to make you more sensitive to the needs and hurts of those around you. *And when He answers your prayer and puts someone into your path, don't be too busy to care. In other words, "be there!"*

COMMIT YOURSELF TO GROWTH!

Let the wise listen and add to their learning.
Proverbs 1:5 NIV

*H*ere are 3 reasons why growth should matter to you: *(1) Gifting without growth produces ineffectiveness.* Albert Schweitzer said, "The secret of success is to go through life as a person who never gets used up." But how do you do that? The answer lies in how you approach talent. If you draw on your talent but never sharpen it, you're headed for trouble because nobody's that talented. But if you take the time to sharpen your axe, God can call on you at a moment's notice. *(2) Growth prevents stagnation.* Do you feel stuck spiritually, relationally, career wise, or at home? You won't get unstuck by making external changes, looking for a different job, leaving your family or changing churches. The truth is, nobody's keeping you down but yourself. The lid on your life—is you! In order to do more, you've got to grow more. So, if you're serious about getting unstuck, stop looking for quick fixes, take a long hard look at yourself, accept responsibility for what you see, pray, then commit yourself to doing something about it. *(3) Continuous improvement guarantees success!* The Tartar tribes of central Asia used to pronounce a certain curse over their enemies. They didn't hurl words calling for their enemy's swords to rust or their people to die of disease. No, they said, "May you stay in one place forever." If you don't work on improving yourself every day that could be your fate. You'll be stuck in the same place, doing the same things, hoping the same hopes, but never gaining new ground or developing spiritually. So, commit yourself to growth!

TAKE GOD TO WORK (1)

The Lord himself goes before you and will be with you.
Deuteronomy 31:8 NIV

$\mathcal{S}$urely God would only send those He could trust into enemy territory. Understand this: God cares about where you are. He has selected you for your work environment. He has already, or is currently equipping you. You wouldn't send your child off to camp without packing his bags or making provision for everything he would need while he's away. And God wouldn't either. Sometimes hostile environments can be overwhelming—but by God's grace we can thrive in them! If you'll take God to work with you and keep your identity intact, the enemy will lose ground. Don't let him keep you focused on everything that's problematic: gossip, office politics, the too-heavy workload, the too-low pay, the micro-managing super-visor, the injustice of a system that seems to promote based more on *who* you know, than *what* you know. The danger is that you'll focus on the discomfort of the moment and miss the blessings that lie beyond it. While you're praying for God to change your circumstances and take away your stress, He's saying, "If only you knew what awaited you. Your purpose and destiny are only moments away, and, though not wrapped in shiny paper, they contain all you'll ever need to reach your goal and bring Me glory." God understands us so well. He realizes our tendency to stay too long when things become comfortable, to lean on the arm of flesh. Often He has to trouble the waters so that we'll reach out to Him in desperation, and as a result, tap into strength and success we never knew possible.

TAKE GOD TO WORK (2)

*I can do all things through Christ
which strengtheneth me.*
Philippians 4:13

*W*hether it's doctors in surgical scrubs or fire-fighters in heat-resistant uniforms, proper attire is required to do certain jobs. And as Christians, we also have to dress for work. We don't necessarily need to fuss with our outward appearance (although how we're perceived can go a long way toward helping us achieve) but we must dress up our character by "putting on the Lord Jesus Christ" (See Ro 13:14). After all, we're His representatives!

Secular society is confused about who Christians actually are. And these misconceptions are fed by our inability to step out in our true colors. Your workmates probably don't need another sermon, they can get that in church. Your job is your pulpit! How you conduct yourself should reflect what you *believe* and who you *belong* to. You may protest that it's difficult to maintain Christian integrity when you have to deal with backstabbing, unfair criticism and the misuse of power. Actually, we Christians are supposed to be at our best under pressure (See Isa 59:19). God's power is released in our lives by enemy encroachment. Sometimes we just have to get more creative as challenges enlarge or intensify. You may have to step outside of the situation and remind yourself Who put you there. Leave your office, take a break, or simply go to the restroom and talk to God—your real Boss. God is very present in times of trouble, and learning to call on Him instead of falling into the trap of the enemy is what wins spiritual wars! When adversity and challenges come—as they surely will—remember this, "I can do all things through Christ who strengthens me."

BECOMING MORE TRANSPARENT

Confess your faults one to another.
James 5:16

*W*hen a Sunday school teacher asked her class to define "sins of omission," a little boy replied, "That's easy, they're all the sins we should've committed, but never got to!" How's *that* for honesty? Until you're willing to share your shortcomings as well as your successes, others who are struggling will always wonder, "What's wrong with me that I can't overcome my problems too?" Notice: God didn't tell us to confess our *sins* to each other; we should confess those only to Him and let Him put them under the blood. He said, "Confess your *faults*...[weak areas where we struggle]." We're not as different as we think. Like the old Irish preacher said, "Flesh is flesh is flesh, no matter whose bones it's on!"

Adam was stripped of his covering and forced to stand naked before his wife and his God. Why? Because it's honesty in *both* areas that leads to wholeness. After all, if we can only love somebody when they've attained a certain level of perfection, is it *real* love? On the other hand, if you have people in your life who love you despite your flaws you're blessed. Many relationships thrive only as long as the parties meet one another's expectations. But when one falls short, look out!

You need to love others the way God loves you. And what way's that? (a) He loved you while you were still a sinner (Ro 5:8 NKJV). (b) He made you part of His family, giving you value and identity (1Jn 3:1). (c) Nothing can ever change that (Ro 8:35). In other words, He loved you while you were unlovable, so that unlike Adam, you wouldn't have to hide in the bushes!

SPIRIT FILLED LIVING

They were all filled with the Holy Spirit.
Acts 4:31 NIV

*T*he Holy Spirit can fill your *cup* until it overflows, or be like a *river* flowing through you. It's a matter of capacity, availability, and spiritual hunger. When the disciples were first filled with the Holy Spirit we read that He "sat upon each of them" (Ac 2:3). And doesn't He still work that way? When we were about to show off, He sat on us. When we were about to give in to the flesh, He sat on us. When we were about to throw in the towel, He sat on us. When we were about to have a nervous breakdown, He sat on us. The Holy Spirit can keep us in balance, in peace, and on track.

Here are 3 life-changing things that the Holy Spirit does for us: (a) He gives us direction when we feel lost: "For as many as are led by the Spirit of God, they are the sons of God" (Ro 8:14). (b) When others put us down, He reminds us who we are. "The Spirit itself beareth witness with our spirit, that we are the children of God" (Ro 8:16). (c) He steps in when we don't know how to pray about the situation: "We don't even know what we should pray for…but the Holy Spirit prays for us…in harmony with God's own will" (Ro 8:26-27 TLB).

So what should our attitude be toward the Holy Spirit? "Do not grieve the Holy Spirit" (Eph 4:30 NIV). The Bible likens the Holy Spirit to a dove, and a dove is gentle. It will not land on a nest that's out of order. Think about it!

FULFILLING YOUR GOD-GIVEN ASSIGNMENT

I gave them a mission in the world.
John 17:18 TM

*E*very day you live you're in the process of becoming. *What* you become, however, depends on what you
give yourself to. So consider these 7 steps:

(1) By making a commitment to grow *daily,* it won't be
long before you begin to see real change. (2) Value the process
more than the product. Certain events may be helpful in making
your decision, but it's going through the *process* that matures
you into what God wants you to be. (3) Don't wait for inspira-
tion. Sometimes you can run on excitement, but most times
only commitment will carry you through. (4) If you're willing
to pay now you'll enjoy the rewards later, and those rewards
always taste sweeter. (5) Don't limit God. By focusing on your
limitations you magnify them. The God who lives within you is
able to do "exceeding abundantly above all that we can ask or
think" (Eph 3:20). (6) Learn to master your time. Since you
can't recover lost time, make every moment count. What difference does a few minutes make? A lot! If you save 5 minutes
each day by streamlining your morning routine, 10 by eliminat-
ing things you do to keep from starting your day, 5 by avoiding
talkers or other distractions, and 10 by taking a shorter lunch
break—you'll gain an additional 125 hours a year. That's three
40-hour work weeks to use for anything you want. And you can
double that by watching 30 minutes less of television each day.
(7) Life is filled with decisive moments when you have to trade
one thing for another. Always trade up, not down. Want to
fulfill your God-given assignment? Follow these steps!

"WELL DONE, MOM!"

Many women do noble things, but you surpass them all.
Proverbs 31:29 NIV

*T*he emotions of motherhood are universal, from new mothers stumbling through night feeding and sleep deprivation, to seasoned mothers learning to let their grown children go. Today we honor all the Moms who sit up comforting sick toddlers and crying infants; who turn up at work with shadows under their eyes, stains on their blouses and diapers in their handbags; who organize car pools, bake cookies and sew costumes. Mothers who give birth to babies they'll never see, and mothers who give these children homes. Moms whose only priceless art hangs on refrigerator doors, who brave the cold to sit on hard benches at ball games. Who, when a child asks, "Did ya see me, Mom?" can honestly say, "I wouldn't have missed it for the world." Mothers who go without, so that their family doesn't have to. Moms who taught their children to tie their shoelaces before they started school—and those who opted for Velcro! Mothers who bite their lip when their teens dye their hair green; who automatically turn around when a little voice at the mall shouts, "Mom," even though they know their own children are safe at home or away at college. Mothers who never stop praying for their kids no matter how old they get.

What makes a good mother anyhow? Patience? Compassion? The ability to nurse a baby, cook a meal and sew on a button all at the same time? It's *all* those things—*plus* the God-given assurance that you're doing the most important job in the world. The Bible says, "Many women do noble things, but you surpass them all." "Well done, Mom."

LIVING UNSELFISHLY

Give without expecting a return.
Luke 6:35 TM

If you're serious about becoming like Jesus, pay careful attention to His words: "Ask yourself what you want people to do for you; then grab the initiative and do it for them …give without expecting a return. You'll never—I promise—regret it" (Lk 6:31-35 TM). Love, expecting nothing in return. Give, though they'll never say thanks. Forgive, even though they won't forgive you. Come early, stay late, invest everything you've got even though nobody notices. Paul calls this "the high calling" (Php 3:14). And there's a reason: none of us would set such a standard for ourselves! If you think some people are just naturally more loving than others, think again. Love is a choice —one that costs! You can't love others while you're staring into a mirror or give to others while you're clinging to what you've got. Love will cost you your time, your money and your pre-occupation with self. If you think you'll just go to church some Sunday morning, read a book or attend a 7-step seminar and turn into the kind of person we're talking about—good luck! There are no pre-packaged saints; no "add-and-stir" formula that makes God's love gush forth. To be loving you've got to take up your cross, deny yourself and make *others* your priority.

Remember the woman caught in adultery? Jesus stooped down to reach her, stood by her under attack, then sent her home redeemed and refocused. Do you want to be like Him? Go and find people who are hurting, hopeless, and even wrong. When you do, minister to them until they're redeemed, restored and right. *That's living unselfishly!*

ICEBERGS

Each tree is recognized by its own fruit.
Luke 6:44 NIV

*T*he Titanic received 5 iceberg warnings just before it went down. When the 6th message came during the wee hours of the morning: "Look out for icebergs," the operator wired back "Shut up! I'm busy!" Thirty minutes later the great vessel—whose captain said, "Even God couldn't sink this ship"—was sinking fast. What happened? They forgot the truth about icebergs. What they saw above the water couldn't have sunk the great ship. But unfortunately most of an iceberg is below the water. Do you know what? That iceberg represents your life! The 10% above the water is your reputation, the 90% below is your character. And it's what's below the surface that sinks your ship. What is character? (a) *Self-discipline*— the ability to do what's right, even when you don't feel like it. *(b) Core values*—principles you live by in spite of the pressures around you. *(c) Sense of identity*—a self-image based on who God, not others, says you are. *(d) Emotional security*—the capacity to be emotionally stable and consistent. Your life's greatest impact doesn't come from what you *own,* but from what you *are*. Jesus said, "Each tree is recognized by its own fruit…The good man brings good things out of the good stored up in his heart, and the evil man brings evil things out of the evil stored up in his heart" (Lk 6:44-45 NIV). Whatever's happening today on the outside of your life comes from what's happening on the inside. God puts "being" before "doing." He prioritizes taking care of the inside (your heart) because that will determine what takes place on the outside (your behavior). Think about it!

SIMPLIFY YOUR LIFE

Let us lay aside every weight.
Hebrews 12:1

A stressed-out traveler at an airport was worried about missing his plane so he asked a guy, "What time is it?" The man set down 2 big heavy bags, looked at his watch and said, "Exactly 5:09, the outside temperature is 73°, and it'll rain later. In London the sky is clear with a high of 28° Celsius. And let's see, in Singapore the sun is shining brightly. And…oh, this is interesting, the moon will be full over Los Angeles tonight." "Your watch tells you all of that?" asked the traveler. "Sure. In fact it tells me much more. You see, I invented this watch and I assure you there's no other timepiece on earth like it." The man said, "I simply must have that watch. I'll give you $10,000 for it." "Okay," said the inventor, "it's a deal," and held out his hand for the money. The traveler grabbed the watch and put it on, smiling with delight. But before he could take a step the inventor stopped him. "Wait!" Then he reached down for the 2 big heavy bags and said, "Don't forget the batteries!"

We hope the latest hi-tech gadgetry will be the very thing that will set our schedule free. But in the end it weighs us down, it increases our dependency on something that will eventually break or become obsolete with the next marvel of modern science. It's time we counted the hidden cost before investing more time, money and confidence in the next does-it-all watch. Those batteries get awfully heavy once the novelty has worn off. What's the message? "Lay aside every weight." Simplify your life, get back on track, focus—and run!

LEARNING TO BE STILL

Be still, and know that I am God.
Psalm 46:10

*F*ormer CBS anchor Dan Rather found himself unprepared for a television interview with Mother Teresa. Ron Mehl described the encounter this way: "All of Dan's standard approaches were inadequate. And the little nun from Calcutta didn't seem inclined to make his task easier. "When you pray," asked Dan, "what do you say to God?" "I don't say anything," she replied. "I listen." Dan tried another tack. "Well, okay... when God speaks to you, then, what does He say?" "He doesn't say anything. He listens." Dan looked bewildered. For an instant, he didn't know what to say. "And if you don't understand that," Mother Teresa added, "I can't explain it to you."

It's in the place of silence that the Holy Spirit boils the truth we receive from Scripture down to its essence, reveals specific insights that are pertinent, and then applies them to our most perplexing problems and our most stubborn misconceptions. As He transforms our heart to beat in sync with His, our decisions begin to accomplish His will and we begin to reflect His character. Go ahead, try it. Open the Word of God in a peaceful place and sit in quietness before Him. In time, the Holy Spirit will illuminate a passage and it will come to life in your mind. Before you know it the knotty situation that drove you to distraction will unravel. As you learn to "be still" in God's presence, your greatest problems will suddenly become more manageable. He will reveal Himself to you. He will calm your emotions and relieve your mind. You'll discover new direction, freedom from worry, and a fresh sense of peace.

MARRIAGE MYTHS (1)

May…God…give you a spirit of unity.
Romans 15:5 NIV

*M*any couples struggling with "curable" issues, have bought into 4 common marriage myths. For the next few days let's look at each of them:

If I try, I can change my partner. Give it up! If you think following the "right" plan, struggling harder and refusing to give up will change them, think again. The Bible says, "Do not think you are better than you are" (Ro 12:3 NCV). The truth is, you can only work on yourself. Once you change *your* steps in the marriage dance, your mate will begin to adjust theirs. Plus, by identifying and working on your own shortcomings you'll gain credibility with your mate, and create an environment that's conducive to change. Now, here are some things you can do:

(a) Praise the qualities you admire most (remember when you were dating?) *and build on them.* Anytime you see positive change, recognize and encourage it. *(b) Don't let things escalate.* Make a habit of asking, "Is there anything on your mind we haven't talked about lately?" The Bible says don't go to bed angry (See Eph 4:26), so deal with things before they lead to hard feelings and cause strife. *(c) Try to be more understanding.* When people don't feel understood, they dig in their heels and re-sist change. *(d) Lessen your dependence on your mate.* Remember, no one can meet all your needs all the time. You need friends to talk to and share activities with. *(e) Above all, be patient; neither of you is perfect.* Ask God to "give you a spirit of unity." And bear in mind that self-control is the result of God's indwelling Spirit, not just human effort (See Gal 5:23 NIV).

MARRIAGE MYTHS (2)

May...God...give you a spirit of unity.
Romans 15:5 NIV

We're just not compatible. Marital disagreements fall into 5 categories: money, sex, in-laws, kids, and household responsibilities. Too many couples think if they argue about these things they're automatically headed for divorce. No, conflict doesn't kill relationships. What's important is how you deal with it, not the fact that it exists. One woman said, "My husband hates confrontation so when problems arose in our marriage he just walked away. I went ballistic and nothing got settled. Eventually we learned to talk about handling our disagreements; *he* can't walk away and *I* can't get hysterical. It works...now we work together to resolve problems." Anger is just part of your emotional make-up; God didn't make a mistake when He included it. But He wants you to handle it right (Mt 16:15). Being upset doesn't give you license to yell and slam doors. Solomon said, "A fool gives full vent to his anger...a wise man keeps himself under control" (Pr 29:11 NIV). Hasty words hurt, and they can't be taken back. David said, "In your anger do not sin ...search your hearts...be silent" (Ps 4:4 NIV). In other words, think, listen, and calm down before you react. And never resort to name-calling (See Mt 5:22); it serves no purpose but to intentionally hurt the other person.

We live in a culture of lawsuits and revenge, but a marriage built on retaliation is headed for trouble. God said "Don't insist on getting even...I'll take care of it" (Ro 12:19). You can become physically and emotionally sick by hanging on to bitterness. So release it and ask God to fill your heart with His love. He'll do it!

MARRIAGE MYTHS (3)

May…God…give you a spirit of unity.
Romans 15:5 NIV

We're not in love any more. Did you hear about the woman who ran a newspaper ad that said, "Husband wanted"? She got lots of responses, all saying the same thing: "You can have mine!" Seriously, if negativity and bitterness are eroding your marriage it's time to make some changes by:

(1) Remembering your history. Chances are you started out as good friends. So ask yourself how you'd treat your best friend if you were having relationship issues. Not by being critical and defensive, right? What initially attracted you to one another anyhow? When did you fall in love? How did you act when things were good? Recall and rehearse your best moments.

(2) Keeping your thoughts focused on what God can do. Zero in on your mate's best qualities, then start believing that God can turn your relationship around. Remember, you have more ability than you realize to change your perception of your partner. So concentrate on all the things in your marriage that are "of good report" (Php 4:8).

(3) Building thoughtful behavior back into your relationship. List some of the things you know would make your spouse happy. Be specific. For example, hugging your husband when he comes home from work after a hard day, or helping your wife with the laundry. Show you care! Inject consideration back into your relationship.

(4) Seeing your partner through God's eyes. Trying to love others like God loves you is a good rule for all your relationships, not just marriage. And if you don't love yourself, start by remembering what God says about you: that you're blessed… loved…valued…and wonderfully made.

MARRIAGE MYTHS (4)

May…God…give you a spirit of unity.
Romans 15:5 NIV

*N*othing can fix our relationship. A woman asked her girlfriend, "How come you're wearing your wedding ring on the wrong finger?" She replied, "Because I married the wrong man!" Sound familiar? The biggest mistake you can make is calling it quits because you think you married the wrong person, and that nothing short of a miracle can save your marriage.

The good news today is, God is still in the miracle business! With Him "nothing is impossible" (Lk 1:37 NIV). It's when problems seem insurmountable that God comes through for you. Jeremiah said, "Lord, you…made the heavens and the earth by your great power…Nothing is too hard for you" (Jer 32:17 NIV). The trouble is too many of us live in the realm of the *probable,* thinking things *probably* won't get better…that we'll *probably* always have money issues…or we'll *probably* get divorced. Instead, we should be living in the realm of the *possible.* Paul says, "Faith…is the confident assurance that what we hope for is going to happen…the evidence of things we cannot yet see" (Heb 11:1 NLT). The Bible says God's plans for you "are for good and not for disaster, to give you a future and a hope" (Jer 29:11 NLT). If you're feeling discouraged about your relationship, try praying, and fixing your thoughts on what God can do. The Bible says when you look earnestly for Him you'll find Him (See 2Ch 15:2). He's not some distant deity who's far removed from the challenges of your everyday life. No, He wants to have an intimate relationship with you; to use His power to transform your marriage into something lasting and wonderful.

"IT'S ALREADY IN THE SAUCE!"

I will…put a new spirit in you.
Ezekiel 36:26 NIV

*W*hen a woman becomes pregnant she has cravings she never had before. And when God saves you, He places within you new desires and appetites. This new nature craves fellowship with God; it desires to please Him above all else. These are intense cravings, which is why, when we sin, we can't enjoy it. Oh, you'll still "blow it," but it will cause an intense struggle in your soul because now you have to try and ignore your new appetites. Paul writes: "Walk by the Spirit, and you will not carry out the desire of the flesh" (Gal 5:16 NAS). The order is crucial here, because a lot of us get it backwards. We think that if we can just stop fulfilling the desires of our flesh, then we can begin walking in the Spirit. But it's just the opposite. The Holy Spirit working on the inside produces spiritual victory on the outside. All that we need to walk in victory— is already present within us! One television commercial for spaghetti sauce shows a mom cooking spaghetti. As the aroma fills the house her son asks, "Hey Mom, where are the mushrooms?" "They're already in the sauce" she says. "What about the sausage?" "It's in there too." "And what about the tomatoes?" Once again the mom says, "They're already in the sauce." Are you looking for victory? It's already within you. Are you looking for strength to obey God? It's in there too. Need grace to endure the trial? It's already in the sauce! *Everything* required for victorious Christian living has already been deposited within you. Just tap into it!

AMNESIA

Beware that in your plenty you do not forget the Lord.
Deuteronomy 8:11 NLT

A spider dropped a single strand down from the rafter of an old barn and began to weave his web. Months went by and the web grew. Its elaborate maze caught flies, mosquitoes and other small insects, providing the spider with a rich diet. Eventually it became the envy of all the other spiders. Then one day the spider noticed a single strand stretching up into the rafters. "I wonder why it's there? It doesn't catch me any dinner." Concluding it was unnecessary, he climbed as high as he could and severed it. In that moment the entire web began to fall in upon itself, tumbling to the floor, taking the spider with it.

Could we as a people make that same mistake? Can a country spin a great web, then sever it? Can we grow so successful, so smug, so self-sufficient that we forget the strong strand that supports us? Could we look at our prosperity and respond not with gratitude, but with arrogance? Recent actions make us wonder. A movement to remove God from all public life is gaining momentum. An emboldened portion of our population stares at the strand of faith upon which our country hangs and asks: "Why is that there?" Are we forgetting the hand that holds us? We're not the first nation to suffer from amnesia. Israel did it too, and Moses warned them: "Beware that in your plenty you do not forget the Lord your God and disobey his commands…I assure you of this: if you ever forget the Lord your God…you will certainly be destroyed" (Dt 8:11 & 19 NLT).

IDENTITY THEFT

Christ lives in me.
Galatians 2:20 NIV

*Y*our identity has great value not only to you, but also to the thief who wants your name and credit card to run up a stack of bills. Some of us will go to great lengths to try and gain an identity we think will make us more acceptable to a certain group—like wearing designer clothes or driving a certain car. Some think it's in their looks and opt for plastic surgery. Some identify themselves by their profession or trade. Maybe you've heard about the guy who went to the psychiatrist with a severe identity crisis, saying, "Doctor, I'm convinced I'm a dog." When the psychiatrist asked how long he had this problem, he blurted out, "Ever since I was a puppy!" Too many of us are confused or basically uninformed about our true identity as redeemed children of God. This leads to false growth, or no growth. Paul bottom-lined his identity like this: "Christ lives in me." Then he added: "I can do all things through Him who strengthens me" (Php 4:13 NAS). With the fingers of Mozart there's no musical piece you couldn't play. With the brain of Einstein there's no mathematical formula you couldn't unravel. With the life of Christ within you there's no victory you cannot win. Your new identity also solves your self-worth problem. When you understand who you are in Christ you realize that you've already been accepted by God—and you can't improve on that! So who are you? You're a totally forgiven, fully accepted, deeply loved, daily-empowered child of God. Once you fully grasp that, you'll have joy you've never known and grow like you've never grown.

FAITH SAYS, "IT'S SO"

Without faith it is impossible to please God.
Hebrews 11:6 NIV

*T*ony Evans writes: "A practical definition of faith I like, is acting like it's so even when it's not, in order that it might be so, just because God said so." Maybe you're saying, "That sounds like I'm supposed to pretend something's real when it isn't." No. We're talking about believing that what God says is true, even when there's no evidence available. And the way you know you believe—is when you act on it. Maybe you think people like Noah and Moses had it easier than we do because God spoke to them directly. True, God did speak to them, but that didn't make their obedience any easier. Remember, Noah worked for 120 years with no water around him, and kept announcing a coming flood based solely on what God had told him. Moses didn't get to attend a showing of *The Ten Commandments* and find out how the Red Sea would part. Actually, we have the advantage because we have God's completed Word. But we still experience the turbulence of life. Ever been on an airplane when it started shaking or dropped? Remember how you felt when the captain spoke over the intercom, calmly explaining that this was no big deal. Your options were to have faith in the captain—or believe what you saw and felt. Depending on your choice, you either white-knuckled the rest of your flight, or relaxed and enjoyed it. Faith takes you beyond the limits of your logic, reason and senses. It enables you to believe that if God said it, it's true. Simply put, faith is *acting* as if God is telling the truth.

A DAILY DOSE OF SCRIPTURE

It felt like a fire burning in us when Jesus...
explained the Scriptures to us.
Luke 24:32 NCV

*T*he two Emmaus-bound pilgrims discovered the power of the Scripture that first Easter Sunday. They were broken-hearted from the crucifixion: "Sadness [was] written across their faces" (Lk 24:17 NLT). They allowed their pain to blind them to the presence of Jesus. He'd risen from the dead, and though they didn't yet recognize Him, He'd come to take their sorrow. How would He do this? "Jesus took them through the writings of Moses and all the prophets, explaining from all the Scriptures the things concerning himself" (Lk 24:27 NLT). He opened their eyes, lifting their heavy hearts with the Scriptures. He chose the one thing that never fails—God's Word! Did it make a difference? For those two it did: "It felt like a fire burning in us when Jesus talked to us on the road and explained the Scriptures to us." Trying to live a victorious Christian life without a daily dose of the Scriptures is like trying to run your car on an empty tank, work all week on an empty stomach, or pay your bills on an empty checking account.

Steve Farrar writes: "I need to be reminded of what is true. God's Word gives me a dose of reality. My morning briefing in the Word gives me a perspective that I don't get in the world. I need God's commentary on my life every day. A Christian...in this society is swimming upstream. Without the constant nutrition of the Word, he will soon tire and be dragged off by the sheer force of the current." So, spend time each day in the Scriptures!

INTOXICATED

Do not get drunk on wine…
Instead, be filled with the Spirit.
Ephesians 5:18 NIV

A drunk man doesn't get that way by just talking about alcohol, or looking at advertisements for liquor. No, he gets drunk by drinking! And the more he drinks the more the alcohol controls him. We say he's "under the influence." Another power takes over which transforms him into someone he was not before. One minute he's nice and quiet, the next he's loud and boisterous. He may even think he's Pavarotti and start to sing. When a police officer stops him and tells him to walk a straight line he can't do it. Why? Because something else is running the show. And what alcohol is to your body negatively, the Holy Spirit is to your new nature positively. When you're under His control He makes you walk in ways you wouldn't normally walk, and talk in ways you wouldn't normally talk. That's why, rather than spending our time and energy trying to change, we need to concentrate on being—and staying—filled with God's Spirit. A sober man doesn't have to try and stagger, all he has to do is get drunk; the alcohol will take care of the staggering. Now you see why Paul drew the analogy between someone who's drunk and someone under the Spirit's control. But a word of caution: those under the influence of the Holy Spirit will not be offensive or rude, self-serving or "show-boating" in an attempt to impress others. No, the Holy Spirit is a gentleman. The power He provides is *controlled* and *channeled* towards a life that's not possible by any other means. And that power is available to *you* today.

WHO DO YOU HAVE? (1)

Two are better than one.
Ecclesiastes 4:9 NIV

*E*dward Farrell said, "Listening is rare. There are certain people to whom we feel we can talk because they have such a deep capacity for hearing, not just our words, but hearing us as a person. They enable us to communicate on a level we've never reached before. They enable us to be as we've never been before. We will never truly know ourselves unless we find people who can listen, who can enable us to emerge, to come out of ourselves, to discover who we are. We cannot discover ourselves by ourselves." Note the words "there are certain people...who enable us to be as we have never been before." Those are the people you need most. Consider these questions: *Who coaches you?* What older, wiser, and more experienced person stands on the sidelines of your life and watches with the big picture in mind? A coach doesn't try to run the race for you. No, he sets the standard for the race and makes a judgment on your performance. Who does this for you? *Who stretches your mind?* Who makes you wince as they expose the many faces of your ignorance; who will not let you get away with spiritual and intellectual superficiality. *Who listens to and encourages your dreams?* Dreams are not intellectual propositions that must be proven. They are the work of visionaries; they are out-of-the-box, frequently awful and occasionally good. These are the folks who, when others laugh and say you're trying to build castles in the air, remind you that God "calls those things which be not, as though they are" (See Ro 4:17). These are the people you need!

WHO DO YOU HAVE? (2)

Two are better than one.
Ecclesiastes 4:9 NIV

Who protects you? When the Christians in Jerusalem wanted nothing to do with the newly converted Saul of Tarsus, Barnabas acted as his advocate. You don't have enough voices. You need others to speak up for you. *Who shares your tears?* Mary of Bethany was the only person in the room who understood what Jesus was going through as He came closer to His hour of death. She alone shared His tears. Who's close enough to you to pick up on the signals, to sense when fears and tears need to be shared? Yes, there are times when we need a pep talk or a shot in the arm, but there are also times when we need to be encouraged to lie low, to process our emotions. Who does that for you? *Who rebukes you?* Even with 20/20 vision, one pair of eyes is not enough. You have blind spots. Satan is always ready to remind you of your good qualities. But a true friend is the one who exposes and challenges your self-seeking, self-pleasing and self-dependence, and helps you to restore to God the authority you've robbed Him of. *Who plays with you?* Does this sound unimportant, even carnal? No! You must never let the seriousness of life override your need for recreation, a word that's only understood when it's hyphenated, re-creation. *Who seeks God with you?* Praying together keeps us honest. It also keeps us dependent on God. We're reluctant to open up, to get real about our areas of struggle. Yet it's only in the honesty of shared prayer that we draw closer to God—and to one another.

KEEP YOUR SENSE OF HUMOR

He will yet fill your mouth with laughter.
Job 8:21 NIV

*O*ne of the best ways to reduce stress is to keep your sense of humor. Don't panic, don't overreact, and don't use unnecessary force. If you do people will avoid you. Happy people get more done than their oh-so-serious counterparts. Actually, being joyful can make you laugh all the way to the bank. Would you rather buy a car from a stressed-out, verbally abusive salesman, or someone whose company you enjoy? Would you rather work around someone who's congenial, or someone moaning and groaning about what ought to be done? "A cheerful heart is good medicine" (Pr 17:22 NIV). However, keep in mind 2 things when it comes to humor: *(1) Make sure your humor is at no one else's expense.* Avoid jokes about things others might be sensitive about. Weight, bad hairdos and cheating husbands might make some people laugh, but to others it's not funny. No one likes to be the butt of the joke. Be careful with teasing someone else. Make sure that their personality can handle your humor. It's always wise to let the joke be on you; you know you're not going to offend yourself! *(2) Remember that timing is everything.* "There is a time for everything... a time to weep and a time to laugh" (Ecc 3:1, 4 NIV). If people don't believe you truly care about them, your humor will produce only a shallow and strained response. Every relationship, every path you cross, every conversation you have can ultimately be used by God to further His purposes. Whether at work, at home or at play, always keep these things in mind.

STARVING BAKERS

I am the bread of life.
He who comes to me will never go hungry.
John 6:35 NIV

*I*magine finding a new bakery. You love going there because the baker creates new recipes, better than any you've ever tasted. Soon word gets out and crowds start coming. The baker doesn't have enough help and ends up trying to serve all the customers himself. Gradually you see a change. He's getting thin. Very thin! What's up? You decide to sit and observe. Suddenly the problem becomes obvious. He's busy serving everyone else but never stops long enough to feed himself. With food all around him, he's starving. Can you relate? A lot of us, particularly leaders, fail to take care of ourselves spiritually, emotionally and intellectually, and eventually we end up being unable to take care of others. And when we do read our Bible or listen to CDs, it's always for others. And what's the result? We end up busy but barren, going through the motions without taking time to feed our souls on the bread of life. And we keep promising ourselves to do better: "when the kids are raised... when I go on vacation...when things slow down...when I retire." Solomon wrote: "They made me caretaker of the vineyards, but I have not taken care of my own" (SS 1:6 NAS). The only way things are going to change—is if you change them! Otherwise you'll simply exchange one set of demands for another. Learn to walk away. Jesus did: "After He had dismissed the multitudes, He went up into the hills by Himself to pray" (Mt 14:23 AMP). Start doing what Jesus did, otherwise you'll end up like the starving baker!

YOUR GROWTH—GOD'S GLORY!

To him be glory.
2 Peter 3:18 NIV

After writing, "Grow in the grace and knowledge of our Lord," Peter adds: "To him be glory." Your *biggest* reason for wanting to grow spiritually should not be to "get it right," or look good personally. No, it should be that God may be glorified in your living. Paul writes, "Glorify God in your body, and in your spirit" (1Co 6:20). Why should we keep our flesh in check, or watch our attitudes? To glorify God before others! The problem is, our emphasis is on what *we* are doing, instead of focusing on God and His glory. The word glory refers to something or someone of great worth. So what are we supposed to do? Draw attention to God. Promote Him. God wants to go public. Since He's invisible, He's created people whose full time job is to make Him visible so that the world might be drawn to Him. A company intent on promoting itself doesn't settle for a small ad buried in the yellow pages. It may start that way, but the idea is to grow into something bigger so that more people will be reached. We are billboards advertising God's grace to a lost world. He wants us to grow so that we can display Him more. In fact, God has entrusted His public image to us. Glorifying Him is our most awesome privilege and responsibility. Unless you think this is overstating the case, Paul writes, "Whether you eat or drink or whatever you do, do it all for the glory of God" (1Co 10:31 NIV). God is passionate about His glory. "Why grow?" you ask. Because spiritual growth increases your capacity to bring God glory.

DO YOU PRACTICE HUMILITY?

But it is not this way among you.
Mark 10:43 NAS

*I*t would be wonderful if just being around humble people automatically made us humble. The disciples proved it didn't. Mark describes an incident involving James and John, two brothers. The story makes most parents nod and smile. It took place before John grew into maturity—still a disciple, still young, and still looking out for John: "James and John...came up to Jesus, saying...'Grant that we may sit, one on Your right, and one on Your left, in Your glory.'" Jesus replied: "You do not know what you are asking" (Mk 10:35-38 NAS). Then He called the disciples together and said, "Those who are recognized as rulers of the Gentiles lord it over them; and their great men exercise authority over them. But it is not this way among you" (Mk 10:42-43 NAS). Our modern world is run by chain of command. In the military, generals command colonels, who command majors, who command captains, all the way down to the lowly private on the end of a mop handle. Jesus barely took a breath after contrasting the two kingdoms, then added, "But it is not so among you." In God's Kingdom there's no privileged rank. The lowly don't pamper the privileged—quite the opposite. Once He got their attention, Jesus spelled it out, "Whoever wishes to become great among you shall be your servant" (Mk 10:43 NAS). Genuinely humble people have one thing in common—they don't think of themselves as humble. As a matter of fact, they rarely think of *themselves* at all! They're too occupied with God's purposes and the well-being of others. So, do you practice humility?

FOCUS ON THE NEW, NOT THE OLD!

The old has gone, the new has come!
2 Corinthians 5:17 NIV

*T*oo many of us are busy trying to repair our old nature and make it look good, when God's in the business of throwing out the old and crafting something brand new. When your car's been declared a loss in an accident, if you're insured you receive a new car. But if it isn't totaled, you get it repaired and hope it runs well. God has declared our old nature a total loss. He wants you to concentrate on the new nature He has given you. If you've spent years trying to fix up what God says cannot be fixed up, allow the truth of God's Word to liberate you from a very frustrating way of life. To understand this, think of caterpillars and butterflies. Caterpillars are not very pretty. But once they break free from the cocoon of their old nature and become butterflies, the transformation is incredible. What was once ugly is now beautiful. A creature that could only crawl can now soar. But this transformation requires a growth process, and it isn't always easy. There's a lot of struggle involved. But the result is worth the effort. A butterfly is not just a fixed up caterpillar, but a new creature with a new capacity for life. And the good news is, we don't become butterflies in our own strength. From God's perspective, willpower is no power. Paul writes, "For it is God who works in you to will and to act according to his good purpose" (Php 2:13 NIV). Our job is just to draw close to, submit to, and cooperate with God in this work.

THE MOST INCREDIBLE BOOK
EVER WRITTEN (1)

The word of the Lord will live forever.
1 Peter 1:25 NCV

*W*illiam Gladstone, Prime Minister of England, stated: "I have known 95 great men in my time. And of these, 87 were followers of the Bible." President John Quincy Adams declared: "The Bible is the book above all others, to read at all ages, and in all conditions of human life." Suppose a museum of art commissions a painting to be painted by 40 different artists. They work in their respective studios knowing nothing of each other's efforts. Yet when all these many canvasses are assembled on one wall they create the perfect landscape. What are the odds? Or suppose 40 architects set out to design one building. Some know what others are doing—others are unaware anyone else is doing anything at all. When they gather to compile notes, the result is a magnificent blueprint. Could it happen? It did with the Bible. No publisher commissioned it. No committee outlined it. No earthly editor oversaw it. Though separated by 16 centuries, and penned by an unlikely assortment of kings, soldiers, shepherds, farmers and fishermen, from Moses in the Arabian desert to John on the windswept island of Patmos—one theme threads the Bible together. That theme is salvation through Jesus Christ. Your Bible is the most incredible book ever written. Every passing day validates Peter's prophecy: "The Word of the Lord will live forever." The question is: does it live in your heart? Does it determine your conduct? Does it set your priorities? Do you hunger for it? Can you say "Oh how I love your law! I meditate on it all day long" (Ps 119:97 NIV)?

THE MOST INCREDIBLE BOOK
EVER WRITTEN (2)

The word of the Lord will live forever.
1 Peter 1:25 NCV

$\mathcal{V}$oltaire, the famous French atheist, once wrote from his Paris office: "I will go through the forest of Scripture and girdle all the trees so that in one hundred years Christianity will be but a vanishing memory." In a twist of divine irony, the room in which he penned those words was later purchased by the British and Foreign Bible Society and packed with Bibles. What rivals the durability of the Bible? We applaud the Number One Best Seller. We award the book that remains on the top for weeks at a time. If one claimed the lead for several years, we would bronze each page. But what if a book is Number One for *300 years?* Your Bible is the most widely published and translated book in history—available in over 2000 different dialects. Why? Because it works! Apply its principles to any part of your life and see what happens. (a) Apply it to your finances. Manage your money the way the Bible says: tithe, save, provide for your family, give to the needy. Test God's Word and prosper. (b) Test God's Word on your job. Follow the Bible's code of work conduct. Be honest. Be on time. Be efficient. You may get a promotion. (c) Test the Bible on your relationships. Forgive your enemies. Refuse to gossip. Do all you can to be at peace with all. Be quick to listen and slow to speak. (d) But most of all, apply the Bible to your soul. "There's nothing like the written Word of God for showing you the way to salvation" (2Ti 3:15 TM).

HOW DO YOU TREAT HURTING PEOPLE?

Feed the hungry! Help those in trouble!
Isaiah 58:10 TLB

*D*on't get sidetracked by the pain or problems of others. After all, it's probably just the result of their sin. Just get them converted and the problem will solve itself. Anyway, feeding the hungry and helping those in trouble is something 'liberals' do! Who thinks like that? Sadly, some folks who claim to be following Christ! Why can't we be committed and still be compassionate? Jesus wouldn't give an inch when it came to the truth, but watch Him around hurting people. He was "moved with compassion" (Mt 9:36). Unfortunately, a lot of us are only moved with indignation. But then that's easier, isn't it? That way we don't have to get our hands dirty, take risks, feel what it's like to hurt, or deal with the "thorny side" of an issue that has no easy answers. Look out! People don't care how much you know, until they first know how much you care!

A conversation took place many years ago between God and some very religious people. These folks asked God, "Why don't you see our sacrifices? Why don't you hear our prayers?" (Isa 58:3 TLB). God's answer should make us sit up and do some real soul-searching. He said, "Feed the hungry! Help those in trouble! Then the Lord will guide you continually, and satisfy you with all good things, and keep you healthy too." Guidance. Security. Satisfaction. Health. And there's more! Jesus said that we'll all be evaluated and rewarded according to how we treat hurting people (See Mt 25:34-40; Col 3:12-14; Jas 5:11). So ask yourself today: "How do I treat them?"

WISE UP!

I fear that…I myself might be disqualified.
1 Corinthians 9:27 NLT

$\mathcal{L}$et's take another look at Samson! *He broke the rules!* The relationships he formed destroyed him. The Bible warns: "Be ye not unequally yoked together with unbelievers" (2Co 6:14). An ox and a donkey can't work in the same harness. Why? Because their natures are different! When God says "no" to certain things He's not being difficult, He's being protective. Heed Him! *(2) He lived by his impulses!* He thought he was in love when he was only in heat. When confronted about his relationship choices he replied, "She pleaseth me well" (Jdg 14:3). Before it was over he became a laughing-stock. Peter writes: "Abstain from sinful desires, which war against your soul" (1Pe 2:11 NIV). In war the strongest side wins, so keep your impulses in check. *(3) He misused his gift!* Samson exploited his God-given strength for personal gain. Listen to these words spoken to his Philistine buddies, concerning a bet he'd made with them: "Then shall ye give me" (Jdg 14:13). God gives us gifts to fulfill His purposes, not ours. When we misuse them we end up in trouble. *(4) He was blind to his weaknesses!* You may not like to believe that your private imperfections will have public consequences, but you can't escape what you are. If Satan attacked Jesus 3 times in the wilderness, he's not going to give you a free pass! Protect yourself! Satan always attacks those who are in line for God's blessing. Why does God make such a big deal of this? Because sin hurts us, and anything that hurts one of His children makes Him angry.

SENSITIVITY TRAINING

*Who because of practice have their senses
trained to discern good and evil.*
Hebrews 5:14 NAS

$\mathcal{T}$he writer to the Hebrews says, "Solid food is for the mature, who because of practice have their senses trained to discern good and evil." With maturity comes the increased capacity to see things from God's angle. What an advantage! Seasoned believers can filter everything that comes their way through the grid of God's Word, discerning His will, obeying what He tells them to do. As a result they walk in God's blessing. They pick up on signals that immature believers don't have the capacity to receive, grasp or interpret, even though they may be able to communicate certain doctrinal facts.

Here's an illustration from everyday life. Suppose you want your daughter to respond with love and trust, but you also want to teach her not to come running when a stranger offers her candy to get in their car. Your challenge is, your daughter's reasoning powers aren't mature enough to distinguish between someone who loves her and someone who may want to harm her. She may be able to repeat the information you teach her, but without maturity she's unable to apply it correctly in a real life situation. So you keep reinforcing the lesson because your child can't always discern a good situation from a bad one. Are you getting the idea? The writer to the Hebrews states, "Who because of practice have their senses trained to discern good from evil." To mature, you must spend time daily in God's Word. But you must do more; you must *practice* its principles in all your affairs. Only then can you know and enjoy what's good for you.

HOW'S YOUR PRAYER LIFE?

Pray without ceasing.
1 Thessalonians 5:17

 $\mathscr{P}$ rayer is not a monologue where one person does all the talking, or a ritual where we must say things in the right order, or a chore to get out of the way like brushing our teeth before going to bed. Jesus rejects this performance-based understanding of prayer: "Find a quiet, secluded place so you won't be tempted to role-play before God. Just be there as simply and honestly as you can manage. The focus will shift from you to God, and you will begin to sense his grace" (Mt 6:6 TM). For many, prayer has little to do with the realities of life. They think of it like the National Anthem at a game: a nice opening, but nothing to do with what happens on the field afterwards. Other people treat prayer like a rabbit's foot you pull out and rub when things are tough: "A prayer a day keeps the devil away." Paul writes, "Pray without ceasing." That doesn't sound like something you do once in a while, or a flare you shoot up during a crisis. Try substituting the word *breathe* for the word *pray:* "breathe without ceasing"—doesn't that sound like a good idea to you? We don't breathe only when we feel like it. Or decide, "I'm not into oxygen today," and stop breathing. Or get frustrated and say, "This isn't getting me any-where. I'm not going to do it any more." No, we cling to the breath in our bodies like it's life. So, just as breathing is an indispensable part of your natural life, prayer is an indispens-able part of spiritual life. Without it you die spiritually. So, how's your prayer life?

THRIVING IN TOUGH CIRCUMSTANCES

He grew up…like a root out of dry ground.
Isaiah 53:2 NIV

*I*saiah points out that Jesus sprang up "like a root out of dry ground." Talk about tough circumstances! God dressed up in a man's body, living among those who wanted to kill him simply because He wanted to save them. He left Heaven—which we're hard-pressed to even imagine—to enter earth, a hostile environment filled with betrayers and religious stiff-necks, to go toe-to-toe with the devil. So, He pulled away a lot. What a consecrated, set-apart life He had to live in order to survive among His own who despised, rejected and finally crucified Him. He spent much time in prayer and came back from those visits with His Father encouraged and empowered. Jesus always kept one thing in mind: He came to do His Father's will. Just that! And He said that as the Father had sent Him, "So send I you" (Jn 20:21). So we too should keep God's will in mind at all times as we endeavor to survive our struggles. We need to remember that He sent us, and that we have a job to do. When we know that we are not our own, that our well-being and identity are not dependent upon the recognition of others, we can experience a level of peace, joy and contentment even in the toughest of circumstances. When we know that God appreciates us we can have a healthy self-esteem, not a weak dependent ego that constantly needs propping up like a loose signpost. Tough times produce strong character, and strong character brings God's blessing. "For to everyone who has, more will be given, and he will have abundance" (Mt 25:29 NKJV).

YOU NEED THE CHURCH

Not forsaking the assembling of ourselves together.
Hebrews 10:25

*T*he Church is God's life-support system for individual Christians. Nobody expects a baby to grow on its own, and God never meant for us to grow and develop spiritually in isolation. Spiritual growth is a group project, which should be good news to you because that means you don't have to do it all by yourself. You need to be surrounded by spiritual fathers, mothers, brothers and sisters who can help you. Adam's aloneness was the only part of creation that God said was "not good" (Ge 2:18). The universal church is made up of believers *everywhere,* the local church is made up of believers *somewhere.* The writer in Hebrews states, "Let's see how inventive we can be in encouraging love and helping out, not avoiding worshiping together as some do" (Heb 10:25 TM). You say, "But I don't need encouragement and I don't need help." Perhaps not today, but what about next week or next month? And what about the people who need your help and encouragement?

There are 2 kinds of growth: *(1) Symbiotic growth,* which occurs when 2 organisms both benefit by the relationship. *(2) Parasitic growth,* which occurs when one organism feeds off another without giving anything back. Paul describes the church as "God's household" (Eph 2:19 NIV) in which the members grow by being "fitted together" and by being "built together for a dwelling place of God" (Eph 2:21-22 NKJV). We are all to be part of something bigger than any one of us. There is no mention in Paul's words of individual growth apart from the church. We only grow as we connect, relate, contribute, and receive one from another.

STAY SHARP!

If the axe is dull and he does not sharpen its edge,
then he must exert more strength.
Wisdom has the advantage of giving success.
Ecclesiastes 10:10 NAS

*D*id you hear about the 2 lumberjacks who challenged each other to see which one could cut down more trees in a day? At daybreak the first one began furiously chopping down trees. He worked up a sweat and by noon he had cut down 16 trees. Meanwhile the other lumberjack had only cut down 4, because he took the first 2 hours to sharpen his axe. As he sharpened it his challenger laughed at him thinking he was doomed to lose the bet because of all that wasted time. That's when things got interesting. By early afternoon the first lumberjack was slowing down. It took him almost an hour to cut down one tree, while his friend was picking up speed. How could this be? Certainly he was as strong as his friend. Unfortunately, strength had little to do with it. It was all about whose axe was sharper. The sharper the axe—the quicker the trees came down. By late afternoon the second lumberjack, who'd sharpened his axe, had passed his friend by several trees and won easily. There's an important lesson there for you. Your ceaseless activity may feed your ego and satisfy your need to be needed, but eventually: (a) it will leave you dull spiritually, emotionally and mentally; (b) the people who need and applaud you now, will discover it and go looking for someone sharper, leaving you feeling "used" and unappreciated; (c) because you've lost your edge you'll be unprepared for what God has for you next! So, stay sharp!

TWO PHASES—ANTICIPATION AND REALITY!

But the hour cometh, and now is.
John 4:23

*P*hase one: anticipation. This woman had lived through 5 failed marriages, become the talk of the town, and lost her capacity to trust others or respect herself. Then Jesus showed up and said, "The hour cometh." What a message: "Your time has come. Things in your life are about to change. What you're weeping over today you'll rejoice over tomorrow." God's grace turns the failures of our past into fertilizer. Like a lily springing up in a mud marsh, God offers us: "Beauty for ashes, and the garment of praise in exchange for the spirit of heaviness." (See Isa 61:3). Notice, when Christ mentioned this woman's past He wasn't a Pharisee pointing an accusing finger. No, He was the Good Shepherd walking for miles to find one lost sheep; the great Physician pouring healing love into her deepest wounds; and "the door" that leads out of misery and into the life she always longed for.

Phase two: reality. "And now is." The waiting is over. Anticipation turns to reality and she seizes her moment. When Jesus said, "Whosoever drinketh of the water that I shall give... shall never thirst" (Jn 4:14); she replies: "Sir, give me this water, that I thirst not" (Jn 4:15). She reaches by faith and receives what He has for her. Then redeemed, recycled and redirected, this woman with a questionable past goes all over town introducing others to Christ. What a story! And what Jesus did for her He'll do for you. What He said to her He says to you: "Your time has come. Your breakthrough is at hand. Believe it, receive it and walk in it."

A WORD TO TEACHERS (1)

You, however, know all about my teaching,
my way of life.
2 Timothy 3:10 NIV

*I*f you want your teaching to have impact, you must do these 3 things:

(1) Know your students. And that takes commitment and time. This is where we lose a lot of teachers. There's no magic formula. Good teaching has a price tag: you've got to be willing to pour out your life for others. If your students have to trip you up on your way out of class in order to have a moment with you, you're not going to reach them. People don't care how much you know, until they first know how much you care. *(2) Earn the right to be heard.* Walk out on the street and tell the first guy you meet that you know what his problem is—and he'll probably give you a bit of his mind he can't afford to lose. Even if you know what his problem is, you won't get through to him. Credibility must precede communication. And our celebrity society has never figured that out. You must win a hearing! *(3) Be willing to become vulnerable.* It's the broken who become masters at mending. Don't be afraid to let people know what you're struggling with, and what you've struggled with through the years. People tend to see us in terms of where we are now, rather than in light of where we've come from and what we've been through. They didn't see the process. So tell them about the God you know personally, and what He's brought you through. That'll impact them every time! Want to be a teacher who "gets through to people"? Practice these principles.

A WORD TO TEACHERS (2)

Everyone who is fully trained will be like his teacher.
Luke 6:40 NIV

*I*f you stop growing, you stop teaching! The truth doesn't change, but your understanding of it should. Peter writes: "Grow in…grace and knowledge" (2Pe 3:18 NIV). This requires the attitude that you haven't yet "arrived." Those who apply this principle are always asking, "How can I improve?" Dr. Howard Hendricks writes: "When I was a college student… I worked in the dining hall. On my way to work at 5:30 each morning I walked past the home of one of my professors. Through a window I could see a light on at his desk. He was poring over his books. One day he invited me home for lunch and I said: 'Would you mind if I asked you a question? What keeps you studying? You never seem to stop.' He answered 'Son, I would rather have my students drink from a running stream than a stagnant pool.' He was one of the best professors I ever had—a man who marked me permanently." Do you teach others? From which wells are you drinking? Jesus said, "Everyone who is fully trained will be like his teacher." Those words should either excite you—or drive you to your knees. If you want to touch others you must first ask God to touch you! He desires to work *through* you, but He can't until He works *in* you. He'll use you as His instrument, but first He wants to sharpen and cleanse that instrument so it becomes a more effective tool in His hands. So, if you want to strengthen your teaching, do everything in your power to strengthen the teacher!

A WORD TO TEACHERS (3)

I press on toward the goal.
Philippians 3:14 NIV

*I*f you want to become a change agent, *you* yourself must change! And you're never too old to do that. Change has nothing to do with your age and everything to do with your attitude. "Well, I'm just getting too old," you say. How old is too old? Have you died? "No," you say, "I'm still alive." Good! Then learn—or you'll die mentally. Older people can be excellent learners. Somewhere along the line we've taken in the mistaken idea that you can't teach an old dog new tricks—which is true if you're teaching dogs and if you're teaching tricks. But you are not in the business of either one, are you? Some folks in their 20's are dead in the head, while others in their 80's are plugged in, turned on, and going places. The apostle Paul was one. Near the end of his life, when most of us are looking for rocking chairs, he wrote: "Forgetting what is behind and straining toward what is ahead, I press on toward the goal to win the prize for which God has called me" (Php 3:13-14 NIV). Paul was neither impressed by his successes nor intimidated by his failures. He learned from his past, but he refused to live in it. His goal was always before him. And he was just as properly related to the present. He said, "I press on." Every day when Paul's eyes opened he thought, "It's a new day full of possibilities; Lord help me to max every moment!" As they say, "The older the fiddle the sweeter the tune"—but only if you keep practicing and stay in shape!

A FATHER'S MEMORY

The righteous man walks in…integrity;
blessed…are his children after him.
Proverbs 20:7 AMP

*M*ax Lucado writes: "Today's my first [Father's Day] without a father. For 31 years I had one of the best, but now he's…buried under an oak tree in a west Texas cemetery. Strange he isn't here…because he was always available. His words were nothing novel; his achievements, though admirable, were nothing extraordinary. *But his presence was*. Because he was there, life went smoothly…the future was secure…and my growing up was what God intended. He taught me how to shave and how to pray. Helped me memorize verses for Sunday school, taught me that wrong should be punished…and that rightness has its own reward. He modeled…the elusive balance between ambition and self-acceptance. I knew if I ever needed him he'd be there. Like a warm fireplace. Maybe that's why this Father's Day's a bit chilly. The fire's gone out. The winds of age swallowed his splendid flame leaving only golden embers. But there's a strange thing about those embers, stir them…and the flame will dance…and knock just enough chill out of the air to remind me that he's still…present."

Compare that to an interview with actor Gene Hackman who recalls: "I was just 13, but that Saturday morning is still vivid. I was playing down the street…when I saw my father drive by and give me a light wave. Somehow I knew that gesture meant he was going away forever. To this day the memory's a ghost that never seems to fade." Solomon said, "The righteous man walks in integrity…blessed are his children after him." Attention father! What memories will *your* kids have when you're gone?

WHEN WE PRAY—GOD WORKS!

Therefore I tell you, whatever you ask for in prayer,
believe that you have received it, and it will be yours.
Mark 11:24 NIV

*T*wo things about prayer are truly amazing: *(1) God listens when we pray.* "If you believe, you will receive whatever you ask for in prayer" (See Mk 11:24). You may not have much clout anywhere else, but when you pray God listens. *(2) We seldom pray.* We have the greatest privilege imaginable—access to the control center of the Universe—yet we rarely use it. And our lack of prayer surprises God. Through the prophet Ezekiel He lamented: "I sought for a man among them who would... stand in the gap before Me on behalf of the land, that I should not destroy it; but I found no one" (Eze 22:30 NKJV). Upon learning that Sodom and Gomorrah were going to be destroyed, Abraham didn't rush to warn the cities. No, he chose to "[remain] standing before the Lord" (Ge 18:22 NIV). When God said the golden calf warranted a nationwide death penalty for Israel, Moses interceded and saved them. One translation of Exodus 32:11 says, "Moses soothed the face of his God." An obscure priest by the name of Phinehas begged God not to send the plague, and it was checked. (See Ps 106:30 NIV). You say "Why place such a premium on prayer?" Simple. Because when we work, *we* work. But when we pray, *God* works! Scripture attaches breathtaking power to prayer. "When two of you get together on anything...and make a prayer of it, my Father in heaven goes into action" (Mt 18:19 TM). Does any other activity promise such results? Did God call us to preach without ceasing? Or have committee meetings without ceasing? No, but He did call us to "pray without ceasing."

"SEEING IT!"

How many loaves do you have? he asked. Go and see.
Mark 6:38 NIV

Learn to look for the extraordinary, within the ordinary moment! Opportunities for growth and blessing are constantly coming your way—or passing you right by. James writes, "If any of you lacks wisdom, he should ask God, who gives generously to all without finding fault, and it will be given him" (Jas 1:5 NIV). Before you act, stop and pray: "Father, show me what I'm not seeing. Your Word says You can turn a curse into a blessing. If I can't change this right now, how can I use it to grow wiser and do better next time? Have You permitted this problem because You have the solution, and You want me to seek You and draw closer to You before You reveal it to me?"

Before Jesus fed the five thousand He told His disciples (who'd decided to send the crowd away to find their own food), "You give them something to eat" (Lk 9:13 NIV). They replied, "That would take eight months of a man's wages!" (Mk 6:37 NIV). That's when Jesus asked, "How many loaves do you have?...Go and see" (Mk 6:38 NIV). Sending the problem away is the easy way out. He's challenging them to look for the extraordinary, within the ordinary moment. When you do that you invite God into your situation—and with Him all things are possible! The key to this miracle was Christ's words, "How many loaves do you have?...Go and see." They already *had* the solution; they just didn't know it. When you consult God you begin to see things in a new light, and find answers you never dreamed possible.

DISCOVER WHAT'S INSIDE YOU

Let's just go ahead and be what we were made to be.
Romans 12:6 TM

*F*orty years ago *The Golden Buddha* was discovered in the city of Bangkok, Thailand. For years a huge, ugly, concrete Buddha sat in the middle of town. Visitors put empty soda cans and other trash on it. Then one day a priest decided to take the old statue to his temple. In the moving process it cracked. As the pieces crumbled the priest noticed something underneath the concrete shell. He gathered some helpers. They pulled the shell away and inside they found the world's largest chunk of sculptured gold, standing 8 feet high. For years it had been there—but no one knew it. And *you* are a lot like that statue. Your real value is inside, if you'd only stop and take inventory of it. You cannot consistently perform in a manner that's inconsistent with the way you see yourself. You'll perform at a level that reflects your perspective of yourself. If you think you're average, you'll perform in an average way. Once in a while you may have a really great day and perform higher. You might even think, "That was awesome, I really outdid myself!" However, unless you discover your God-given gifts, value and potential, you'll retreat to your old level of living because you think: "That's not the real me." What a loss. Paul writes, "Since we find ourselves fashioned into all these excellently formed and marvelously functioning parts in Christ's body, let's just go ahead and be what we were made to be, without enviously or pridefully comparing ourselves with each other, or trying to be something we aren't" (Ro 12:6 TM).

SURRENDER IT!

Trust in the Lord.
Proverbs 3:5 NAS

*E*ver notice how much energy it takes to keep a tight grip on something? Come on, you know what you're holding on to, don't you? You're in turmoil because you can't control the people or circumstances in your life. Hey, release your grip. Go ahead: surrender it to God. You'll be amazed at how much more energy you'll have, and how much easier life will be. Once you make the choice to surrender it to God, your hardest days become your easiest. A.W. Tozer wrote: "Father, my cowardly heart fears to give up its toys. I cannot part with them without inward bleeding, and I do not try to hide from you my terror of the parting. I come trembling, but I do come. Please root from my heart those things which I have cherished so long and which have become a very part of my living self, so that you may enter and dwell there without a rival." You say, "Surrender what?" *(1) Your position!* Place it all before your God. Find your security, your identity and your contentment in Him. *(2) Your plans!* Plan wisely, but be ready for God to rearrange things and take you along paths that may be uncomfortable for you. *(3) Your relationships!* Nothing this side of Heaven is permanent, including relationships. Enjoy the time you have with your loved ones, but avoid the temptation to cling. *(4) Your anxieties!* If your emotions are wrapped around some issue involving a possession, a job, a particular expectation or a relationship, you aren't fully relying on God. No, you're still clinging to lesser things. Stop. Let it go! You're delaying the surprise God has waiting for you.

SEED-FORM BLESSINGS

That which is conceived in her is of the Holy Ghost.
Matthew 1:20

You must learn to recognize seed-form blessings. Why? Because for a period of time it may not be clear to others (or even you) that the Lord is with you. Look at Mary: "In the sixth month, God sent the angel Gabriel to Nazareth…to a virgin pledged to be married to a man named Joseph…The virgin's name was Mary. The angel…said, 'Greetings, you who are highly favored! The Lord is with you.' Mary was greatly troubled at his words and wondered what kind of greeting this might be. But the angel said to her, 'Do not be afraid, Mary, you have found favor with God. You will be with child and give birth to a son, and you are to give him the name Jesus.'…'How will this be,' Mary asked the angel, 'since I am a virgin?' The angel answered, 'The Holy Spirit will come upon you…So the holy one to be born will be called the Son of God…For nothing is impossible with God.' 'I am the Lord's servant,' Mary answered. 'May it be to me as you have said'" (Lk 1:26-38 NIV).

Notice the following things about Mary: (a) She was capable of conceiving what God wanted. (b) She could carry it full-term. (c) She could deliver it in health. (d) She could trust God with her unanswered questions. (e) When the time came she could release it to fulfill God's plan, even though it meant the breaking of her heart. The seed that went into the ground on Good Friday sprang to life on Easter Sunday and produced a harvest that changed the world. So, learn to recognize your seed-form blessings.

WE ARE MANAGERS, NOT OWNERS

The earth is the Lord's, and everything in it.
Psalm 24:1 NIV

*I*t seems like the last part of us to surrender to God is our checkbook. The extent to which this is true explains why more of us are not growing into maturity faster than we are. Your attitude towards giving is like the lights on your car's dashboard. When one of those lights comes on, something under the hood needs attention before there's a breakdown. When God turns on the indicator light of *money* and *giving* in your life, it's not because He's hurting for cash. No, He's looking at something in your heart that you can't afford to ignore. And He wants to deal with it. Many Christians suffer from a disease Dr. Tony Evans calls "cirrhosis of the giver." It's been around since the earliest days of the church, first diagnosed around 34 A.D. in a couple named Ananias and Sapphira who became greedy with God's gifts and suffered some really bad consequences (See Ac 5:1-11). It's an acute condition. Those who have it show symptoms that include sudden paralysis and inability to reach for their purse or wallet at offering time. This strange symptom often disappears in stores, on golf courses, or when dining in fine restaurants. Some have attempted to treat this condition by offering tax deductions for charitable giving. But judging from the prevalence of the problem this incentive has not had great effect. What's the answer? Realizing that you are a manager—not an owner. You're simply overseeing what belongs to God. So when He asks you to give, regardless of how much, remember, He's just asking for what He already *owns*.

BEING SPIRITUALLY DISCIPLINED

Discipline yourself for the purpose of godliness.
1 Timothy 4:7 NAS

$\mathcal{D}$isciplined people don't need cheering crowds to feed their hunger for excellence. Jascha Heifetz, perhaps the greatest violinist of the 20th century, practiced 4 hours every day, until his death at 87 years of age. That's more than 100,000 hours of practice, punctuated by occasional public performances! The great painter, Leonardo da Vinci, desired nothing less than anatomical perfection for his paintings. He spent countless hours studying the human body. For one commission he became so frustrated by his inability to paint the body as he wished that he drew thousands of hands until he felt it was just right. Centuries later we gaze in awe at his work but forget the hours of preparation. We're barely aware of the diligent training of da Vinci's hand, mind and heart for the sake of those magnificent canvas images. It's easy to forget that it's the discipline we didn't see, that made our most gifted people the best at what they did.

And what's true of them is also true among the godly. If there's an individual you respect because of their spirituality, you can be certain that person has cultivated certain disciplines. They weren't born that way. The life you respect and hope to emulate didn't automatically come with age, or a promotion to some position. No! They paid dearly for their spiritual depth— hours of trying, failing, and trying again; suffering through hardship; learning to rely on God; yielding to the spiritual disciplines because they found life works better that way. This is why Paul encouraged Timothy, his protégé, "Discipline yourself for the purpose of godliness."

CONTROL YOUR EMOTIONS (1)

Cain, Why are you angry?
Genesis 4:6 NIV

*U*nless you learn to discipline your emotions you'll lose credibility, alienate others, and miss great opportunities. Your emotions are like a car: properly understood and directed it can take you places; out of control it can destroy you. When God asked Cain, "Why are you angry with your brother?" He was saying: "Listen up, Cain! Your emotions are sending you a message. If you don't get a handle on this you'll create a mess you won't be able to live with. Yes, you'll repent and regret it, but you won't be able to undo it." But Cain wouldn't listen. The situation seemed unfair; he felt unappreciated. He thought his brother's blessing had come at his expense. What emotions were at work here? Jealousy. Resentment. Competitiveness. A sense of victimhood. These unchecked forces caused him to murder his brother Abel and cross a line he couldn't come back from.

Most of us have an inner response mechanism that isn't necessarily controlled by the rational side of our brain. It reacts to people and events, and like a sudden storm rises with strength from within, sometimes overwhelming us. Gordon McDonald writes: "I used to pride myself on the fact that I kept my emotions to myself. I never saw myself as an angry person …Then I got married and my wife informed me that I had plenty of anger after all. While it rarely came out in words it showed itself in full color in facial expressions (the gift of glare, we called it) I never knew I had. I had work to do. I had emotions that needed to be disciplined." How about you?

CONTROL YOUR EMOTIONS (2)

Refrain from anger...it leads only to evil.
Psalm 37:8 NIV

*M*ike Singleterry, who played for the Chicago Bears football team, was a star player—and a Christian. One day, however, while they were losing, the hometown fans became ugly and threw insults at him. He didn't like it. The TV cameras trained on Singleterry's face as he glowered at the crowd. Suddenly he lost his temper and started toward the stands, shouting back. It wasn't his finest hour. But after the game may have been one of Mike's finest hours. That's when he met with the press and apologized. No excuses, no blaming: just an apology. His emotions had gotten out of control and he took responsibility. Perhaps Singleterry had read these words: "A man's wisdom gives him patience; it is to his glory to over-look an offense" (Pr 19:11 NIV). As you go through life people will offend you. Sometimes it will be deliberate, other times it will be inadvertent. The question is—what are you going to do about it?

Spiritually mature people discipline their emotions and make sure they accurately reflect reality. They can be sad, joyful, angry or elated in appropriate ways at appropriate times. They refuse to allow their emotions to determine their conduct, attitude, or choices. One Christian author writes: "When I feel things going against me, when feelings of anger and resentment begin to rise, it's time to stop and ask what's happening. Is this for the greater good, or not? Is God speaking to me, or isn't He? Will my flesh rule this moment, or my spirit?" That's good advice for you too!

CONTROL YOUR EMOTIONS (3)

He had compassion on them and healed their sick.
Matthew 14:14 NIV

$\mathscr{B}$efore you congratulate yourself on having your emotions in check, understand that there's *another* side to the coin—control but no compassion, moral indignation over human suffering yet no corresponding action. James talks about these folks. And they were church folks too. They see the pain and unmet needs of others. They have the ability to do something about it. But they lack the willingness or care, so they walk away muttering about being too busy. Or they try to assuage their conscience with a token gift. James asks, "How dwelleth the love of God in him?" (1Jn 3:17). How indeed? If we are not responsible, who is? If we don't do something, who will? "Faith without works is dead" (Jas 2:20).

You're truly disciplining your emotions—when you translate them into responsible action. And your "somebody ought to do something about this" sentiments won't get you off the hook. William Barclay wrote: "There is nothing more dangerous than the repeated experience of a fine emotion with no attempt to put it into action. It is a fact that every time a man feels a noble impulse without taking action, he becomes less likely ever to take action. In a sense it is true to say that a man has no right to feel sympathy, unless he at least tries to put that sympathy into action. An emotion is not something in which to luxuriate; it is something which at the cost of effort and of toil, of discipline and of sacrifice, must be turned into the stuff of life." That just about says it all—doesn't it?

WE HAVE ONE!

The Lord is my shepherd; I shall not want.
Psalm 23:1

*J*esus said, "Suppose one of you had a hundred sheep and lost one. Wouldn't you leave the ninety-nine in the wilderness and go after the lost one until you found it?" (Lk 15:4 TM). Do you recall when *you* were that one lost sheep? Do you remember when Jesus found you? Where would you be without Him?

Eighty percent of Jesus' listeners made their living off the land. Many were shepherds living on the mesa with their sheep. No flock ever grazed without a shepherd, and no shepherd was ever off duty. When the sheep wandered the shepherd found them. When they fell he picked them up and carried them. When they were wounded he healed them. Sheep aren't smart; they tend to stray into running creeks for water, then their wool grows heavy and they drown. They need a shepherd to lead them to "still waters" (Ps 23:2). They have no natural defense —no claws or horns. They need a shepherd with a rod and staff to protect them (Ps 23:4). They have no sense of direction. They need someone wise enough to lead them "in paths that are right" (Ps 23:3). So do we. We tend to drown in circumstances we should have avoided. We have no natural defense against our enemy who goes about as a "roaring lion, seeking someone to devour" (1Pe 5:8 NAS). We, too, lose our way, don't we? No doubt about it, we need a shepherd. We don't need a cowboy to herd us, we need a shepherd to care for us and guide us—aren't you glad we have one!

HE'LL BE WITH YOU!

*Yea, though I walk through
the valley of the shadow of death.*
Psalm 23:4 NKJV

*S*pringtime grazing leaves the pasture bare. So with no companion other than his sheep and no desire other than their welfare, the shepherd leads his flock to the rich grasslands of the mountains. The journey is long. The valley is dark and deep. Poisonous plants can infect. Wild animals can attack. But the shepherd knows the path because he's walked it many times.

Before David led Israel, he led sheep. So he writes: "Yea, though I walk through the valley of the shadow of death, I will fear no evil; for You are with me." And what the shepherd does with his flock, our Lord does with us. Some day He'll take each of us to the rich grasslands of the mountains by way of the valley. He'll guide us to His house where we'll feel more at home than any place we've ever been. Jesus spoke about it in John, Chapter 14. The disciples didn't know it was His farewell address. No one did—but it was. So He spoke about death: "Don't let your hearts be troubled. Trust in God, and trust in me. There are many rooms in my Father's house; I would not tell you this if it were not true. I am going there to prepare a place for you. After I go and prepare a place for you, I will come back and take you to be with me so that you may be where I am" (Jn 14:1-3 NCV). What an arrangement—with Jesus as your Shepherd, you get the best of *both* worlds.

A LIFETIME GUARANTEE

*Goodness and mercy shall follow me
all the days of my life.*
Psalm 23:6

Goodness and mercy. Not just goodness alone, for we all are flawed and in need of mercy. Not just mercy alone, for we all are fragile and inadequate, in need of God's goodness. So He guarantees both. And if that doesn't impress you, try this phrase: *"all the days of my life."* Think of the days that lie ahead of you: tough days raising children, days in a dead-end job, underpaid and financially strapped, days of loneliness, days of ill health, days of care giving. Listen: "Goodness and mercy shall follow me all the days of my life." All of them!

And what will the Shepherd do during those days? He will *follow* you. What a surprising way to describe God. We're accustomed to a God who remains in one place; who sits enthroned in the heavens and rules. But no, like a Shepherd who comes behind, gently coaxing His sheep forward, our Lord follows us. Pursues us. Tracks us down and wins us over. Have you sensed Him pursuing you? So often we miss Him; we don't know our Helper when He's near. Yet He's always there; through the kindness of a stranger; through the question of a child or the commitment of a loved one; through a word of encouragement spoken or a touch well timed we sense His presence. Even when we choose our hovel over His house and our efforts over His grace, still He follows. Never forcing us. Never leaving us. Using all His power to convince us that He is who He is, and that He can be trusted to lead us home. What more could we ask for?

YOU'RE NOT HOME YET

I will dwell in the house of the Lord for ever.
Psalm 23:6

Where will you live forever? In the house of the Lord. So what does that make your present house? Temporary accommodation. "Our homeland is in heaven" (Php 3:20 NCV). This explains the homesickness you've felt ever since your husband or wife died, you learned about the lump in your breast or the spot on your lung, or when your family fell apart. The twists and turns of life have a way of reminding us—this world is not our homeland. We aren't fluent in its language. Its culture confuses our heart. Its stress disrupts our sleep. It promises much but delivers so much less. But that's okay—we have an eternal address fixed in our hearts: "[God] has...set eternity in the hearts of men" (Ecc 3:11 NIV). But even though our eyes are fixed on heaven, for some of us the journey has been long, very long and stormy. We've been robbed of lifelong dreams. We've been given bodies that can't sustain our spirits, or spouses who can't tolerate our faith, or bills that outnumber our pay checks, or challenges that outweigh our strength—and we get tired. It's hard to see the city in the midst of the storms. The desire to pull over to the side of the road and get out, entices us. We want to go on, but some days the road seems so long. Remember this: God never said the journey would be easy, but He did say the arrival would be wonderful. So trust Him. He'll get you home. Soon the trials of the trip will be forgotten in the joys of the feast.

FOR COFFEE DRINKERS

Taste and see that the Lord is good.
Psalm 34:8

*I*n "A Box of Delights," J. John and Mark Stibbe share this hilarious article. "You know…you're addicted to coffee when:

You're employee of the month at the local coffee house and you don't even work there…your eyes stay open when you sneeze…you chew on other people's fingernails…you can type sixty words per minute with your feet…you can jump-start your car without cables…you don't sweat, you percolate… you've worn out the handle on your favorite coffee mug…you walk twenty miles on your treadmill before you realize it's not hooked up…you've worn the finish off your coffee table… you're so wired, you pick up radio signals…your birthday is a national holiday in Brazil…you'd be willing to spend time in a Turkish prison…you go to sleep just so you can wake up and smell the coffee…you name your cats 'Cream' and 'Sugar'… your lips are permanently stuck in the sipping position…you have a picture of your coffee mug on your coffee mug…you don't tan, you roast…you don't get mad, you get steamed… your coffee mug is insured by Lloyd's of London…you introduce your spouse as your coffee mate…you think CPR stands for 'coffee provides resuscitation'…you ski uphill…you get a speeding ticket even when you're parked…you haven't blinked since the last lunar eclipse…you just completed another sweater and you don't even know how to knit."

The Bible says, "Taste and see that the Lord is good." Here's an idea. Why not turn your coffee break into a time with God. Carry a "Scripture for Today" with you (or this Devotional). Meditate while you sip, talk to God while you savor. Doing this could transform your spiritual life!

THINK LIKE A FARMER (1)

He who sows bountifully will also reap bountifully.
2 Corinthians 9:6 NAS

*Y*ou'll never see a farmer who *refuses* to plant seeds, sitting around expecting a harvest. He may go to church regularly, be a good family man, have his devotions every day and share his faith with others, but he's not going to get a harvest without first planting. That's because the law of sowing and reaping is built into creation. "As long as the earth endures, seedtime and harvest…will never cease" (Ge 8:22 NIV).

And there's something else a farmer won't do; he won't *eat* the seed he should be planting. He knows he must start with his seed, not his need, if he's to reap a harvest. Some of us approach God from a need standpoint, "I can't give to the Lord because I have to pay these bills." That's like a farmer saying, "I can't plant this seed even though it'll yield a good crop, because I'm hungry right now." This is where your faith must kick in. When a farmer plants his seed instead of eating it, it's an act of faith that his seed will turn into a harvest. Now, he won't get his harvest right away. He must wait for the right season. But he's putting his faith in an unfailing law that God's placed in the universe, the law of sowing and reaping. Are you getting the idea? When you give, you're demonstrating faith in God's Word. When He tells you to sow generously so that you can reap generously, your willingness or reluctance to do what He says, tells you whether or not you hold God and His promises in high esteem.

THINK LIKE A FARMER (2)

This most generous God…
gives you something you can then give away.
2 Corinthians 9:11 TM

$\mathcal{T}$he thing you want to reap, must be the thing that you sow. Why? Because the seeds you plant will reproduce after their own kind, whether for good or for bad. "Whatsoever a man soweth, that shall he also reap" (Gal 6:7). Notice, you don't necessarily reap *when* you sow or *where* you sow, but you always reap *what* you sow. Some of us want to plant weeds and get roses. We're quick to judge others, yet we ourselves are the first to plead for mercy and understanding when we mess up. A farmer doesn't sow corn and expect to reap potatoes. Sometimes we shake our heads and wonder why God isn't blessing us with a harvest, forgetting that we haven't sown the right seed in the first place.

And there's one more principle of sowing and reaping we need to understand. We not only reap what we sow, we always reap *more*. "For God, who gives seed to the farmer to plant, and later on, good crops to harvest and eat, will give you more and more seed to plant [not to hoard] and will make it grow so that you can give away more and more fruit from your harvest. Yes, God will give you much so that you can give away much" (2Co 9:10-11 TLB). Some people live by the philosophy "get all you can, can all you get, then sit on the can." But *why* would you want to do that when God has offered you something much better, backed up by the warranty of His Word?

GROWING IN 4 AREAS

Jesus grew in wisdom and stature,
and in favor with God and men.
Luke 2:52 NIV

$\mathcal{G}$rowing is something even Jesus did. He grew in 4 areas: (1) He grew "in wisdom"—intellectual development. (2) He grew "in stature"—physical development. (3) He grew "in favor with God"—spiritual development. (4) He grew "in favor with men"—social and emotional development. Your spiritual growth should not be compartmentalized, but integrated into every other aspect of your life. This is where we've been missing it! You cannot neglect one of these areas without endangering your growth in all of them. So don't limit Jesus to some religious compartment of your existence and say, "A chapter a day keeps the devil away." Wake up to the realization that you can give the Lord of your life greater control over *every* aspect of your being. This is what makes the Christian life dynamic, not static.

But notice something: this is a highly individualized process. We are each in different stages of our development. That's why comparison is foolish. Don't spend your life comparing yourself to others, because you're not them. You are *you!* Each day examine these 4 major areas and ask, "Lord, how am I doing?" In some areas you'll show up well, in others you'll have a long way to go. When it comes to your values and your habits you'll discover that: (a) some are good and just need to be reaffirmed; (b) some are inconsistent and need to be reinforced; (c) some are underdeveloped and need to be refined; (d) some are harmful and need to be repented of. Bottom line? You'll grow if you commit yourself to it!

LET'S PRAY FOR OUR NATION

I will forgive their sin, and I will heal their land.
2 Chronicles 7:14 NCV

*I*n 1888 a noted chess master named Paul Morphy attended a dinner party in Richmond, Virginia. During the dinner his attention was drawn to a painting on the wall. The scene portrayed a young man locked in an intense chess match with the devil. The devil's next move would surely claim victory—entitling him to the young man's soul. The devil wore a triumphant expression. After dinner the chess champion walked over to the painting, studying the board and the pieces portrayed on it. Suddenly he turned to his host and said, "I can take the young man's game and win!" "That's not possible!" his host replied. "Not even you can retrieve that game." The chess master answered, "Yes, I think I can. Suppose we place the men and give it a try." To the surprise of everyone Morphy bested the smug opponent in the painting. Victory was snatched from the devil and the young man was saved.

Sometimes we feel like that young man. We see Satan poised to claim victory. We feel something near despair as we watch our nation make wrong turn after wrong turn. Yet in the darkest moment God whispers, "I have good news for you. He hasn't won yet. If my people who are called by my name are sorry for what they have done, if they pray and obey me and stop their evil ways, I will hear them from Heaven, I will forgive their sin and I will heal their land." God gets the final move. *And we can urge Him to take it—when we pray!*

BE A THERMOSTAT!

Don't become so well-adjusted to your culture
that you fit into it without even thinking.
Romans 12:2 TM

*D*on't be a thermometer, be a thermostat. Thermometers just reflect the climate around them—thermostats set it. Actually, they lift it! Most of us are like thermometers reflecting the culture around us. We buy things others buy, say things others say, wear things others wear, and value things others value. Oh, there are slight variations, but most of the time we don't set the climate for the world we live in; we simply adjust to it. But not overcomers! No, they take life to the next level. They become thermostats and change the environment in which they're placed. For instance, you may know people who raise the spiritual temperature of a group, or determine the attitudes of others just by being present. They're pacesetters. They influence others, rather than allowing others to influence them. Paul's challenge to the Romans was to move from being a thermometer to being a thermostat. Listen: "Don't become so well-adjusted to your culture that you fit into it without even thinking. Instead, fix your attention on God. You'll be changed from the inside out. Readily recognize what he wants from you, and quickly respond to it. Unlike the culture around you, always dragging you down to its level of immaturity, God brings the best out of you, develops well-formed maturity in you" (Ro 12:2 TM). God calls us to be authentic. The word *authentic* comes from the Greek word "to author." It means to read God's script for your life and write your story accordingly, not copy somebody else's. That's living. That's being a thermostat, not a thermometer!

GROWTH—DON'T RUSH IT!

They go from strength to strength.
Psalm 84:7 NIV

Child development experts have identified a problem called "hurried child syndrome." It's the tendency of parents in our fast paced society to rush their children into adulthood. There are numerous reasons: they want their child to excel to the point of never giving them a chance to enjoy their childhood. Activities that are supposed to be fun become hotbeds of competition and pressure. Jam-packed schedules with no relaxed family time also contribute. Some parents want their children to hurry and grow up because they don't want to be bothered with the inconveniences. But you can't skip the stages of childhood and produce healthy adults. Each stage is important.

The same's true of our spiritual growth. Spiritual birth, childhood, and adolescence are all necessary stages to our becoming mature. Although, unlike physical development, you can grow spiritually as fast as you want to. But you have to work at it. The first tree to go down in the storm is the one with shallow roots. So don't get in a hurry. And don't covet something because it looks good in somebody else's life. God tailors His blessings to your size. If you try wearing a suit you haven't grown into, you look foolish. Speaking of leaders, Paul writes, "He must not be a new believer, lest the position go to his head and the Devil trip him up" (1Ti 3:6 TM). God will give you all the blessing and responsibility you can handle—but not one bit more. And He'll do it based on your stage of growth. So, enjoy where you are, on your way to where you're going!

IS YOUR GIFT BIGGER THAN YOU?

O Lord…who may dwell on your holy hill?
He who walks with integrity.
Psalm 15:1-2 NAS

*Y*ou wouldn't give your 5-year-old a 12-gauge shotgun or a big Harley-Davidson motorcycle. Shotguns and motorcycles are for adults. You need maturity to handle them. Giving such gifts to your child would endanger them, and everybody else around them. The gifts just don't fit the person. Perhaps you're a talented individual. God's given you some large gifts like the ability to speak well, or organize things, or create and design. But we sabotage ourselves when our gift becomes bigger than we are. How does this happen? When we begin to lean on the talents God gave us and don't mature emotionally and spiritually, we ruin our chance to use those talents as God designed them. When our character doesn't keep up with our talent, we learn to "wing it" through life. We live on the surface but lack real strength underneath. And it shows up when the crisis hits, the storm comes, or we are under pressure. You can't "wing it" when it comes to character building. The greater the size of your gifts, the more you must dedicate time to developing your character. Eugene Peterson paraphrases the Psalmist in *The Message:* "God, who gets invited to dinner at your place? How do we get on your guest list? Walk straight, act right, tell the truth. Don't hurt your friend, don't blame your neighbor; despise the despicable. Keep your word even when it costs you, make an honest living, never take a bribe. You'll never get blacklisted if you live like this" (Ps 15:1-5 TM). So, do you live that way?

BE A FRIEND WHO PRAYS

When a believing person prays, great things happen.
James 5:16 NCV

*M*ark records: "Four men arrived carrying a paralyzed man on a mat. They couldn't get to Jesus through the crowd, so they dug through the clay roof above his head...they lowered the sick man on his mat, right down in front of Jesus. Seeing their faith, Jesus said to the paralyzed man, My child, your sins are forgiven" (Mk 2:3-5 NLT). The word "prayer" doesn't show up once in this paragraph. But look closely and you'll see it in action; four men lowering their sick friend through the roof into the presence of Jesus. He stops preaching, looks at the man and then announces, "My child, your sins are forgiven." What stirred Jesus? Mark answers, "Seeing their faith." The faith of 4 friends triggered Christ's power on his behalf. Notice, he has no movement, no treatment, no answers, and no hope. But what he does have is friends who know how to lift him into the presence of Christ. The paralytic might be gulping ("don't drop me!"). The homeowner might be groaning (de-roofing is decidedly antisocial). But Christ? He's smiling! Their faith stirs His strength. He heals the man. The paralytic leaves the house with a clean soul and strong body. Faithful friends carry those they love in prayer, into God's presence. And when they do God responds. How? When? The four men didn't know. And we don't know either, but we know this: "When a believing person prays, great things happen." So be that kind of friend. Go ahead, carry your loved ones into the presence of Jesus, then watch what happens!

LIMITED BY OUR SENSES

We walk by faith, not by sight.
2 Corinthians 5:7 NAS

*T*he reason many of us aren't growing spiritually is because our faith doesn't reach beyond our sight. Real faith begins where our senses end. When we can see something, we usually don't feel the need to *trust* God for it. And since we can't see very far, living by sight keeps us living small.

Think of the African impala, a marvelous animal that can soar 10 feet high and 30 feet out with just one jump. But did you know that you can put that impala in a 3-foot cage with no roof and it will not attempt to escape, even though it has more than enough power to clear the cage. That's because the impala won't jump if it cannot see where its feet are going to land. The impala lives by sight, so it's easy to keep it caged. The same goes for you!

But let's add an all-important truth here. Some children believe in the Tooth Fairy. The problem with that is, their faith is ineffective because the object of their faith isn't real. Scriptural faith says, "God, I know that whenever You speak You're telling the truth, and that I can stake my life on it." Faith establishes what we believe about God. Too many of us act like we've more confidence in ourselves than we do in Him. If faith is the action by which we lay hold of the power and promises of God, then if our faith is lacking we won't see the supernatural work of God in our lives—and we'll live in the natural with all its limitations.

BE YOURSELF

I have finished my course.
2 Timothy 4:7

$\mathcal{B}$e yourself. Life's too short to be anything else. Paul said "I have finished my course." You can only win if you run on the track God gave *you*. To run any other kind of race is to lose. Perhaps you remember the movie *Catch Me If You Can*. It's based on a true story. Frank Abagnale, Jr. lived a wild and crazy life as a doctor, airline pilot, banker, investor, attorney and celebrity. The irony is, he wasn't any of those. And even though he deserves an academy award for his portrayal of them, he was a fake, a fraud and a pretender. It all began early in his life when he realized he'd the talent to convince people he was "somebody" through his sheer confidence and acting ability. He began to make money at his game and soon found himself addicted to role playing. Before it was over he'd helped perform surgery in an operating room, conned banks out of thousands of dollars, flown an airplane as a pilot, and gone places most people only dream of going. The problem was—it was all a show. A few years into it he wanted out. The glamour was gone. He was desperate to come clean. But he had created such a web of deceit that it wasn't easy. The FBI was onto him, and he ended up spending years in prison. Frank had a great talent, but he wasted it pretending to be someone else. God can only bless you when you're committed to being what He redeemed and called you to be. To live any other way is a lonely, fearful, unfulfilled life. So, be yourself!

THE GYMNASIUM OF THE SOUL (1)

Training yourself for spiritual fitness.
1 Timothy 4:7 NLT

*W*hen Dallas Cowboys' coach, Tom Landry, was asked how to build a winning team he said: "My job is to get men to do what they don't want to do, in order to achieve what they've always wanted to achieve." What did those football players want to achieve? Victory at the Super Bowl. What did they not want to do? The hard work necessary to get there! Achieving greatness requires discipline—determined, deliberate, daily, definable actions with a clear goal in mind. Paul coached Timothy, saying: "Spend your time and energy in training yourself for spiritual fitness." Timothy was the Pastor of the Church in Ephesus, a Las Vegas sort of city. It was a busy, rich, sensual place to be a Christian. Paul knew that succeeding there wouldn't be easy, so he used the Greek term from which we get our word gymnasium. In other words, becoming Christ-like requires a daily workout. So Paul writes, "Training yourself for spiritual fitness." Notice two words: *(1) Training*—which calls for repetitive exercises so that your mind and appropriate muscle groups work together reflexively and automatically. It combines endurance and skill. It's what turns game-winning abilities into habits. *(2) Yourself*—Nobody else can do it for you. Look through the telephone directory; you don't find "Lease-a-Dieter," or "Rent-a-Runner." No, it's up to you!

So, why train yourself? To become like Christ! By living life as He lived it, allowing the Holy Spirit to shape you by His disciplines from the inside out, you'll become more like Him. In other words, spend time each day in the gymnasium of the soul.

THE GYMNASIUM OF THE SOUL (2)

Train yourself to be godly.
1 Timothy 4:7 NIV

*G*odliness was *central* to Paul's advice to Timothy. Go ahead, try asking your friends what they think "godliness" means. They see a monk removed from the world, praying, meditating and humming hymns behind monastery walls. Others see squeaky-clean, Bible-toting do-gooders, naïve, moralistic, annoyingly innocent. Wrong! One scholar defines godliness this way: "Not just outward worship, nor a mere concept of God, nor a virtue, nor an ideal over against a Gnostic philosophy of self-deprivation that regards creation as bad. True godliness that's born of faith covers everyday conduct in honoring God as Creator and Redeemer." Some well-meaning people seem to think that becoming like Christ means that we should strive to be perfect. For them, spiritual disciplines are like push-ups and sit-ups, religious exercises to beat their bodies and minds into submission. This is more Gnostic than Christian. If you just want to have control over your lusts or become more serene, *any* meditative religion will do. What sets Christianity apart from other religions is knowing and be-coming like Christ is our goal: not moral perfection (although you will grow in character), not tranquility (although your life will become remarkably more peaceful). Because of the grace we have in Christ, the disciplines will do nothing to make us more accepted by the Father, since Jesus has already done it all for us. No, a "godly" person is one who ceases to be self-centered in order to become Christ-centered. Christ became a man, and as a result of His earthly ministry we see how God intended for us to live. Jesus is our unblemished example of godliness. Therefore, being "godly," simply means becoming more Christ-like.

MIND MANAGEMENT

A man reaps what he sows.
Galatians 6:7 NIV

*M*anaging your mind should be one of your top priorities. Your mind is like a computer, it only spits out the data you feed it. Winners work hard at investing the right material inside themselves. Dr. Hans Selye researched and popularized a tiny membrane in the back of our head known as the RAS: Reticular Activating System. Your RAS has a primary function: it moves you in the direction of your dominant thought at that moment. We naturally act on what fills our minds. When we become preoccupied with a thought, eventually we want to act on it. This explains a lot of things—like why so many rapes happen after guys have watched pornography night after night. It also explains the huge amount of violence among young people between the ages of 12 and 24. By then the average young person has seen more than 4,000 murders on TV, not to mention video games. Indiana University School of Medicine studied how the images we see impact our brains. For instance, adolescents who'd a higher level of exposure to violence, had reduced levels of cognitive function. The more violence they saw the less thinking, learning, reasoning and emotional stamina they had. The garbage they fed their minds affected what came out. Their computer stored the wrong information —now they could only retrieve the wrong stuff. The apostle Paul didn't know about computers. But he knew about agri- culture: "The one who sows to please his sinful nature, from that nature will reap destruction; the one who sows to please the Spirit, from the Spirit will reap eternal life" (Gal 6:8 NIV). So, manage your mind!

SET YOUR SAILS!

That I may…become more deeply and
intimately acquainted with Him.
Philippians 3:10 AMP

*E*lla Wheeler Wilcox wrote: "One ship drives east and another drives west, with the selfsame winds that blow. 'Tis the set of the sails and not the gales, that decides the way to go. Like the winds of the sea are the ways of fate, as we voyage along through life; 'Tis the set of the soul that decides its goal, and not the calm or the strife." Have you noticed that the same difficult circumstance that lays one person low, lifts another to incredible heights? "'Tis the set of the sails and not the gales, which tells us the way to go." Clearly, Paul had set his sails: "That I may…become more deeply and intimately acquainted with Him." And he refused to compromise or be sidetracked. Intimacy with God was his all-consuming goal. Is such a goal reached easily? No! It means never quitting, giving yourself ample time. You can't put godliness on a schedule. Spiritual disciplines must be worked with until they become enduring habits. Your mind needs time and experience to assimilate them. And like any new model of behavior they must be wrestled with, talked through, come to terms with, and tried on. With time, a few of them will begin to settle in and become a consistent lifestyle. Looking back, you'll discover you've actually changed. How? You set your sails in a new direction and you are no longer hopelessly blown by the winds of impulse, circumstance, expediency, popular opinion or self-interest. Christ-likeness is a journey, not a destination. So plan on a lifetime of travel. And while you're at it, be sure to enjoy the journey.

YOU'LL NEVER KNOW UNTIL YOU TRY IT!

You cannot serve both God and Money.
Matthew 6:24 NIV

*R*ichard Foster writes: "We had a swing set, a real custom-made job—huge steel pipes and all. But our children would soon be beyond swing sets, so we decided to sell it. I went out in the back yard and looked it over. 'It should bring a good price,' I thought to myself. 'In fact, if I touched up the paint I could charge even more.' All of a sudden I began to monitor a spirit of covetousness within me. I asked my wife, Carolyn, if she would mind if we gave the swing set away rather than selling it. 'No, not at all!' I thought to myself 'rats!' But before the day was out we'd found a couple with young children who could make good use of it, and we gave it to them—and I didn't even have to paint it! This simple act of giving crucified the greed that had gripped my heart—at least for the time being."

When was the last time you just gave something away? Something that meant something to you. Not easy, is it? It requires trust that God will look after your needs in ways that you'll never see until you give Him the opportunity. Dallas Willard said, "The cautious faith that never saws off the limb on which it is sitting, never learns that unattached limbs may find strange, unaccountable ways of not falling." Is it possible that you don't have the intimacy with God you desire, because you haven't given enough away? The truth is—you'll never know until you try it!

DON'T GIVE UP HOPE

*The plans I have for you…are…good…
to give you a future and a hope.*
Jeremiah 29:11 TLB

A few years ago the Soviet submarine *Kursk* went down in the Barents Sea. When the diving crews finally reached it they heard SOS signals coming from inside. Desperate sailors wondered "Is there any hope?" Sadly, for them there wasn't.

Do you feel trapped in an impossible situation you can't seem to change or escape? If so, God is saying to you today, "The plans I have for you…are…good…to give you a future and a hope." Now, hope is not just the absence of despair, it's the presence of something greater; something only God can give. Hope is not passive; it's the most active force in the world because it's derived from the most powerful being of all—God. And it's never further away than He is. Clint Eastwood became famous for starring in a movie called *The Good, the Bad and the Ugly*. Four decades later some of us still use those words when describing certain aspects of life. But here's the good news: through His amazing grace God can take the good, the bad and the ugly experiences in your life and use them to make you unbelievably better at what He created you for, whatever that might be! In God's economy all is redeemed and nothing is ever lost. He can take the good things we remember fondly, the bad things we might like to forget, and the ugly things that shaped us into people we didn't start out to be, and use *all of them* to facilitate His purpose for each and every one of us. So, don't give up hope!

AFTER YOU'VE FAILED

When you have turned back, strengthen your brothers.
Luke 22:32 NIV

$\mathcal{G}$od can turn your failures into stepping stones to success. Look at Peter. Jesus told him, "Satan has asked to sift you as wheat. But I have prayed for you, Simon, that your faith may not fail. And when you have turned back, strengthen your brothers" (Lk 22:31-32 NIV). Notice: (1) Christ warned him about it but He didn't stop it from happening. There are certain things we only learn the hard way. (2) Jesus told Peter that he'd deny Him, not once, but 3 times. Most of us are stubborn; we don't get it the first time. (3) Peter thought he was stronger than he was: "Lord, I am ready to go with you to prison and to death" (Lk 22:33 NIV). We usually start out with an exaggerated opinion of our own strength. (4) Jesus told him, "I'm praying for you that your faith may not fail." Isn't that amazing? When we're so low that we can't pray for ourselves, Jesus handles the enemy and intercedes with the Father on our behalf. What did Jesus pray for? Peter's faith! Faith in God's grace is the rope that pulls us back up again. (5) Jesus believed in Peter even when Peter didn't believe in himself. That's because we evaluate ourselves by our present circumstances, but Jesus sees us in the fullness of our potential. So He tells Peter, "When (not if) you get back on track, do something good with what's happened." Now, if temporary failure happened to Peter, how much more likely is it to happen to you? And when it does, what do you suppose the Lord wants to accomplish through it?

GRIT, NOT GLAMOUR!

Prepare your minds for action; be self-controlled.
1 Peter 1:13 NIV

$\mathcal{T}$oday there seems to be greater emphasis on the glamour of achievement than the grittiness of it. Jamie Clark writes about the grit that's required in preparing to climb Mount Everest: "In order to get yourself up for the climb, you spend several hours a day walking on a treadmill with a heavy back-pack. You look goofy, you smell. It's an ugly scene. That's always true. The road to success is not pretty." The winners in life know this and it doesn't alarm them. They understand the words of Peter, "Prepare your minds for action; be self-controlled." And Paul adds: "Everyone who competes in the games goes into strict training" (1Co 9:25 NIV). Note the word "strict." If you're not strict with yourself you won't make it. The prize is great, but the process can be grueling. Gratification and achievement are usually postponed for a long time. The disciplined person doesn't pursue ways that are likely to make him or her popular. It's only *after* the season of discipline is over and the payoff comes, that the world offers applause. The runner, the wrestler, the swimmer all push their bodies to heightened levels of performance by demanding of themselves longer, faster, and stronger episodes of physical output. They don't stop because there's a feeling of fatigue or even pain. They understand that these are mental barriers that must be overcome. They insist that their bodies behave in accordance with their commitment, not their comfort level. And the same is true of the follower of Christ who responds to a call from heaven to undertake a great task.

LEFTOVERS

I will repay you for the years the locusts have eaten.
Joel 2:25 NIV

*S*ome of you reading this are old enough to remember hard times, shortages on cash, and limited menus. You lived on a food budget, which meant you sometimes saw the same dish more than once. Although, due to your Mom's incredible talent in the kitchen it didn't always have the same face. It might show up as mashed potatoes and peas on Monday, then shepherd's pie on Tuesday. It might even come back a day or two later as something no one but your Mom herself could recognize. She'd chop it, dice it, mix in some cheese, splash Cream of Mushroom soup over the top, dress it up with some parsley, put it on a fancy tray, give it a French-sounding name and you thought it was something brand new! Couldn't Mom work miracles with leftovers?

Well guess what? God works the same way too! If you bring Him what you have left over, He can turn it into somthing you never would have thought possible. You just need to step away, turn it over to Him and let Him do His thing. You didn't hover over your Mom when she was reinventing your dinner. You were smart enough to know that everything would come out a lot better if you just kept your hands off it. This is not to say you should keep your hands entirely off your own life. You just need to step back far enough to let God work without hindrance. When you do, the promise that "All things work together for good" suddenly becomes a reality in your life.

"MAKE YOURSELF AT HOME, LORD!"

That Christ may dwell in your hearts through faith.
Ephesians 3:17 NAS

*T*he word *dwell* means more than just to move in and take up residence. It means to make yourself comfortable, to spread out and have the run of the house. When it comes right down to it, how many of us are willing to give Christ *complete control?* You see illustrations of this in popular television programs where people allow someone else to come in and redo their homes or yards. Sometimes two sets of friends or family members agree to trade houses and redo a room in each other's place, without any prior approval or guarantees. The participants give their house keys to the show's host, and they hand them over to the other party. Then they go to work and tear out the other family's carpet, take down the drapes and pictures, discard furniture, repaint, and do whatever they decide needs to be done. One show called "Radical Home Makeover" even demolishes the house and rebuilds it from the ground up. The family is sent on vacation while this takes place. When they return it's a scene of wild celebration as the neighbors gather and the family breaks down weeping with joy at the result.

Now, if we can demonstrate that kind of faith in other people, surely we can allow Christ to come in and make Himself at home in our hearts. One thing's sure, we won't be unhappy with the results. When you give Jesus the keys to your heart He "decorates" it with love, joy and peace, etc. He rewires it to tap you into the Holy Spirit's power. What could be better?

MISSION ACCOMPLISHED!

Having accomplished the work
which You have given Me to do.
John 17:4 NAS

*I*f Satan can't buy you with what's illegitimate, he'll attempt to bury you with what's legitimate. Either way, his objective is to drive a wedge between you and God. When Christ came to the end of His earthly ministry, though only 33 years old He could say: "I glorified You on the earth, having accomplished the work which You have given Me to do." Jesus could have gotten much more involved with the 12 disciples, or taken advice from some program committee and chosen 24 disciples to double His outreach. He could have traveled to Rome, the seat of power at the time. Or to Athens, where He could touch great minds in order to extend His influence and reputation. But He chose only 12 disciples. He mentored them slowly and intimately, and never traveled far from the place of His birth. Some might say that if you're going to revolutionize the world you need to carry your cause to as many parts of it as possible. But Jesus deliberately limited His itinerary. He kept it simple. At the end, just before breathing His last He said, "It is finished." Jesus was ready to die—because there was nothing left for Him to do. His work had been completed, from the training of the disciples to providing redemption for us. And you'll detect no hint of resignation or regret in any of His last words. Mission accomplished! How long are you going to keep promising yourself that you'll draw closer to God, that you'll put His Kingdom first? If you *ever* plan to do it, do it *now!*

ARE YOU BEING TESTED? (1)

Test me, O Lord…examine my heart and my mind.
Psalm 26:2 NIV

*A*re you going through a test? Tests demonstrate what you've learned. Until you're tested you really don't know what you know—and what you don't know. Tests are opportunities to prove your maturity and discover your potential. So remember: (a) you'll experience tests at each stage of your growth; (b) your goal in each case should be to pass the test, otherwise you get to take it again and again until you get it right; (c) testing always precedes promotion. Actually, it prepares you for it and demonstrates you're ready to handle it. If you cheat, or try to copy somebody else's answers you may temporarily seem to succeed. But eventually time and circumstances will reveal you for what you are—someone who can't handle what you manipulated your way into getting; (d) self-promotion can never replace divine promotion. So don't rush ahead of God; wait, allow Him to open the door; (e) a product cannot be safely and profitably used until it's been thoroughly tested. Neither can you. God's not a hard-hearted parent who enjoys seeing His children struggle through life's tests. If He were to visit you in person He'd probably say: "I don't enjoy making you go through this, but it's the only way to prove you're ready for what's ahead. Before I can use you greatly—I must test you thoroughly." Generally God's tests are about your character. And like any good actor in a stage play that doesn't go according to the script, your job is to "stay in character!" Regardless of what anyone else does, follow God's script for your life.

ARE YOU BEING TESTED? (2)

Test me, O Lord...examine my heart and my mind.
Psalm 26:2 NIV

*L*et's look at some of the tests God uses to develop us: *(1) The test of small things*. This test comes when we're asked to do something beneath our ability and potential. It proves how faithful we are to our commitments. It also reveals whether or not we're ready for greater responsibilities. Jesus said, "Whoever can be trusted with very little can also be trusted with much" (Lk 16:10 NIV). *(2) The motive test*. This test comes to us when we are doing all the right things—but not necessarily for all the right reasons. It's right to pray. Yet Jesus warned: "When you pray, do not be like the hypocrites, for they love... to be seen by men" (Mt 6:5 NIV). Sometimes we don't even know our own hearts. That's why we need the mirror of God's Word: "For the word of God is...able to judge the thoughts and intentions of the heart" (Heb 4:12 NAS). When you stand before Christ to be evaluated and rewarded, the question will not just be *what* did you do, but *why* did you do it? *(3) The stewardship test*. Jesus said, "Give, and it will be given to you" (Lk 6:38 NIV). Only when your hand is open, can you receive more from God. The practice of giving on a regular basis prevents you from being owned by what you own. Money is called currency because it's supposed to flow through you. When you withhold out of fear or greed, you limit what God wants to give you. Want to keep the flow of blessing going in your life? Become a river, not a reservoir.

ARE YOU BEING TESTED? (3)

Test me, O Lord...examine my heart and my mind.
Psalm 26:2 NIV

*L*et's take a look at 3 more tests: *(1) The wilderness test.* This test comes when we feel spiritually dry and our joy level is low. It reveals our ability to adapt to adversity and change, and as a result enter a new level of growth. It proves we're able to perform even when life isn't fun. "He led you through the vast and dreadful desert...to...test you so that in the end it might go well with you" (Dt 8:15-16 NIV). The wilderness test is where we submit to short-term pain, confident that in the end it'll produce long-term gain. *(2) The credibility test.* Nothing matters more than your confidence before God—and your credibility before people. When Lot tried to rescue his sons-in-law from the destruction of Sodom: "He seemed as one that mocked" (Ge 19:14). Had they seen his selfish treatment of his Uncle Abraham and heard about some of his business dealings? One thing is sure, he lost his credibility when it mattered most. Is that happening to you? *(3) The authority test.* Before Paul took the Gospel to the Gentiles he first went to Jerusalem and submitted his plan to the apostles, asking for their blessing. He didn't have a "nobody is going to tell me what to do" attitude. God placed David under a flawed leader called Saul. It's pretty bad when your boss wants to kill you. But you can learn as much from the mistakes of a failure as you can from the achievements of a success. Because David submitted, he qualified to sit on Saul's throne. Want to be a leader? Learn to be a follower. Submit!

ARE YOU BEING TESTED? (4)

Test me, O Lord…examine my heart and my mind.
Psalm 26:2 NIV

*L*et's look at 2 more tests: *(1) The offence test.* Jesus said, "Offences will come" (Lk 17:1). So be ready! Those who lead always take the worst of the flack. The front line is no place for the weak-willed or the weak-kneed. So, what are you going to do when offences come? Get mad and get nowhere? Get even and get into trouble? Or get over it by practicing forgiveness. "If you hold anything against anyone, forgive him, so that your Father in heaven may forgive you your sins" (Mk 11:25 NIV). *(2) The warfare test.* This test is for those who claim to be strong in faith, but prove to be weak in fight. "When Pharaoh let the people go, God did not lead them on the road through the Philistine country, though that was shorter. For God said, 'If they face war, they might change their minds and return to Egypt'" (Ex 13:17 NIV). Now, you haven't been called to be insensitive and abrasive, but if your destiny is worth pursuing—it's worth fighting for! So toughen up! It's a battle-field, not a bed of roses. You must engage the enemy each day using each spiritual weapon at your disposal. If you don't he'll try to steal every God-given blessing you've got, including your identity, your testimony, your integrity, your family, your calling and your future. This test demonstrates your ability to continue in your vision even while you're experiencing dis-appointment and opposition. So remember, the level of attack is the best indicator as to the level of blessing that waits for you beyond the attack!

ARE YOU BEING TESTED? (5)

Test me, O Lord…examine my heart and my mind.
Psalm 26:2 NIV

*L*et's examine the last 2 tests: *(1) The test of time*. This test has two dimensions. One reveals the strength of your life's impact, the other reveals the length of it. Each calls for signing your signature with excellence on all you put your hand to. The electric light still burns even though Edison has left the world. The needy are still being cared for even though General Booth is in heaven. Now, your legacy may not reach those heights, but your influence can outlive you. And the test of time has a second dimension—an eternal one. How you live your life today, determines your rewards and status in Heaven. "Eventually there is going to be an inspection. If you use cheap or inferior materials, you'll be found out" (1Co 3:12-13 TM).

(2) The Lordship test. Simon Peter passed this test by obeying a command that seemed to make no sense at all: Jesus said to him, "'Put out into deep water, and let down the nets for a catch.' Simon answered, 'Master, we've worked hard all night and haven't caught anything. But because you say so, I will let down the nets.' When they had done so, they caught such a large number of fish that their nets began to break" (Lk 5:4-6 NIV). First Peter tried fishing alone and failed. Then he tried it with Jesus and succeeded. Same fisherman. Same boat. Same nets. What changed? He was willing to do it God's way! If you want to succeed, talk to God, listen to what He has to say—and do it!

IN THE END, IT'S WORTH IT

God intended it for good.
Genesis 50:20 NIV

*W*hat happened to Joseph wasn't *fair!* When your own family sells you as a slave and your boss' wife has you wrongly imprisoned on rape charges, you tend to ask, "Lord, what's going on?" Before God promoted Joseph to the palace he wanted to know how he'd hold up under pressure. And the same goes for you. Joseph was called to save his family and lead his nation. But big assignments call for big tests of character. You don't always understand this when you're going through the fires of refinement. When Joseph's brothers finally stand before him as ruler of Egypt he tells them "You didn't do it to me, God orchestrated the whole thing." Talk about seeing things clearly! Someone else's action against you is not the bottom line. And the reason is simple: God knows that somewhere down the line He'll be able to use all that painful stuff to bring your life into focus and accomplish His purposes. With God it's never too late! Have you ever been to a *real* pizzeria? Not the kind where everything is pre-packaged and a 13-year-old can do it. No, the kind of place where they take a ball of dough, slam it down, twirl it around, flatten it, then put it into a 1000° oven. That's what's required for the pizza to hold all that good stuff they plan to put on top. Think of yourself as pizza dough and God as the person working it. He's got some good stuff He wants to lay on you, but before He can do it He's got to knock you into shape.

EVERYBODY'S WELCOME

[Come]...be my disciple...
So Matthew got up and followed him.
Matthew 9:9 NLT

*A*ccording to the Jews, tax collectors ranked barely above plankton on the food chain. So everybody kept his distance from Matthew the tax collector. Everyone except Jesus. "[Come]...be my disciple...So Matthew got up and followed Him." Then it gets interesting. "[Matthew] gave a big dinner for Jesus at his house. Many tax collectors...were eating there, too" (Lk 5:29 NCV). What a party! Salty language. Mardi Gras morals. These guys keep the phone number of their bookie on speed dial. But a friend is a friend. What can Matthew do? Invite them to meet Jesus. Great idea! Then the door opens and an icy breeze blows in. "The Pharisees...began to complain...'Why do you eat and drink with tax collectors?'" (Lk 5:30 NCV). Matthew doesn't know whether to get mad or get out. But before he has time to choose Jesus intervenes, "I have come to call sinners...not to spend my time with those who think they are already good enough" (See Mt 9:13 NLT). And Matthew is just like you, isn't he? Maybe you've never taken taxes, but you've taken liberty with the truth, taken credit for what wasn't yours, taken advantage of others. And to you He says "Follow me." But what if you have a bad reputation? So did Matthew. Come, you may end up, like him, writing a book. Furthermore, you don't have to be weird to follow Jesus. And you don't have to stop liking your friends to follow Him. Just the opposite: a few introductions would be nice. Think of all Christ has done for you—then share Him with your friends, for everybody's welcome.

YOUR CIVIL WAR

Walk by the Spirit.
Galatians 5:16 NAS

*F*ritz Ridenour writes: "You want to do right, but you do wrong. You want to choose obedience, but you choose sin. Sometimes you'd almost swear you were a split personality, a regular 'walking civil war'." Sound familiar? Most of us fight our civil war in the shadows, out of sight, feeling all alone. And when we're at our lowest Satan whispers, "Face it, you'll never be good enough. Why not just give up and accept the inevitable?" Any time we mix this flawed world with our failed nature, we've got the right combination for spiritual defeat. But we can win! Paul writes, "Walk by the Spirit and you will not carry out the desire of the flesh." What a profound statement! God's Spirit and our flesh are completely opposite. But when we're walking in the Spirit we cannot possibly carry out the desires of the flesh. So, we're either operating from the realm of the Spirit and we're under His control, or we're operating in the realm of the flesh and we're under its control. And that's a choice we must make each day.

Everything that tempted you as a lost person can still defeat you because you have that same old nature. It doesn't improve. The cutting remarks you used to make, you'll still make. You can still throw temper tantrums, right? Lustful thoughts will still invade your mind. Therefore, in the power of the Spirit you must throw up your hands and say, "Lord, get this stuff out of me. I can't conquer it on my own!" It's at this point that He takes over and the battle goes your way!

PRAYER IS MORE THAN JUST WORDS

When you pray…close your door.
Matthew 6:6 NAS

esus said "when you pray, go into your inner room, close your door and pray to your Father who is in secret, and your Father who sees what is done in secret will reward you" (Mt 6:6 NAS). With these few words, Jesus set the common perception of prayer on its ear. He said prayer was not to be a public demonstration of how "spiritual" we are. No, the intimate nature of our communication with God calls for getting alone, away from all interruptions and distractions. Why? Because it's just you and your Father in a family discussion.

When people say they don't know how to pray what they usually mean is that they don't know how to pray like some of us. They don't know how to use our "Christian jargon." Jesus said you don't need to worry about getting all the words right because "your Father knows what you need before you ask Him" (Mt 6:8 NAS). God is listening to our heart more than our words. We don't have to be self-conscious about our praying; God isn't grading us on how well we express ourselves.

Again, compare prayer to breathing. Our breathing is done without our conscious attention to it, or even awareness that we're doing it. It is the natural expression of our moment-by-moment dependence on oxygen. That's how God wants us to treat our communication with Him. He wants prayer to be the air we breathe, the environment in which we live. Isn't that wonderful? Through prayer we can live in continuous contact with God. Just think how much that can change us and improve the quality of our lives.

WHY YOU NEED THE CHURCH

The many parts make up only one body.
1 Corinthians 12:12 TLB

*T*here's a wonderful story about Jimmy Durante, one of the truly great entertainers. He was asked to do a show for World War II veterans. He told them he was very busy, but if they wouldn't mind his doing one short monologue and immediately leaving for his next appointment, he'd come. They agreed. But when Jimmy got on stage he went through the short monologue—then stayed, and stayed. Soon he'd been on stage 15, 20, then 30 minutes. Finally he took a last bow and left. Backstage someone stopped him and said "I thought you had to go after a few minutes. What happened?" Jimmy answered, "You can see for yourself if you look on the front row." In the front row were two veterans, each of whom had lost an arm in the war. One had lost his right arm and the other had lost his left. Together, they were able to clap, and that's exactly what they were doing, loudly and cheerfully.

That's a picture of what happens in church: "But the many parts make up only one body when they are all put together. So it is with the 'body' of Christ." But to enjoy its benefits you have to go, and when you get there you must reach out to others so that you can know and be known, strengthening and being strengthened. Pew-sitting, back-of-the-head fellowship won't cut it! Someone sitting next to you has 20/20 vision where you have blind spots. You need their counsel, correction and comfort. And they need yours. When that happens, the church is working like it's supposed to.

WHAT YOUR SPEECH SAYS ABOUT YOU

You are one of them…your speech shows it.
Mark 14:70 NKJV

You can try to disguise your identity by changing your looks, your social circle and your address—but how you speak will give you away every time. It happened to Peter. When a servant girl saw him warming himself by the fire, she said, "'You…were with Jesus of Nazareth.' But he denied it… And the…girl saw him again and began to say to those who stood by, 'This is one of them.' But he denied it again…later those who stood by said to Peter again…'you are one of them…your speech shows it'" (Mk 14:67-70 NKJV). So in order to convince his accusers that he wasn't a friend of Jesus, Peter "Began to curse and swear, 'I do not know this Man of whom you speak'" (Mk 14:71 NKJV). And it worked! After that nobody else accused him of knowing Jesus. Isn't it interesting how public profanity in *any* language, has a way of making others question the quality of your relationship with Christ?

Paul says, "Do not let any unwholesome talk come out of your mouths, but only what is helpful for building others up…that it may benefit those who listen" (Eph 4:29 NIV). If you want to win people to Jesus, be careful how you talk. Paul said, "Let your speech always be with grace…that you may know how you ought to answer each one" (Col 4:6 NKJV). Words are powerful things. They either build up or tear down, add to or take from. It's not important that people can tell from your accent where you're from, but when they can't tell by the way you talk that you're Christ's disciple, something's seriously wrong.

LIFE'S FULL OF "CHICKENS"

These blessings shall come on thee…
if thou shalt hearken unto the voice of the Lord.
Deuteronomy 28:2

*J*ack London's classic, *White Fang,* is about an animal, half dog, half wolf, who learns to live among men. White Fang is very fond of chickens. Once he raided a chicken-roost and killed 50 hens. His master, Weedon Scott, whom White Fang "loved with single heart," scolded him, then took him into the chicken yard. When White Fang saw his favorite food walking around in front of him, he obeyed his natural impulse and lunged for them. Immediately he was checked by his master's voice. He stayed in the chicken yard quite a while, and every time White Fang made a move toward a chicken his master's voice would stop him. In this way he learned what his master wanted—he learned to ignore the chickens. Weedon Scott's father argued "You couldn't cure a chicken killer," but Weedon challenged him and they agreed to lock White Fang in with the chickens all afternoon: "Locked in the yard, White Fang lay down and went to sleep. Once he walked over to the trough for a drink. The chickens he calmly ignored. So far as he was concerned they did not exist. At 4 o'clock he executed a running jump and leaped to the ground outside, whence he sauntered gravely to the house. He had learned the law." Out of love and a desire to obey his master's will, White Fang overcame his natural, inborn tendencies. He may not have understood the reason, but he chose to bend his will to his master's. *Life's full of "chickens." What you have to settle is—whom will I serve?*

RUN TO WIN

Run in such a way that you may win.
1 Corinthians 9:24 NAS

*P*aul writes, "Run in such a way that you may win." The Isthmian Games to which Paul referred, were open to everyone. Obviously the object of running any race is to win! But it's not just a matter of putting on your Nike's, wearing the outfit and enjoying the scenery: "Run in such a way that you may win." So, what's the secret to winning? "Everyone who competes in the games exercises self-control in all things" (1Co 9:25 NAS). Athletes who run to win, exercise restraint over their impulses, emotions and desires. They watch their diet, get sufficient sleep and train their bodies in just the right way. They're not doing things that could limit their performance on the track. They measure the consequences of every indulgence according to whether it will help or hinder them. Paul says that those who ran in the Isthmian Games did so to win "a perishable wreath." Actually, the victors were treated like royalty. Often their debts were cancelled and they were allowed to live tax free for the rest of their lives. In some cases they were given a lifetime supply of food so that they could rest on their laurels. So Paul points out that, as valuable as that leafy crown was, it can't compare to the eternal rewards for which we strive. In other words, run with *eternity* in view. Obedience to God, even in details, enhances your heavenly reward. At the end of a life of deep commitment and detailed obedience, Paul could say, "There is laid up for me a crown." So, live each moment with that crown in view!

DITCH THOSE OLD WINESKINS!

New wine must be put into new wineskins.
Matthew 9:17 CEV

*I*n Bible times animal skins were cured and made into wine containers. At first they were flexible and easy to work with, but over time they grew rigid and lost their ability to expand. That's why Jesus said, "No one pours new wine into old wineskins. [It] would…burst the old skins…[and] the wine would be lost…New wine must be put into new wineskins." Likewise, God can't put fresh ideas into fossilized minds, or change your situation till you're ready to change your thinking.

God's Word says: "Don't keep going over old history… I'm about to do something brand-new" (Isa 43:18-19 TM). So if you're asking Him to enlarge your vision, you first need to make room *mentally*. Isaiah said, "Clear lots of ground…Make your tents large. Spread out! Think big" (Isa 54:2 TM). Remember, dreams always come a size too big so you can grow into them, so don't settle for mediocrity in your work, your relationships and your walk with God. Mark Twain said, "Twenty years from now you'll be more disappointed by the things you didn't do, than by the ones you did. So throw off the bowlines. Sail away from the safe harbor. Catch the wind. Explore. Dream. Discover." Maybe you come from a background of addiction, poverty, depression, abuse and low self-esteem. Well, God can enable you to rise up and put an end to that old mind-set of defeat. He's ready to fill you with "new wine," but first you need to ditch those old wineskins!

FAMILY SECRETS

He is not ashamed to call them his brothers and sisters.
Hebrews 2:11 NCV

$\mathcal{M}$ost families like to keep their family secrets a secret. Yet amazingly, you've barely dipped a toe into Matthew's gospel when you realize that Jesus hails from a less-than-perfect family. Rahab was a Jericho harlot. Grandpa Jacob was slippery enough to warrant an electric ankle bracelet. David had a personality as irregular as a Picasso painting—one day writing Psalms, another day seducing his captain's wife. But did Jesus erase their names from the list? Not at all. Why did He hang His family's dirty laundry on the neighborhood clothesline? Because your family has secrets too. A cousin with a prison record. A dad who left and never came home. A grandparent who ran away with a co-worker. If your family tree has damaged fruit, Jesus wants you to know "I've been there." The phrase "I've been there" is Christ's theme song. To the lonely He whispers "I've been there." To the discouraged, He nods His head and sighs "I've been there." The absence of Joseph in the adult life of Jesus suggests that Mary may have raised Him and the rest of their children alone. Jesus was not reluctant to call His ancestors His family—and He's not ashamed of you either! Jesus, who makes people holy, and those who are made holy, are from the same family. "He's not ashamed to call them his brothers and sisters." That means He's not ashamed of you; nor is He confused by you. Your actions don't bewilder Him. Your family secrets don't trouble Him. So come to Him. After all, you're part of the family.

AIM THEM IN THE RIGHT DIRECTION (1)

Train up a child…
in keeping with his individual gift or bent.
Proverbs 22:6 AMP

$\mathcal{A}$s a parent, you either accelerate or stifle your child's giftedness. They will spend much of their life benefiting from, or recovering from your influence. "Train up a child in the way he should go, and when he is old he will not depart from it." "Does that mean if I put my kids on the right path, they'll never leave it?" No, salvation is the work of God (See 1Co 3:6). So what does this passage teach us? To view your child as a book, not to be written but to be read. The Amplified Bible reads, "Train up a child in the way he should go [and in keeping with his individual gift or bent], and when he is old he will not depart from it." Note the word "bent." You hold the bow, your child is the arrow. Aim him (or her) "in the way he should go." God prewired your infant. He preprogrammed your toddler's strengths. He set your teen on a trajectory. God gave you an 18-year-plus research project. Ask yourself, "What sets this child apart?" Childhood tendencies forecast adult abilities. Read them. Discern them. Affirm them. Cheerlead them. Look at Joseph. At 17 he saw dreams and envisioned himself as a leader (See Ge 37:2-10). As an adult he interpreted the dreams of Pharaoh and led the nation (See Ge 40-41). As a boy David displayed two strengths: fighting and music. He killed a lion and a bear (See 1Sa 17:34-37) and played skillfully on the harp (See 1Sa 16:16-18). And what two activities dominated his adult years? Fighting and music. Think about it!

AIM THEM IN THE RIGHT DIRECTION (2)

Train up a child…
in keeping with his individual gift or bent.
Proverbs 22:6 AMP

$\mathcal{R}$aising your child "in the way he should go" means recognizing 4 things: *(1) Strengths*. At 2, Van Cliburn played a song on the piano as a result of listening to teaching in the adjacent room. His mother noticed, gave him lessons, and the kid from Kilgore, Texas went on to win the first international Tchaikovsky piano competition in Moscow. *(2) Topics*. John Ruskin said, "Tell me what you like, and I'll tell you what you are." What do your children like? Numbers? Colors? Activities? Study them! The greatest gift you can give them is not your riches, but revealing to them their own. *(3) Optimal conditions*. A cactus thrives in different conditions than a rose bush. What soil does your child grow best in? Some kids love to be noticed. Others prefer to hide in the crowd. Some do well taking tests. Others excel with the subject, but stumble through exams. Winston Churchill repeatedly failed tests in school, and he turned out okay. We each have different optimal conditions. What are your children's? *(4) Relationships*. What phrase best describes your child? "Follow me, everyone…I'll let you know if I need some help…Can we do this together?…Tell me what to do and I'll do it." Don't characterize loners as aloof, or crowd seekers as arrogant. They may be living out their story. What gives your children satisfaction? What makes them say "yes!" Do they love the journey or the destination? Do they like to keep things straight or straighten things out? What thrills one child, bothers another. Parent, resist the urge to label before you study. Understand the uniqueness of your child!

FOOTPRINTS

I will never leave thee, nor forsake thee.
Hebrews 13:5

*T*ake a moment and reread these timeless words by Margaret Fishback Powers: "One night I dreamed I was walking along the beach with the Lord. Across the sky flashed scenes from my life. For each scene I noticed two sets of footprints in the sand. One belonged to me and other to the Lord. When the last scene of my life flashed before me, I looked back at the footprints in the sand. I noticed that many times along the path there was only one set of footprints. I also noticed that it happened at the lowest times in my life. This really bothered me and I questioned the Lord about it. 'Lord, you said that once I decided to follow you, you would walk with me all the way. But I notice that during the worst times in my life there was only one set of footprints. I don't understand why in times when I needed you most, you should leave me.' The Lord replied, 'My child, I love you and would never leave you during your times of trial and suffering. When you saw only one set of footprints...they were mine. *It was then that I carried you!*'"

Need reassurance? "The Lord, he it is that doth go before thee; he will be with thee, he will not fail thee, neither forsake thee: fear not" (Dt 31:8). Need more reassurance? "For he hath said, I will never leave thee nor forsake thee. So that we may boldly say, the Lord is my helper, and I will not fear what man shall do unto me" (Heb 13:5-6). Today you're not alone—God is with you!

THINK OUTSIDE THE BOX!

Waters to swim in.
Ezekiel 47:1-5

*H*ave you heard about the frog that was born at the bottom of a well? He thought life couldn't get any better till one day he looked up and saw daylight. Climbing up to investigate he was amazed to find a much larger pond than the one he lived in. And going further afield he discovered a lake that was bigger again. When eventually he came to the ocean and all he could see was water, it dawned on him just how limited his thinking had been. He thought everything he needed was down in the well, but that was a drop in the bucket compared to the things that were out there for him to enjoy.

Maybe you're living today in your own little "well," reluctant to leave your comfort zone, settling for a limited and safe existence while God has rivers deep enough "to swim in." Wouldn't you like to step out in faith, experience new depths in Him and go where you've never been before? Remember, the enemy will do everything he can to keep you focused on your background, your lack of formal education, your appearance and your limited resources. But Bruce Wilkinson says, "It doesn't matter whether you're short of money, people, energy, or time. What God invites you to do will always be greater than the resources you start with." You don't have to let fear limit your vision when *God* is your source, because His supply is unlimited! One idea from Him, just one, can change your life and the lives of others. He's got great things in store for you today—so start thinking outside the box!

SITTING, STANDING, BOWING!

Regard one another as more important than yourselves.
Philippians 2:3 NAS

$\mathcal{C}$oncerning General Robert E. Lee, J. Steven Wilkins wrote: "The degree to which Lee was indifferent to his own honor was astonishing. After the civil war Lee received distinguished visitors from the north into his home in Lexington. Assuming that the Lees, like many prominent families in the north, had household servants, the guests, after retiring to bed, would leave their boots outside their bedroom door to be cleaned and 'blacked.' Many a night it was the old General himself who stayed up after the others retired, and—in order not to embarrass his guests—collected the boots, cleaned and polished them himself." Paul writes, "Do nothing from selfishness or empty conceit, but with humility of mind regard one another as more important than yourselves; do not merely look out for your own personal interests, but also for the interests of others" (Php 2:3-4 NAS). Paul points out that walking in humility means practicing 3 things: *(1) Sitting* on the temptation to promote yourself. Trusting God to promote you when He, not you, determines the time's right. *(2) Standing* up for others. Like who? Whoever popped into your mind as you read that last sentence. Think of the least liked person you know, or the one who's made a royal mess of life. Stand up for them. Ask, "How can I serve them?" Then do it—and keep doing it. *(3) Bowing* low before God. Accepting His discipline. Acknowledging your dependence. Giving Him all the glory. The path to greatness in God's Kingdom leads through the valley of selflessness. Why? Because some things only grow there—like humility!

BOUNDARIES AND BURNOUT

Follow the Lord's rules for doing his work.
2 Timothy 2:5 TLB

*A*re you so eager to stay in everybody's good graces that you're complying with their every demand, even though it's draining you? Good people burn out every day because they lack discernment when it comes to setting boundaries. And once that happens it's hard to fix, because none of us (not even those "ordained by God!") can break His natural laws without consequences. A well-known Bible teacher writes: "Once when I was complaining about my heavy schedule I heard God's Spirit say, 'You're the one who makes the schedule; if you don't like it, do something about it.'"

Paul told Timothy: "Follow the Lord's rules for doing his work...as an athlete...follows the rules or is disqualified." Not every problem is spiritual, some are physical. Furthermore, you can't blame the devil for things that are *your* fault. We resent people who pressure us, yet we keep doing what they want: and it feeds our silent anger. You're allowing yourself to be pressured by not taking responsibility for your own life! The fact is, many well-intentioned folks are walking around burned out and depressed because they can't say no. They forget that Jesus is our example; that even He made time for rest and renewal. The answer lies in: (a) putting your life under the guidance of the Holy Spirit; (b) learning to put first things first; (c) not expecting everybody to understand when you set boundaries. Remember, Solomon said, "A friend loveth at all times" (Pr 17:17), not just when you comply with their wishes. So if saying no costs you the friendship, it wasn't a healthy friendship to start with!

KNOWING YOU'VE BEEN "CALLED"

*One day as they were worshiping God…
the Holy Spirit spoke.*
Acts 13:2 TM

*I*n Acts 13 we read, "The congregation in Antioch was blessed with a number of prophet-preachers…One day as…they waited for guidance—the Holy Spirit spoke: 'Take Barnabas and Saul and commission them for the work I have called them to do.' So…they laid hands on their heads and sent them off" (Ac 13:1-3 TM). Notice the following things:

(1) God called out Paul and Barnabas by name. God knows your name and where you live. Whether you're hiding in a cave like Gideon or gone fishing like Peter, God knows where to find you. He doesn't play hide and seek with His purpose for your life. *(2) Their calling was confirmed by trustworthy leadership.* Those who laid hands on Paul and Barnabas, confirming their calling, were leaders who took the time to pray, fast and seek God's will. Such people are a gift. They won't tell you what you want to hear, they'll tell you what you need to hear. They'll cover you, counsel you, correct you, and confirm God's direction for your life. Do you have such people in your life? If not, get busy and find some. *(3) They found their calling in church.* Why is that important? Because God gave us the "pastor-teacher to train [us for service], working within Christ's body, the church" (Eph 4:12 TM). The Holy Spirit still speaks to us today as we gather to pray, worship, and hear God's Word. One reason so many of us lose our way is that we aren't in the place where God can speak to us objectively through His Word, and subjectively through His Spirit.

PUT ON YOUR ARMOR (1)

Put on the full armor of God.
Ephesians 6:11 NAS

*L*et's take a look at the 6 pieces of God's armor described by Paul in Ephesians 6:14-17. The first 3 are things we wear all the time. The last 3 are things we pick up as needed for the moment. Let's check out the first 3:

(1) The belt of truth. "Stand firm therefore, having girded your loins with truth" (Eph 6:14 NAS). During World War II, a plane flew many miles past its destination because the crew didn't realize they had a strong tail wind and refused to believe what the plane's instruments were telling them. All on board perished. Sadly, when the plane was found years later the instruments were still in perfect working order. God's Word is your infallible instrument panel. Read it daily. Believe it no matter what your senses or the devil may be telling you. *(2) The breastplate of righteousness.* The breastplate covers your heart, which must beat in sync with God's Word. When it doesn't, God sets off a warning beeper that something's wrong—it's not wise to ignore those signals. *(3) The shoes of peace.* Shoes mean that you're going somewhere. Don't expect to hear from God if you remain frozen in the same spot. When you move ahead for God He confirms the rightness of your direction by the peace He gives you. That puts a firm foundation under you. But why does God say, "Stand firm" instead of "Go fight?" Because the battle has already been won! We're not fighting *for* victory, but *from* victory. Jesus has already conquered the big 3—the world, the flesh and the devil. All we're doing is mopping up!

PUT ON YOUR ARMOR (2)

Put on the full armor of God.
Ephesians 6:11 NAS

*L*et's look at the last 3 pieces of armor:
(1) The shield of faith. Paul says that the shield of faith allows us to "extinguish all the flaming arrows of the evil one" (Eph 6:16 NAS). Do you remember in the old western movies, the battles between the Indians and the settlers? The settlers would circle the wagons, then the Indians would shoot flaming arrows into them. Smart thinking! You can't fight fires and foes at the same time. Flaming arrows are a huge distraction. And Satan uses the same tactic against us. But faith (and focus) snuffs out those flaming arrows. *(2) The helmet of salvation.* This helmet protects your mind, which has to do with your new identity as a Christian. Your salvation isn't just a ticket out of hell, it's everything you are in Jesus Christ—a blood bought, Spirit filled, totally forgiven, absolutely redeemed, heaven-bound child of God. *(3) The sword of the Spirit.* Paul says that the sword of the Spirit is the Word of God. This is rich, because the word for Scripture here is not *logos,* but *rhema,* which means an "utterance." This refers to our speaking God's Word to defeat Satan in battle; using the right Scripture at the right time to deal with the problem at hand. Three times Satan came at Jesus in the wilderness and 3 times Jesus answered, "It is written" (See Mt 4:4-10). He carved Satan up with the Word! The devil can outargue and outdebate you, but he has no answer for the Word of God. So memorize the Scriptures, then use them as a weapon against your enemy.

PUT ON YOUR ARMOR (3)

Put on the full armor of God.
Ephesians 6:11 NAS

*A*n important key to the effectiveness of a soldier's armor is putting it on correctly so that the pieces fit together and provide maximum protection. So, how do you "put on the full armor of God?" By prayer: "Pray at all times in the Spirit" (Eph 6:18 NAS). Praying in the power of the Spirit clothes us for spiritual warfare. You need to pray specifically at the start of every day, asking God to clothe you with each piece of His armor. Don't go into battle spiritually underdressed. Again Paul writes: "Put on the Lord Jesus Christ, and make no provision for the flesh" (Ro 13:14 NAS). This is one of the best verses in the Bible regarding how to win over temptation. Don't give Satan an inch or he'll take a mile.

Trainers who want to train dogs to listen to them and obey their commands no matter what, start by throwing a juicy piece of red meat in front of the dog. The untrained dog goes for the meat immediately, but eventually the trainer teaches the dog to keep its attention on *him* no matter what's put in front of him. When the process is successful the dog will not take its eyes off its master, even when the "temptation" of meat is right under its nose. There's an important lesson here for you. If you keep your eyes on Jesus it won't matter what kind of meaty lie or temptation Satan throws your way. Every now and then you may want to "go for it," but if you keep your eyes on Jesus and listen to His voice alone, you'll be victorious every time.

AMAZING, TRULY AMAZING GRACE!

By grace you have been saved.
Ephesians 2:5 NAS

*H*ave you any idea of the mess you were in, or moving toward, when God reached down and saved you? Perhaps an illustration may help you get the picture. If you took your children to a petting zoo and a little lamb came running towards you, you probably wouldn't be afraid at all because lambs are harmless. You might even reach out your hand and let the lamb lick it. But let's say you're at the zoo and the alarm goes out that a lion has escaped from its cage. If you're standing there and that lion comes running towards you, you'll be terrified and start to run because you know what lions can do. But just suppose that the runaway lion corners you in one part of the zoo and comes up to you—but instead of attacking you it gently licks your hand the way the lamb did. If that happened whose gentleness would you appreciate more, the lamb's or the lion's? You'd appreciate the lion's gentleness more because you know that he could just as easily have destroyed you without violating his nature as a lion. Well, grace is God's kindness and gentleness to us when He could have backed us into a corner as guilty sinners and destroyed us without violating His holy character. But God wanted to make us His children, so instead of expressing His wrath against us He poured it out upon His own sinless Son on the cross. Jesus took our punishment so God could embrace us. Hence, we have a brand-new relationship with God through grace. Isn't that amazing!

KNOW YOUR ENEMY—HE KNOWS YOU!

I am afraid that just as Eve was deceived by the serpent's cunning, your minds may somehow be led astray.
2 Corinthians 11:3 NIV

*T*emptation begins in your mind. *Satan* gave Eve the idea of eating the forbidden fruit. Eve wasn't just standing there trying to figure out how to disobey God. You must understand that the initial thought to do evil, is not from you. The new nature you have from God would not come up with that. The devil studies you the way a coach studies the game film of his opponents. Satan knows your weak spots. He knows which temptation has the best chance of success against you. How often have you ended up saying "I promised God and myself that I'd never do that again," yet you did it. That's because Satan knows what works on you.

But before you feel defenseless and get discouraged, God gives us this assurance: "No temptation has overtaken you but such as is common to man [we're all cut from the same bolt of cloth]; and God is faithful, who will not allow you to be tempted beyond what you are able, but with the temptation will provide the way of escape also, so that you will be able to endure it" (1Co 10:13 NAS). God builds a back door into every temptation with a lighted "exit" sign over it. The key word in this Scripture is "with." The way of escape comes *with* the temptation. So while you will never be exempt from temptation, you can be victorious over it. And the Good News is, when Satan discovers that his strategies against you are not working, he goes looking elsewhere.

LOOK FOR ADDITIONAL STREAMS

A river went out of Eden to water the garden...
and became...four [streams].
Genesis 2:10

*T*he vision God has given you may need to be funded by more than one stream. God gave Adam 4 streams of provision, and you are no different. Before your feet hit this planet God had placed dreams, gifts, talents and destiny deep within you. All of that came from Him, so surely He will enable you to put them to work. That may mean having various streams of revenue available. Your job should not be your only financial river, but one of several. Paul writes: "I know how to live on almost nothing or with everything" (Php 4:12 TLB). Sometimes Paul was well supported by the churches, other times he used his skill-set as a tent maker to fund his ministry. You might just be realizing that there's another gift surfacing in your life. If so, embrace it, develop it, pray over it, use it, then watch God make it flourish!

Don't let people label or compartmentalize you; you're not *just* a teacher. You may teach, but you may also have a remarkably strong gift of money management and be able to counsel those who struggle with budgeting and investment. You may be a factory worker, but also be handy enough to build furniture or fix cars, so you create a side business. There is so much you can do to make your talents work for you. It's never too late to pray, "Lord, I know there's more. Show me the extra streams of supply you have entrusted to me, that I might be a blessing to you and others. In Christ's name, Amen."

LOOK IN THE MIRROR (1)

A hearer of the word and not a doer.
James 1:23 NAS

*Y*our Bible is a mirror that shows you what you really look like in God's eyes: "If anyone is a hearer of the word and not a doer, he is like a man who looks at his natural face in a mirror; for once he has looked at himself and gone away, he has immediately forgotten what kind of person he was" (Jas 1:23-24 NAS). This word "man" is the Greek word for a male, so we're talking about the way *men* use the mirror. They glance just long enough to get the basics done—then they're gone. But not women. They're so intent on knowing how they look that they carry a mirror in their purse. They can find out any time of the day how they look. The point here is not the difference in the way men and women use a mirror, but the difference between taking a quick glance at yourself and hanging out in front of the mirror until you have fully seen who you are in God's eyes.

As we read God's Word the Holy Spirit holds up a mirror before us. He wants us to see ourselves so that we can make whatever adjustments are necessary. James continues: "One who looks intently at the perfect law, [the word of God], and abides by it, not having become a forgetful hearer but an effectual doer, this man will be blessed in what he does" (Jas 1:25 NAS). In what area of your life do you desire a greater measure of God's blessing? Take care of the "doing" and God will take care of the "blessing."

LOOK IN THE MIRROR (2)

One who looks intently at the perfect law…
and abides by it…will be blessed in what he does.
James 1:25 NAS

*P*aul writes, "We all…beholding as in a mirror the glory of the Lord, are being transformed into the same image" (2Co 3:18 NKJV). A mirror is a reflector. And the more time you spend in God's Word, the more you'll begin to reflect your Heavenly Father's likeness.

Now this is no overnight change, and it doesn't happen by just grabbing a Bible verse here and there, or skimming through a passage. No, it calls for soaking yourself in the Scriptures until the Holy Spirit connects with your spirit and produces the nature and ways of Christ in you. Jesus said, "If ye abide in Me, and My words abide in you, ye shall ask what ye will, and it shall be done unto you" (Jn 15:7). If you've ever left dishes in a sink until the food has dried on, you know those dishes need to "abide" in some hot, soapy water so that all the junk can be removed. We need to soak our minds in God's Word until the junk that James calls "all filthiness and all that remains of wickedness" (Jas 1:21 NAS) begins to melt away. This is not just gross sin, but hardened inner attitudes that keep us from growing in grace.

Our new nature has been "programmed" to want to obey God in much the same way that a calculator is programmed to compute numbers. All you have to do is feed a calculator the right information to get the right response. Your new nature has been set up to give you the right response when you feed it with the Word of God. That's why your enemy will do anything to keep you from spending time in God's Word. Don't let him do it!

THERE'S ALWAYS SOMETHING LEFT TO LOVE

Be ye kind one to another.
Ephesians 4:32

*T*ony Campolo writes: "Some years ago I saw Lorraine Hansberry's play, *A Raisin in the Sun*, and heard a passage that still haunts me. In it an African-American family inherits $10,000 from their father's insurance. The mother sees the chance to escape ghetto life. The brilliant daughter sees a chance to go to medical school. But the older brother begs for the money so that he and his friend can go into business together, and make things good for the rest of them. The mother gives in. Well, the 'friend' skips town with the money, and the desolate son has to break the news to the family. Immediately his sister lashes him with ugly words. Her contempt has no limits. Suddenly the mother interrupts her, 'I thought I taught you to love him.' The daughter answers, 'Love him? There's nothing left to love.' The mother responds: 'There's always something left to love. And if you ain't learned that, you ain't learned nuthin'! Have you cried for that boy today? I don't mean for yourself and the family. I mean for him: for what he's been through and what it done to him. Child, when do you think is the time to love somebody the most? When they done good? Well then you ain't through learning, because that ain't the time at all. It's when he's at his lowest and can't believe in himself 'cause the world has done whipped him so. When you starts measurin' somebody, measure him right, child, measure him right. Make sure you've taken into account what hills and valleys he's done come through before he got to wherever he is.'"

A NEW APPROACH TO OBEDIENCE (1)

Serve the Lord with gladness.
Psalm 100:2

*P*aul says, "God…is at work in you, both to will and to work for His good pleasure." Most of us don't connect obedience with pleasure. We're used to obeying out of necessity or fear. Perhaps we had parents who made us obey "just because I said so." Now it's not wrong for parents to demand obedience from children, or bosses to demand cooperation from their employees. But it's not the best definition or the highest motivation for obedience. The element that's missing is the "want to" factor that God built into each of us at the point of salvation. This takes the "ought to, have to, better do it or else God will zap you" element out of it. It elevates obeying God to a level of joyful response because of all that He's done for you. Obedience is not something you have to manufacture. It's something you have to *cultivate,* then *activate,* because the desire is already present in you. This is called "serving the Lord with gladness." Anything else is merely outward compliance. It's like the boy who misbehaved and was told by his mother to go and sit in the corner. After a few minutes she called to him from the other room, "Are you still sitting down?" He replied, "Yeah, I'm sittin' down on the outside, but I'm standin' up on the inside." You could call that obedience, but actually it's nothing more than outward compliance without the inward response of eager and joyful obedience. Biblical obedience is gladly doing on the outside, what you really want to do on the inside.

A NEW APPROACH TO OBEDIENCE (2)

Serve the Lord with gladness.
Psalm 100:2

*J*esus said, "Take My yoke upon you and learn from Me, for I am gentle and humble in heart, and you will find rest for your souls. For My yoke is easy and My burden is light" (Mt 11:29-30 NAS). Some of those who heard these words were farmers who used oxen to plow. They understood Jesus because they wouldn't dream of putting an ill-fitting harness on their oxen that caused them to chafe. Nor would God! And these farmers understood something else: without a harness oxen can't be directed and won't fulfill their highest purpose— to be productive. "But if I'm supposed to have this desire deep down to obey God, why can't I find it?" you say. First, because you still live in a body of flesh. And until God gives you a new body you'll contend with the impulses of your old one. The second reason many of us don't feel this inbuilt desire to obey, is that it's been covered by calluses built up over years of doing things because we *had* to. It's like the hard dry skin that builds up on your feet. That hard layer has to be removed to get to the soft skin underneath. That's usually the first thing a doctor does when treating your feet. In the same way, the Holy Spirit has to remove the calluses from our hearts as part of the softening process that makes us receptive to God's will. And how does He do that? Through love! Our love for Christ in response to what He's done for us.

A NEW APPROACH TO OBEDIENCE (3)

Serve the Lord with gladness.
Psalm 100:2

A man trying to win a woman will do anything for her. She'll call him and say, "I know it's late, you're tired and it's raining, but could you come over and change my flat tire?" "Sure, I'll be right over," he says. And over he comes with a smile. Now, fast forward. They've been married 20 years; he's in the same house with the same woman he courted and won. She asks him to get up off the couch and do something for her. She has to say it 3 or 4 times, and you'd think she'd asked him to cut off his leg the way he moans and groans. Then she gets upset. What's happening? What was once a delight has become a drudgery—because the love motivation has cooled off!

Our problem isn't really obedience, it's keeping our love for Christ strong, for love makes obedience a joy. Less obedience is simply less love. Often we replace grace with law, and love with rules. But we don't enjoy the rules because we don't exercise the love. Our new nature functions best when motivated by relationship, not rules. Rules without love lead to coldness. Christ said to the Christians at Ephesus: "I have this against you, that you have left your first love" (Rev 2:4 NAS). In other words, "You don't love Me like you used to." Then He commanded them to return to the point where they had fallen, which is where they let their love for Him slip. Is Christ saying the same thing to *you* today?

RENEWED DESIRE

In pain you shall bring forth children,
yet your desire shall be for your husband.
Genesis 3:16 NRS

*I*n the Garden of Eden God told Eve, "In pain you shall bring forth children." But He didn't leave it there, He went on to say, "Yet your desire shall be for your husband." God promised to restore the relationship between the man and the woman and that its return would be signified by rekindled desire. That's because He knows *there's no cure for past pain like present desire.* When the longing for something is powerful enough, it can wipe out the pain of the past, making the wounded and weary rise again with renewed energy and purpose. Ask any woman who's just given birth to a much-anticipated child if it was worth all that she went through. Chances are she'd do it again in a heartbeat just to experience the joy of holding that little one in her arms.

Maybe you've experienced a tragedy that's left you feeling indifferent about the future, or a heartbreak that has you still reeling in pain. You may even have tried to rationalize it by telling yourself, "As long as I don't care, it won't hurt." The fear of being wounded again is very real; a burned child dreads the fire. But you can't live the rest of your life in fear. God wants to revive your passion and give you a future filled with hope (See Jer 29:11 & Job 11:18). Are you willing to let Him renew your desire and wipe out the pain of the past? He will! All you have to do is surrender to His love today, and He'll do the rest.

TELL THEM

I try to find common ground with him
so that he will let me tell him about Christ.
1 Corinthians 9:22 TLB

*J*osh McDowell writes: "An executive head hunter who goes out and hires corporate executives for other firms once told me, 'When I get an executive I'm trying to hire for someone else, I like to disarm him. I offer him a drink, take my coat off, then my vest, undo my tie, throw up my feet and talk about baseball, football, family, whatever, until he's all relaxed. Then when I think I've got him relaxed I lean over, look him square in the eye and say—what's the purpose in your life?' It's amazing how top executives fall apart on that question.' Well, I was interviewing this fellow the other day, had him all disarmed with my feet up on my desk talking about football. Then I leaned over and said—what's the purpose in your life, Bob? Without blinking an eye he said 'To go to heaven and take as many people with me as I can.' For the first time in my career I was speechless."

There are basically 5 reasons why we don't share our faith more often, and not one of them will hold up when we stand before Christ: (1) We think it's the preacher's job. (2) We aren't sure of our salvation. (3) We fear being rejected. (4) We've never taken responsibility for learning how. (5) Our love for Christ has grown cold. But not Paul: he said, "Whatever a person is like, I try to find common ground with him so that he will let me tell him about Christ and let Christ save him." Can you say that?

HOW TO KEEP YOUR JOB

*Be quick to listen, slow to speak
and slow to become angry.*
James 1:19 NIV

*E*ighty percent of the time people don't lose their job because of technical incompetence, but because of relational incompetence—they don't know how to get along with other people. If you master the 3 instructions that James gives, the likelihood of that happening to you will go down to just about zero.

(1) Be quick to listen! By staying calm and refusing to react, you gain insight—and respect! "A fool gives full vent to his anger, but a wise man keeps himself under control" (Pr 29:11 NIV).

(2) Be slow to speak! If you tend to talk too much or too fast, here are 3 tips to slow you down: (a) Stop. Just stop talking. Inhale. Count up to 10. Excuse yourself and go to the bathroom. (b) Practice not interrupting. Allow the other person to continue what they're saying until they're through. (c) Ask yourself: Why am I talking so much? Is it insecurity? Anxiety? The need to control? A desire to impress? The reason most of us try to convince, impress or control others is because we have a hard time trusting God to work things out. In other words, "our talk issue, is a trust issue."

(3) Be slow to anger! If you observe the first two principles you'll generally come out all right on number three. It'll just happen. You can make progress on these three things—and you can start today. And if you do it consistently year after year you'll get to the end of your life and say to yourself, "I'm so glad that I took the wisdom of God seriously."

WHILE YOU'RE WAITING

Multiply there and do not decrease.
Jeremiah 29:6 NAS

$\mathcal{G}$od tells His people "I know the plans I have for you...plans to prosper you...plans to give you hope and a future" (Jer 29:11 NIV). But hope needs a nurturing environment. God didn't give them permission to take that hope, then just sit back and do nothing. No, He told them exactly what He wanted them to do while He was working out some of the details for their future: "Build houses and settle down; plant gardens and eat what they produce...Also, seek the peace and prosperity of the city to which I have carried you...Pray unto the Lord for it, because if it prospers, you too will prosper" (Jer 29:5-7 NIV). In other words, while you're waiting for God to turn things around, seize the moment. Become as productive as you possibly can. Maximize your present. A lot of us, while we wait for God to work, think we can do nothing when there's plenty around to do. God said, "Pray for the prosperity of those around you, because when they prosper you will too." A lot of us don't understand this. We've become concerned about one person only—ourselves. When we mess up, the only person we tend to see is ourselves. But God says "While you're waiting on me to do something good for you, begin doing something good for others." That's what Paul meant, "It is more blessed to give than to receive" (Ac 20:35 NAS). Then he added: "The Lord will reward everyone for whatever good he does" (Eph 6:8 NIV). You see, by blessing others you literally open up a channel for God to come through when He blesses you.

TURN AROUND!

Then will I…heal their land.
2 Chronicles 7:14 NIV

$\mathscr{S}$olomon's temple was finally complete. The work of 70,000 laborers, 80,000 stone cutters, and 3600 foremen—finished. Pure gold covered parts of the interior. Precious inlaid stones sparkled. The Ark of the Covenant inhabited the Holy of Holies. Only the presence of God was missing. So Solomon prays "Arise, O Lord God, to Your resting place" (2Ch 6:41 NJKV). And how did God respond? "And the glory of the Lord filled the temple" (2Ch 7:1 NIV). The people fell on their faces declaring, "He is good; his love endures forever" (2Ch 7:3 NIV). After 15 days of celebration Solomon retreated to his palace.

But God wasn't finished speaking. God knows our tendency to forget His blessings and go our own way. Look around you. The conditions that preceded the fall of every great civilization are in place. Can our country be saved? Yes! By whom? God said: (1) "If my people, who are called by my name." We must turn from self-promotion to God promotion. (2) "Will humble themselves and pray." We must turn from self-reliance to God reliance. (3) "And seek my face." We must turn from self-direction to God direction. (4) "And turn from their wicked ways." We must turn from self-indulgence to self-examination. When will God heal our land? When His people turn back to Him!

If the terrain tells you you've made a wrong turn, it's time to make a right one. As a country we've been traveling through some rough terrain. And it's getting rougher every day. What can be done? God's people can turn it around! And that turn begins with—you!

GET RESULTS WHEN YOU PRAY

When a believing person prays, great things happen.
James 5:16 NCV

*S*andra P. Aldrich says, "Early in my widowhood as I prayed…about a possible move, I ended with, 'Thank you God that you'll show us what to do.' My 12-year-old said, 'Mom, you didn't say *Amen.'* I nodded, 'That's because God and I are going to talk about this all day.' And we did. Eventually my family made a cross-country move that opened a new career for me. But more importantly, I began a new adventure with God. Here's what I learned:

"*(a) You don't pray into thin air:* where I live, Pike's Peak rises above the city…but when clouds obscure it we don't say, 'The Peak's gone!' It's there even when we can't see it…and God's working even when you don't see Him. *(b) Just jump in:* James says, 'When a believing person prays, great things happen,' so while reading about prayer and learning about great intercessors can be helpful, you've got to start talking to God yourself. *(c) There's no 'right' way to pray:* one lady remembers her grandparent's prayers being filled with 'Thee's' and 'Thou's,' that made her feel unfit to pray. Then one day as she wrestled with a stubborn lawnmower she simply said, 'Lord, I really need your help.' Suddenly the responding roar of the engine gave her a fresh awareness of God's presence. *(d) Pray like you'd talk to a friend:* Jesus said, 'Be direct. Ask for what you need' (Lk 11:10 TM)." Aldrich continues, "My grandmother talked to God so naturally that I'd meander into the kitchen expecting to see a neighbor." That's how to get results when you pray.

FINDING THE RIGHT CHURCH!

Understanding our lives together as a church.
1 Corinthians 12:25 TM

*W*hat should you look for when trying to find a church? The first is Christ-centered worship, the celebration of God for who He *is,* and what He has *done* for us. A biblically sound church places a high priority on praising God. Second is quality Bible instruction. Does the church you are considering believe, honor, and teach God's Word in such a way that you understand the Bible and see how it applies to your life? Remember, you can't grow beyond what you know. A third characteristic of a good church is fellowship—the sharing of the life of Christ among the members. This goes far beyond Sunday morning attendance or coffee and donuts in the fellowship hall. True fellowship occurs when we are involved in each other's lives—caring, encouraging, correcting, loving and engaging with one another. The church should provide us with a meaningful sense of belonging. Fourth is the church's ministry of outreach. A church that wants to grow, cannot be ingrown. There's nothing wrong with being a small church—as long as you are not a small-minded church. The church you identify with should provide you with opportunities to use your gifts and talents to touch other lives, emphasizing the importance of demonstrating your faith in word and good deeds. In other words, the church's impact should extend well beyond its walls.

When you find a church where these priorities and experiences are regularly offered in an environment that's saturated in grace and charged with faith, you have found the right church. Join it! And don't ask what your church can do for you—ask what you can do for your church!

BREAKING THE APPROVAL CYCLE (1)

If God is for us, who [can be] against us?
Romans 8:31 AMP

*E*ssayist Joan Didion says, "Self respect has nothing to do with reputation or the approval of others." Know what? People-pleasing is a miserable way to live. You turn yourself inside out for them and just when you think you've succeeded, they change their minds. Apart from stealing your peace of mind, approval-seeking makes it impossible to follow God's directives, and ultimately that's your greatest loss. But changing the habits of a life time isn't easy; it requires an act of real faith and asking God for the courage to follow through. David said, "I know…you are with me…I…am not afraid. No one can harm me" (Ps 56:9-11 CEV). And Paul asks, "If God is for us, who [can be] against us?" Understand two things:

(1) Breaking the approval cycle means risking rejection by saying no when others expect to hear yes. When people are used to meek, compliant responses, they'll react negatively till they get used to the "new you." Certainly navigating uncharted waters is intimidating, but is it *really* any worse than living the rest of your life in fear of other people's reactions? (2) You may have to explain to others that in the past you sought their approval because you felt insecure, but that's no longer the case. The important thing is to act *now*. Breaking any addiction involves discomfort and suffering, but the only other option is spending your life feeling trapped. You can choose to suffer short-term on the way to freedom, or long-term by continuing to engage in the struggle to please others. So, which will it be?

BREAKING THE APPROVAL CYCLE (2)

I saw…the people…slipping away from me.
1 Samuel 13:11 NRS

*A*pproval seeking cost Saul his kingdom. God had told him to wait for Samuel to come before offering the evening sacrifice, but because Samuel was late and the people were getting impatient, Saul disobeyed. And when Samuel questioned him, "He replied, 'When I saw…the people… slipping away from me…I…offered the burnt offering… Samuel said…'You have done foolishly…The Lord would have established your kingdom…now [it] will not continue'" (1Sa 13:11-13 NRS). Saul compromised his future because he feared man more than God.

Paul says, "Express truth [in all things]" (Eph 4:15 AMP). Approval seeking is basically dishonest, because people pleasers aren't candid about their feelings. You are telling people what *they* want to hear, rather than what *you* need to say! You don't have to be rude, but you don't have to be a wimp either. Just because somebody doesn't want to hear the truth doesn't negate your responsibility to speak it.

Have you often felt torn about things people are asking you to do? One way God leads is through a sense of peace. Isaiah talks about being "led forth with peace" (Isa 55:12), and Paul says, "pursue…things which make for peace" (Ro 14:19 NKJV). When you don't have peace about doing something it's OK to say so. In fact, people shouldn't expect you to proceed till you do. But that rarely happens when people want *your* help to fulfill *their* agenda! Jesus told His disciples that when people won't "receive…nor listen to your message, as you leave…shake the dust…from your feet" (Mt 10:14 AMP). So, when somebody's reaction threatens to stop you from doing what you feel God wants you to do, be courageous, shake it off and move on.

LET GO AND LET GOD

*If you love someone…You will always believe in him,
always expect the best of him.*
1 Corinthians 13:7 TLB

*T*o let go doesn't mean to stop caring, it just means I can't do it for someone else. To let go is not to cut myself off, it's the realization that I don't control them. To let go is not to enable, but to allow learning from natural consequences. To let go is to admit my powerlessness, which means the outcome is not in my hands. To let go is not to try and change or blame another, I can only change myself. To let go is not to care for, but to care about; not to fix, but to be supportive; not to judge, but to allow another to be a human being. To let go is not to be in the middle arranging all the outcomes, but to allow others to effect their own outcomes. To let go is not to be protective, it's to permit another to face reality. To let go is not to deny, but to accept. To let go is not to nag, scold or argue, but to search out my own shortcomings and correct them. To let go is not to adjust everything to my desires, but to take each day as it comes and cherish each moment. To let go is not to criticize and regulate anyone, but to try to become what I dream I can be. To let go is not to regret the past, but to grow and live for the future. To let go is to fear less and love more. To let go—is to let God!

FIND YOUR PLACE

Our goal is to measure up to God's plan for us.
2 Corinthians 10:13 TLB

*D*a Vinci only painted one Mona Lisa. Beethoven only composed one Fifth Symphony. And God only made one version of you. He custom-designed you for a one-of-a-kind assignment. "How can I discover mine?" you ask. Your *ability* is a key to your *destiny!* "If anyone ministers, let him do it as with the ability which God supplies" (1Pe 4:11 NKJV). When God gives you an assignment, He also gives you the skill-set. To discover your assignment—study your skill-set! Your ease with numbers. Your love of computers. Your gift for interior design. Others stare at blueprints and yawn; you read them and say "I was made for this." Heed the music within! No one else hears it the way you do. Look back. What have you consistently done well? What have you loved to do? Stand at the intersection of your desires and your successes, and you'll find your uniqueness. "The Spirit has given each of us a special way of serving others" (1Co 12:7 CEV). Away with this depreciating "I can't do anything," and its arrogant opposite, "I have to do everything." No, you don't! Paul said, "Our goal is to measure up to God's plan for us." Don't worry about skills you don't have and don't covet strengths others do have. Just use your God-given gifts! "Kindle afresh the gift of God which is in you." If you're not sure what God has called you to do, get down on your knees and ask Him to reveal it to you. And when He does, pour yourself into it!

LEARN TO BE CONTENT

Be relaxed with what you have.
Hebrews 13:5 TM

*D*id you hear about the farmer who grew discontent with his farm so he decided to sell it? A few days later his real estate agent phoned wanting approval for an advertisement she intended to place in the local newspaper. She read it to the farmer. It described a lovely farm in an ideal location— quiet and peaceful, contoured with rolling hills, nourished by a fresh lake and blessed with well-bred livestock. The farmer said, "Read that to me again." After hearing it a second time he said, "I've changed my mind. I'm not selling. I've been looking for a place like that all my life."

Paul would have applauded that farmer. He learned the same lesson: "I have learned in whatever state I am to be content." Before you change your job title, examine your perspective toward life. Success is not defined by position or pay scale, but by this: *doing the most, what you do the best, and doing it as unto the Lord*. Parents, give this counsel to your kids. Tell them to do what they love to do, and do it so well that somebody pays them to do it! Spouses, urge your mate to choose satisfaction over salary. "[It is] better to have little, with fear for the Lord, than to have great treasure [with] turmoil" (Pr 15:16 NLT). Wise up! It's better to be married to a happy person with a thin wallet, than to a miserable person with a thick one. Pursue the virtue of contentment. "Godliness with contentment is great gain" (1Ti 6:6 NIV). When choosing or changing jobs, be careful. Consult your design. Consult your designer. But never consult your greed.

A LITTLE MOTIVATION

It is appointed unto men once to die,
but after this the judgment.
Hebrews 9:27

*Z*ig Ziglar tells the following story. It seems a gentleman worked on the 4 p.m. to midnight shift and he always walked home after work. One night the moon was shining so brightly that he decided to take a shortcut through the cemetery, which would save him roughly a half-mile walk. There were no incidents involved, so he repeated the process on a regular basis, always following the same path. One night as he was walking his route through the cemetery he didn't realize that during the day a grave had been freshly dug in the very center of his path, so he fell into it. Desperately he started trying to get out, but his best efforts failed him. After a few minutes he decided to relax and wait until morning when someone would help him out. He sat down in the corner and was half asleep when a drunk stumbled into the grave. His arrival roused the first guy, since the drunk was also desperately trying to climb out, clawing frantically at the sides. Our hero reached out his hand, touched the drunk on the leg and said "Friend, you can't get out of here"—but he did! Now *that's* motivation!

When you pass 50, if you're wise you'll value time more than money. With hard work you can usually get more money. But when it comes to time—your clock is running out. Maybe a visit to your local graveyard might just be the thing to help you reevaluate and reprioritize, and make the rest of your life—the best of your life!

PROTECT YOUR MARRIAGE

Wives, submit…unto your own husbands…
Husbands, love your wives.
Ephesians 5:22,25

*U*nderstand this: *(1) Every blessing God gives you will be contested by Satan*. Satan was angry that Job's family was a source of delight to God, his provider. Look out, God's blessing on your home invites Satan's attack. He'll place thorns in your nest. He wants to be the third party in your relationship. He wants to agitate and disappoint, using your weaknesses. He inspires unrealistic expectations, diverts your focus from servant-hood to self-absorption. He fuels your imagination through television and unhealthy relationships until God's presence ceases to be the atmosphere of your home or the goal of your union. Beware of his inroads. Become a watchman over your family. *(2) Thoughts have presence*. The moment you walk into a home you sense conflict or contentment, jealousy or joy. Your attitude is contagious. Like a thermostat, it determines the climate. One husband noted that certain television shows nurtured a sexual restlessness within him. He was comparing his wife with the sensuality of the performers. A young wife identified the timing of unexplainable jealousy toward her husband, after watching her favorite soap opera. Every emotion has a birthplace. So be sensitive to any changes in the environment of your home or inner life. *(3) Love is more about listening than talking*. Listen long enough for hidden emotions to be expressed. Listen carefully enough to gain understanding. Listen accurately, so you can assess the true needs of your mate that nobody else has been able to meet. Your questions reveal your caring. So ask them softly, ask them repeatedly, pray and process before you respond, and your marriage can become a masterpiece.

WHO DO YOU SERVE?

The Son of man did not come to be served, but to serve.
Mark 10:45 NKJV

*J*esus entered the world to serve. And we should enter our jobs, our homes and our churches —to serve. Servanthood requires no unique skill or seminary degree. Notice: *(1) To serve is to love the overlooked.* Jesus sits in your classroom wearing thick glasses, outdated clothing and a sad face. You've seen Him. He works in your office. Pregnant again, she shows up late and tired. No one knows the father. Water cooler rumors say even she doesn't. You've seen her. When you love the misfit and befriend the hurting, you love Jesus. "Whenever you did one of these things to someone overlooked or ignored …you did it to me" (Mt 25:40 TM). *(2) To serve is to wave the white flag.* We fight so much: "Where do you think all these appalling wars and quarrels come from?" asks James, "Do you think they just happen? Think again. They come about because you want your own way" (Jas 4:1 TM). Real servants don't struggle, they submit. *(3) To serve is to do something each day that you don't want to do.* Pick up someone's trash. Surrender your parking place. Call that long-winded relative. It doesn't have to be a big thing. Helen Keller once told the Tennessee Legislature that when she was young she longed to do great things and could not, so she decided to do small things in a great way. Don't be too big to do something small. "Throw yourselves into the work of the Master, confident that nothing you do for him is a waste of time or effort" (1Co 15:58 TM).

USE YOUR BUSINESS TO DO GOD'S BUSINESS

Using the boat for a pulpit, he taught the crowd.
Luke 5:3 TM

*L*uke writes: "He climbed into the boat that was [Peter's]...using the boat for a pulpit, he taught the crowd" (Lk 5:2-3 TM). All our boats belong to Christ. Your boat is where you spend your day and make your living. And Christ says to you "You may drive my truck...work on my job site... serve in my hospital wing... preside in my courtroom...edit my newspaper...program my computer." To all of us He says, "Your work is My work."

Later, Peter the boat owner wrote: "You are royal priests. As a result, you can show others the goodness of God" (1Pe 2:9 NLT). And what does a priest do? He represents God to people—and you're supposed to do that too! "Let every detail in your lives—words, actions, whatever—be done in the name of the Master, Jesus" (Col 3:17 TM). Moses prayed, "Let the loveliness of our Lord...rest on us, confirming the work that we do" (Ps 90:17 TM).

Perhaps you see no way God could use your work. Your boss has the disposition of a pit bull. Hamsters have larger work areas; your kids have a better per diem. You feel like you're sentenced to an outpost in Siberia, and hope left on the last train. No! Henry Giles, a 19th century preacher, said, "There is no task so low that we may not elevate it; so dull that we may not enliven it if we understand that what we are doing is service to our Lord Jesus Christ." So, use your business to do God's business!

BE HUMBLE

Do not be wise in your own eyes.
Proverbs 3:7 NIV

A member of the British Parliament took his 8-year-old daughter to visit Westminster Abbey. The awesomeness of it struck the little girl. As she stood looking up at the columns and studying its beauty and grandeur, her father said, "Sweetheart, what are you thinking?" She said, "Daddy, I was thinking how big you seem at home, and how small you look in here."

God's presence has a way of humbling us. And that's good, because when we empty ourselves God has a useful vessel. Your Bible overflows with examples of those who did. In His gospel, Matthew mentions his own name only twice. Both times he calls himself a tax collector. In his list of apostles, he assigns himself the eighth spot. John doesn't even mention his name in his gospel. The 20 appearances of the name "John" refer to the Baptist. John simply calls himself "the other disciple," or "the disciple whom Jesus loved." Luke wrote two of the most important books in the Bible, but never once penned his own name. Paul, the Bible's most prolific author, referred to himself as "a fool" (2Co 12:11). He also called himself "the least of the apostles" (1Co 15:9). Five years later he claimed to be "less than the least of all the saints" (Eph 3:8). In one of his final epistles he referred to himself as "the chief of sinners" (See 1Ti 1:15). As Paul grew older, his ego grew smaller. King David wrote no psalm celebrating his victory over Goliath. But he wrote a public psalm of penitence confessing his sin with Bathsheba (See Ps 51). So, the word for you today is "be humble!"

NOTHING IS EVER LOST!

Gather the leftovers so nothing is wasted.
John 6:12 TM

*D*id you know that what starts as a curse can end as a blessing? When the Mexican boll weevil devastated the southeast Alabama cotton crop, farmers reverted to planting peanuts and ended up producing more than any county in the nation. Consequently the town of Rucker erected a monument bearing this inscription, "In profound appreciation of the boll weevil and what it has done as the herald of prosperity."

When Jesus discovered *Lazarus* was sick he didn't respond till after he'd been dead four days. But because Jesus was waiting didn't mean He wasn't working. He chose to demonstrate His resurrecting power—to prove that nothing's too hard for God. *Joseph* was falsely imprisoned for 13 years. But God was with him and he went on to save multitudes, including his family who'd mistreated him. Joseph's struggles made him better, not bitter. But it could have ended differently if he hadn't maintained the right attitude. God used *Esther* to save her people, but first he put her in the position of living where she didn't want to live and doing what she didn't want to do. Even though a widow, *Ruth* ended up gleaning in a field where she met and married a wealthy man named Boaz. In addition to bearing him children, she became part of Jesus' ancestral bloodline. So if *you're* struggling to see God's purpose in your suffering today, rest assured He *has* one. After feeding a multitude Jesus told His disciples, "Gather the leftovers so nothing is wasted." In God's kingdom nothing is ever lost. When you trust Him He makes "all things work together for good" (Ro 8:28).

LIVING OUT OF THE WRONG BAG

Make sure you understand what the Master wants.
Ephesians 5:17 TM

*H*ave you ever mistakenly picked somebody else's luggage off a conveyer belt at the airport and taken it home? Two seconds after opening it up you discovered—you can't live out of somebody else's bag! You can't wear their clothes or fit into their shoes. So why do we try to? Parents! Dad says, "Son, your granddad was a farmer, I'm a farmer, and some day you'll inherit the farm." Teachers! A teacher warns a young girl who wants to be a stay-at-home mom, "Don't squander your life. With your gifts you could make it to the top." Church leaders! "Jesus was a missionary. Do you want to please Him? Spend your life on foreign soil." Sound counsel or poor advice? That depends on what God packed in your bag. What if God made the farmer's son with a passion for literature or medicine? Or gave that girl a love for kids and homemaking? If foreign cultures frustrate you while predictability invigorates you, what are the chances you'd be a happy missionary? "All the days ordained for me were written in your book before one of them came to be" (Ps 139:16 NIV). God gives us eyes for organization, ears for music, hearts that beat for justice, minds that understand physics, hands that love care giving, legs that run and win races. Secular thinking doesn't buy this. It sees no author behind the book and no purpose behind or beyond life. It says "You can be anything you want to be." Wrong! Don't make their mistake. Don't live carelessly or unthinkingly. "Make sure you understand what the Master wants."

TRUE GIVING (1)

See that you also excel in this grace of giving.
2 Corinthians 8:7 NIV

*P*aul tells the Corinthians "see that you also excel in this grace of giving" (2Co 8:7 NIV). Then he challenges them with the example of the givers in Macedonia: "I want to report on the surprising and generous ways in which God is working in the churches in Macedonia province. Fierce troubles came down on the people in those churches, pushing them to the very limit. The trial exposed their true colors: They were incredibly happy, though desperately poor. The pressure triggered something totally unexpected: an outpouring of...generous gifts...They gave offerings of whatever they could—far more than they could afford!—pleading for the privilege of helping ...This was totally spontaneous, entirely their own idea, and caught us completely off guard. What explains it was that they had first given themselves unreservedly to God and to us. The other giving simply flowed out of the purposes of God working in their lives" (2Co 8:1-6 TM). Notice, the Macedonian givers: (1) First gave themselves to the Lord, with no reservations. (2) Understood that everything they possessed was through God's grace alone. Paul said that the way he knew the Macedonians had given themselves to the Lord, was that they begged him for the offering plate. Wow! When was the last time you sat in church, anxiously waiting for the offering to be taken because you couldn't wait to give? This is not giving because the preacher is begging, or the ministry will go under, or you feel guilty, or you're trying to cut a deal with God. No, this is giving out of the overflow of God's goodness to you. This is true giving!

TRUE GIVING (2)

See that you also excel in this grace of giving.
2 Corinthians 8:7 NIV

$\mathcal{O}$ur giving should be regulated and motivated by—gratitude for what Christ has done for us. Paul writes: "Though he was rich, yet for your sakes he became poor, so that you through his poverty might become rich" (2Co 8:9 NIV). Understanding how gracious and generous God is to us is important, because some of us give Him our leftovers. If we've anything left after we've paid our bills and done everything we wanted to do, we'll give. But even if we give God a million dollars, if it's out of our leftovers, have we given Him our best? (See Mal 1:6-9).

Some people are "re-givers." Re-givers receive a present they don't want, wrap it up and give it to someone else. Some folks have whole closets full of such gifts. That's how some of us approach giving to God—and it's an insult! In the New Testament you don't see preachers begging, selling stuff or using gimmicks to raise money for God's work. What you see are people like the Macedonians responding to God's grace because they understood and loved the God they served.

Everything God created was meant to give. He created the sun to give light during the day and the moon and stars during the night. He created flowers to give seeds. God Himself is a giver: "For God so loved the world, that he gave" (Jn 3:16). When you understand grace, circumstances take a back seat. Your giving is not determined by your debt-to-income ratios, financial indexes, leading economic indicators, or tax brackets. No, your giving is motivated by God's grace!

MONUMENTS

[My] life is worth nothing unless...
Acts 20:24 TLB

$\mathcal{I}$t's said that in Mount Hope Cemetery you'll find several strange gravestones. Farmer John Davis had them erected. He began as a lowly hired hand, then managed to amass a considerable fortune. In the process he didn't make many friends. Nor was he close to his wife's family since they thought she had married beneath her. Embittered, he vowed not to leave them a penny. When his wife died Davis erected an elaborate statue which showed both her and him at opposite ends of a love seat. He was so pleased with this that he planned a second monument, with his wife kneeling at his future grave-side placing a wreath. Then he had a sculptor place a pair of wings on her back. One idea led to another until he'd spent a quarter of a million dollars on monuments to his wife and him-self. Whenever someone from the town asked him to contribute to a hospital or a swimming pool for children, etc., the old miser would say, "What's this town ever done for me?" After using up all his money on statues, Davis died at 92, a lonely, grim-faced resident of the poorhouse. But his monuments...it's strange...each one is slowly sinking into the Kansas soil, fast becoming victims of time, vandalism and neglect. Monuments of spite and self-centered living. There's a certain poetic justice in the fact that within a few years they'll all be gone. Oh, by the way, only one person attended Farmer Davis' funeral: Horace England, the tombstone salesman. What a way to go! But not Paul: "[My] life is worth nothing unless I use it for doing the work assigned me by the Lord Jesus." Can you say that?

LIVE IN GOD'S PRESENCE

I have set the Lord always before me.
Psalms 16:8 NIV

*T*he words "I have set the Lord always before me," are the simplest description of spiritual life. When certain thoughts are present, there's a good chance they're the result of God walking alongside of us. The first thought involves feelings of *reassurance*. Whether it's Joshua taking over from Moses, or Paul going through his worst storm, the message is: "Be not afraid. I am with you." The second thought you'll have when God is present is that you'll get *guidance*. Maybe you're stumped with some issue and then an idea comes to you. It might be a big one or a small one, but it will help. Or you're about to say something that will inflict damage, and suddenly a little voice inside your head says "be quiet." A third indicator of God's presence is *conviction of sin*. You're going down the wrong road and a little stab of pain says, "no, turn around." Heed that voice or you'll violate your values, diminish your influence, and end up guilt-ridden. The fourth kind of thought that will tell you God is present, is *joy!* "You have made known to me the path of life; you will fill me with joy in your presence" (Ps 16:11 NIV). It works like this: you put in an extra effort, something gets accomplished and you feel a surge of satisfaction—that's what happened when God created the world, then said, "That's good!" God can use any of those things to convey His presence. If you "Set the Lord always before [you]" you'll begin to sense Him in your everyday life.

WHY KEEP THE TEN COMMANDMENTS?

God has come to test you.
Exodus 20:20 NIV

We don't hear much about the Ten Command-
ments these days. They've become more like ten suggestions—
for others.

"Thou shalt not steal—from me." Why is this? Because
like children, we want to do what we want to do. Ever watch a
child learning to walk? She totters this way, then the other way,
weaving like a miniature adult who's had too much to drink.
But consider for a moment where that little girl would be with
no adults around; if no doors, gates or fences contained her
wobbly steps. She might stagger into the neighbor's yard where
the Rottweiler has just gotten loose, or fall into a drainage ditch
and be swept away by the current washing down the gutter. It's
vital that she have boundaries. In fact, most children, as well as
adults, feel more secure in knowing their boundaries than in
having unrestricted freedom. The Ten Commandments serve
this purpose. God knows our tendencies like a protective parent
knows how to keep a toddler from wandering into dangerous
places. Although delivered to the ancient Israelites for their
guidance, these commandments remain valid life instructions
for us as His modern day children. Instead of seeing them as a
list of "Thou shalt nots," we should see them in terms of
protection, guidance, and relationship with Him. After Moses
had delivered the Ten Commandments to the people he added
"God has come to test you…to keep you from sinning." God
desires to make us happy—and holy. And the two go together.
Contentment and fulfillment can only be achieved when we
walk straight along the path the Lord has set before us.

LEARNING FROM THE PRODIGAL SON

Father, I have sinned.
Luke 15:18

*T*he Prodigal Son didn't get into trouble until he left the safety of his Father's house. Jesus pointed out 4 things about him:

(1) "He wasted his substance." Satan is a bait-and-switch expert. If you heed his call to come out and play, you'll end up losing the very substance of who you are and what God's called you to be. *(2) "He went and joined himself to a citizen of that country."* Want to know where you are spiritually? Look at who you hang out with and take advice from. Who do you call, who calls you? Solomon writes, "My son, if sinners entice you, do not give in to them" (Pr 1:10 NIV). *(3) "He began to be in want."* Something's wrong! In his father's house he never missed a meal, now he's eating what pigs eat. He's trying to meet a legitimate need in an illegitimate way. Are you doing that? David said, "The Lord is my shepherd; I shall not want" (Ps 23:1). Who's that promise for? Those who live in the safety of the sheepfold and stay close to the shepherd. *(4) "He came to himself."* When his elevator could go no lower he decided to get off. Mercifully, he still could. Some don't get to. The Bible says: "Today, [not tomorrow] if you hear his voice, do not harden your hearts" (Heb 3:15 NIV). It wasn't too late for the Prodigal—and it's not too late for you. The moment he changed his prayer from "give me" to "forgive me," his father opened his arms, welcomed him home and restored him to sonship. And God will do the same for you, if you let Him.

ARE YOU MOVING TOO FAST?

One who moves too hurriedly misses the way.
Proverbs 19:2 NRS

*J*ohn Ortberg writes: "When I first moved to Chicago I called a friend—the wisest spiritual man I know—and asked him, 'What do I need to do to be healthy spiritually?' He said, 'You must ruthlessly eliminate hurry from your life.' There was a long pause, and I finally said 'Okay.' I wrote that one down. 'Now, what *else* do you have to tell me, because I don't have much time and I want to get a lot of wisdom out of this conversation.' He replied 'There is nothing else. Hurry is the great enemy of spiritual life. You can hardly do anything the way Jesus did it if you're in a hurry. Jesus was often busy, but never hurried. Hurry is an inward condition in which you're so frantic and preoccupied that you're unable to receive love from the Father, unable to be present with other people, or to give love to them.'"

Understand this: things will not just "settle down." If you wait to get around to what really matters, you'll *never* do what God's called you to do! Your soul will wither. You must ruthlessly eliminate hurry from your life. Furthermore, no one else can do this for you—not your boss, your pastor, your spouse, your kids, or your best friend. You must do this for yourself. Take a moment and ponder these two scriptures: (1) "The fear of the Lord leads to life: Then one rests content, untouched by trouble" (Pr 19:23 NIV). (2) "Desire without knowledge is not good, and the one who moves too hurriedly misses the way" (Pr 19:2 NRS).

"IN SICKNESS AND IN HEALTH"

Love never fails.
1 Corinthians 13:8 NIV

*R*ichard Selzer writes: "I stand by the bed where a young woman lies, her face post-operative, her mouth twisted in palsy; clownish. A tiny twig of the facial nerve, the one to the muscles of her mouth, has been severed. The surgeon had followed with religious fervor the curve of her flesh; I promise you that. Nonetheless, to remove the tumor from her cheek I had to cut the little nerve. Her young husband is in the room. He stands on the opposite side of the bed, and together they seem to dwell in the evening lamplight, isolated from me, private. Who are they, I ask myself, he and this wry-mouth I have made, who gaze at and touch each other so generously, greedily? "Will my mouth always be like this?" she asks. "Yes," I say, "it will be. It is because the nerve was cut." She nods and is silent. But the young man smiles. "I like it," he says, "it's kind of cute." All at once I know who he is. I understand, and I lower my gaze. One is not old in an encounter with God. Unmindful, he bends to kiss her crooked mouth, and I am so close I can see how he twists his own lips to accommodate her, and to show her that their kiss still works."

A mastectomy, an illness, the loss of a limb that changes life forever by confining you or someone you love to a bed or a wheelchair, can transform the words, "In sickness and in health" into one of love's greatest tests. In such painful moments we discover the truth of Scripture "Love never fails."

CONFESSION

I said, 'I will confess my transgressions to the Lord' —
and you forgave the guilt of my sin.
Psalm 32:5 NIV

Confession does for our soul what working the ground does for the soil. Before the farmer sows his seed he works the land, removing the rocks and pulling the stumps. Why? Because seed grows better in prepared soil. Confession invites God to walk the acreage of our hearts. "There's a rock of greed over here, Father. I can't budge it. And that tree of lust near the fence? Its roots are long and deep. And here's some dry soil, too crusty for seed!" Confession seeks pardon from God, not amnesty. Pardon accepts guilt; amnesty, derived from the same Greek word as *amnesia,* "forgets" the offence without acknowledging guilt.

Remember Peter who denied his Master when he should have defended Him? How did the New Testament writers know the details of Peter's failure? How did Matthew know Peter's accent made him a suspect? How did Luke learn of the glance of Jesus that melted Peter's heart? Who told all 4 Gospel writers about the crowing rooster and flowing tears? Most likely, Peter himself! "Fellows, I've got to get something off my chest." He describes that terrible morning, the fire, the girl, and the look on the face of Jesus. How can we be sure of this? Because Peter couldn't stay away from Christ! Who was the first man to run to the empty tomb? Who was the first to jump out of the boat and swim to Jesus who stood on the shore? Peter! Those who keep secrets from God keep their distance from God. But those who are honest with God, draw near to God.

SMALL DEEDS COUNT

Do not despise these small beginnings,
for the Lord rejoices to see the work begin.
Zechariah 4:10 NLT

*W*hat seems small to you might be huge to someone else. Ask Bohn Fawkes. During World War II he piloted a
B-17. On one mission he sustained flak from Nazi anti-aircraft
guns. Even though his gas tanks were hit the plane did not
explode, and Fawkes was able to land it. On the morning following the raid Fawkes asked his crew chief for the German
shell, to keep as a souvenir of his good fortune. The chief
explained that not just one, but eleven shells had been found in
the gas tank, none of which had exploded. Technicians opened
the shells and found them void of explosive charge. They were
clean and harmless, and with one exception, empty. The exception contained a carefully rolled piece of paper. On it a message
had been scrawled in the Czech language: "This is all we can
do for you now." A courageous assembly line worker was
disarming bombs and scribbled that note. He couldn't end the
war, but he could save one plane. He couldn't do everything,
but he could do something, and he did it.

So, send that e-mail. Make that phone call. Write that
check. David had a sling. Rahab had a string. Dorcas had a
needle. All were used by God. What do you have? John Wesley
said, "Do all the good you can, by all the means you can, in all
the ways you can, in all the places you can, at all the times you
can, to all the people you can, as long as you ever can." With
God, small deeds count!

HOW TO SUCCEED ON THE JOB

With good will doing service,
as to the Lord, and not to men.
Ephesians 6:7

*H*ow do you succeed on the job? *(1) By keeping your eyes on your objective*. Are you selling windows? Then don't walk into someone's house and offer unsolicited advice about their living room décor. Focus on what you're called to do. People can be easily offended, and by speaking about areas outside your expertise—what your customer has solicited your help in—you can jeopardize good opportunities. And learn to appreciate people, even those you don't like. Customers are not friends; friends are friends. Place value on others. Respect them, even if your personal opinions differ from theirs! Remember, your success is not determined by their personality. *(2) By treating everyone fairly and equally.* If you show favoritism by only being kind and respectful to those you like, you're in for trouble—if not now, then down the road. You need to learn how to work with people who aren't your favorites. Why? Because they will remember your attitude, whether good or bad, and not be particularly inclined to help you in the future. *(3) By trying not to take things personally.* You must learn to let go of grudges and to set aside past histories with some of your co-workers. When you find your emotions flaring up and you're tempted to react, stop and remember what's really going on; you're in the midst of a battle and the first shots have been fired. This is the time to say a silent prayer, remember your true calling, and respond with love, patience and a professionalism that will cause those around you to want what you've got!

BE A FOXHOLE FRIEND (1)

Two can accomplish more.
Ecclesiastes 4:9 TLB

*I*t is said that Marines are taught to dig a foxhole big enough for a friend. That's good advice! We all face battles in life, and our "foxholes" come in many shapes and sizes. So let's understand three things: *(1) The foxhole is for you and a friend—not a friend alone.* You can ask a friend to fight with you, but you should never send someone else to fight your battles for you. *(2) Before the battle, you should have developed the friendship.* Foxholes aren't about using people. You first need to be a friend, before asking for the help of a friend. *(3) You have also been in your friend's foxhole with them.* You should be willing to fight for any friend whose help you would request. That's what friends do. Dr. Martin Luther King, Jr. said, "In the end, we will remember not the words of our enemies, but the silence of our friends." Never let it be said you were a silent friend! Here are two important truths about foxholes.

(a) Foxholes without friends are unhealthy. Trying to face the world alone is dangerous and unscriptural: "It is not good for the man to be alone" (Ge 2:18 NLT). (b) Foxholes prove friendships. In tough times you discover who your real friends are. When Pepper Rodgers coached at UCLA, his team had some bad seasons. Recalling one, Rodgers told a reporter "My dog was about my only friend, and I told my wife that a man needs at least two friends. So she bought me another dog." As the old saying goes: "In prosperity our friends know us; in adversity we know our friends."

BE A FOXHOLE FRIEND (2)

Two can accomplish more.
Ecclesiastes 4:9 TLB

$\mathcal{B}$efore you get into a foxhole with someone, understand:

(1) Foxhole friends are few. During the Civil War Abraham Lincoln once received a request to pardon a soldier sentenced to be executed for desertion. The man didn't have a single letter of support vouching for him. Next morning the officer was shocked to hear Lincoln say that the testimony of a friend had sealed his decision to pardon the man. When the officer reminded the President that the request had come with no letter of reference, Lincoln simply stated "I will be his friend" then signed his pardon. If you have such people in your life value them, they are rare indeed.

(2) Foxhole friends provide strength before and during the battle. Even before the battle, simply knowing that someone believes in you and will fight for you is uplifting. Epicurus said "It is not so much our friends' help that helps us, as the confident knowledge that they will help us."

(3) Foxhole friends see things from the same perspective. Five-year-old Tracey asked her dad if she could play at the house of a friend. He told her she could as long as she was home by 6 o'clock for dinner. When 6 o'clock rolled around Tracey was nowhere to be seen. After about 25 minutes, Tracey opened the front door. Her father, working to control his impatience, asked where she'd been. "My friend's doll broke right when I was supposed to leave for home." Her dad said, "And I suppose you were helping her fix it?" Tracey replied, "No, I was helping her cry." What was Tracey? She was a foxhole friend! Are you?

TOUCHING JESUS

[There was] a woman in the crowd.
Mark 5:25 NLT

*M*ark records, "There was a woman in the crowd who had had a hemorrhage for 12 years." She is desperate and her desperation births an idea—"She had heard about Jesus" (v27 NLT). Jesus is coming to town. By invitation of the synagogue ruler. Odd to find the ruler and the woman in the same story. He's powerful. She's pitiful. But his daughter is dying. Tragedy levels social topography. "If I can just touch His clothing, I will be healed" (v28 TLB). So she scurries through the crowd. Knees bump her ribs. "Move out of the way!" someone shouts. She doesn't care and doesn't stop. Jesus' robe is in sight. She extends her hand. "Immediately...she could feel... that she had been healed!" (v29 NLT). She feels power enter. Jesus feels power exit. "Jesus...asked, 'Who touched my clothes'" (v30 TLB). Next we read: "The woman...knowing she was the one...knelt before him, and gave him the whole story" (Mk 5:33 TM). Wow! How long had it been since someone listened to her story? With the town bishop waiting, a child dying and a crowd pressing, He makes time for a woman on the fringe. Using a term He gives to no one else He says, *"Daughter,* your faith has made you well" (v34 NLT). And we have been her, haven't we? Illness took her strength. What took yours? Red ink? Hard drink? Late nights in the wrong arms? Long days in the wrong job? Pregnant too soon? Too often? Is her hand your hand? If so, take heart. Your family may shun it. Society may avoid it. But Christ? He wants to touch it. Yes, yours is the hand He loves to hold!

HELPING "HURTING PEOPLE"

A word of encouragement does wonders.
Proverbs 12:25 TLB

*A*sk yourself, "Do I hurt people, and am I easily hurt by them?" Then consider these truths:

(1) Hurting people hurt other people. The German poet Hermann Hesse wrote: "If you hate a person, you hate something in him that is part of yourself. What isn't part of ourselves doesn't disturb us." Hurting people lash out in response to what's happening inside them. They feel or believe something negative within themselves. Try to remember that.

(2) Hurting people are more often hurt by people. Let's say you've a splinter in your finger and it becomes infected. Then someone brushes against it. You howl with pain, "You hurt me!" No, the real problem is the splinter you neglected to address. Hurting people overreact, overexaggerate, and overprotect. They also overinfluence. Ask any counselor who's dealt with a hurting couple. Emotionally one spouse "throws up," then the other "cleans up." Usually the individual with the most pain does the most damage.

(3) Quick fixes don't work. The kindest thing you can do for hurting people is ask them, "Are you prepared to work through the issues and get beyond your pain?" When a New England pipe cleaning company was working under the streets to clean out a sewer line, they found: sixty-one diamond rings, vintage coins and silverware. It was an unpleasant job—but they were allowed to keep the valuables they discovered in the process! Now, you may have to do some digging and deal with some pretty nasty stuff, but in the process you may discover some treasures you didn't know existed, and at the end of all your hard work, learn to develop healthy relationships.

BE MORE GENTLE!

Be…gentle…bearing with one another in love.
Ephesians 4:2 NIV

*A*braham Maslow said, "If the only tool you have is a hammer, you tend to see every problem as a nail." Face it, because of our strong personalities some of us are inclined to use a hammer when something gentler will do. If that's your problem, try using the following T's: *(1) Total picture.* A middle-aged man walked into a bar. "Do you have anything to cure hiccups?" The bartender slapped him across the face. "Hey! what's the idea?" said the man. The bartender smiled "Well, you don't have hiccups any more, do you?" "I never did," the man replied. "I wanted something to cure my wife, she's out in the car." Do you come to conclusions before the problem has been laid out before you? Slow yourself down; you'll be more likely to respond appropriately. *(2) Timing.* If the parent doesn't get the injured child to the hospital quickly enough, her life might be lost; and if you don't apologize when you've wronged someone, the relationship could be lost. *When* you act, is as important as taking the right action. Also knowing when not to act. Lady Dorothy Nevill observed: "The art of conversation is not only to say the right thing in the right place, but to leave unsaid the wrong thing at the tempting moment." *(3) Temperature.* As tempers flare, we drop bombs when a slingshot would do. In general: (a) if the reaction is worse than the action, the problem usually increases; (b) if the reaction is less than the action, the problem usually decreases. So, be more gentle!

JESUS KNOWS HOW YOU FEEL!

He...experienced...all the pain, all the testing.
Hebrews 2:18 TM

*A*re you financially strapped? Jesus knows how you feel. He said He didn't have a place to lay His head. Do you feel taken advantage of? Jesus paid taxes to a foreign emperor. But what if your problem is the opposite? You have a successful business to run. Can Jesus relate? Absolutely. He recruited and oversaw His own organization. Seventy men, plus an assortment of women who looked to Him for leadership. Do you make budgets and hire personnel? Christ knows leadership is not easy. His group included a zealot who hated the Romans and a tax collector who worked for them. And how about family tension? "When His family heard what was happening, they tried to take Him home with them. 'He is out of his mind' they said" (Mk 3:21 NIV). Have you been falsely accused? The night before His death people "tried to find something false against Jesus so they could kill him" (Mt 26:59 NCV). Oh yes, Jesus has been there. He experienced "All the pain, all the testing." Max Lucado writes: "Jesus was angry enough to purge the temple, distraught enough to weep in public, fun-loving enough to be called a drunkard, winsome enough to attract kids, poor enough to borrow a coin for a sermon illustration, radical enough to get kicked out of town, responsible enough to care for His mother, tempted enough to know the smell of Satan, and anxious enough to sweat blood." But why would Christ endure earth's toughest pain? So *you* would know that "He is able...to run to the cry of...those who are being... tested" (Heb 2:18 AMP). Whatever you're facing today, Jesus knows how you feel!

UNDERSTANDING TEMPTATION

God...does not tempt anyone.
James 1:13 NAS

*T*rials and temptations are very different. Trials are permitted by God to develop character in us. On the other hand, temptations are sent by Satan to bring us down. There's no way a temptation to sexual sin can be called a trial sent from God. He doesn't test our faith by setting us up to sin. Just because your hotel room offers pornographic movies doesn't mean it must be okay with God if you watch them, otherwise He wouldn't have allowed you to check into that room. Get real! James wrote: "Let no one say when he is tempted, 'I am being tempted by God'...each one is tempted when he is...enticed." The word "entice" describes a fisherman putting a worm on a hook to entice a fish to bite. The fish is looking for a snack, not to become dinner for the fisherman. No mouse goes looking for a mousetrap. What the mouse wants is the cheese. But its legitimate hunger for cheese deceives it into thinking that the cheese is there for the taking, and the trap is sprung. The legitimate use of food nourishes your body, the lust for it produces gluttony and sickness. The proper use of money can bless you, the irresponsible use of it can enslave you with debt. Food. Sex. Money. Power. When the desire for these things becomes all consuming, the warning bell is ringing. Pay attention!

But the Good News is, you're not in this fight alone. Peter writes: "The Lord knoweth how to deliver the godly out of temptations" (2Pe 2:9). Victory comes when you draw closer to the One who defeated the tempter both in life and in death. So call on Him today. He's ready to help you!

WORKING WITH DIFFICULT PERSONALITIES

As much as lieth in you, live peaceably with all men.
Romans 12:18

*M*any people dream of being in full time ministry. Their goal is to work where there's praise music playing and co-workers praying. With Scripture verses on the wall and crosses around every neck, they imagine such a place to be holy, always joyful and peaceful. They believe that in such a place one of their primary sources of stress—getting along with difficult people—will disappear. Don't you believe it! Paul and Barnabas, two great Christian leaders, fought so badly over John Mark that they had to split up. The early church experienced financial squabbles, moral scandals and doctrinal disputes. Understand this: until the Lord comes back you'll always experience difficulty relating to certain people. There's very little difference in how people operate when they're under pressure. The mind is not new, it is constantly being renewed—even the minds of Christians. This doesn't mean they're not sincere, it just means they're not as mature as they should be. Pettiness, greed, ambition and favoritism all creep in as the enemy fires his darts and hopes to create a flame. So if we are going to thrive in our hostile environments, we must increase our capacity to work with difficult personalities. How? By preparing yourself spiritually through prayer and the reading of God's Word before you get to work. By committing to be Christ-like on the job in your attitudes and actions. Will you always succeed? No! Will you be stretched? Yes! Can it be done? Absolutely! "My grace is sufficient for thee" (2Co 12:9). How do you become more gracious? By drawing each day on God's grace!

ALL THE GRACE WE NEED

Draw near with confidence to the throne of grace.
Hebrews 4:16 NAS

$\mathcal{H}$ebrews 4:16 says we can "draw near with confidence to the throne of grace." We don't have to hold anything
back in prayer. And we don't have to wonder if we are wasting
our time. We have been authorized to enter His throne room,
using the name of Jesus.

Aren't you glad it's not a throne of judgment? Who
among us could stand it? No, it's a throne of grace, "unmerited
favor." It's a throne because the One who sits on it is the Sov-
ereign Ruler of the universe. It's also where our Father gives
His sons and daughters what we could never give ourselves.
Yes, He gives us what we don't deserve and could never earn,
from a throne that never runs low in its provision—and it is all
tied to our drawing near in prayer. God has all the grace we
need to help us, but we have to go before His throne to ask for
it. *Therefore a prayer-less Christian is also a grace-less
Christian!* Christians who are not praying as a way of life are
not growing in their spiritual life because they are not hanging
around the throne that dispenses grace.

Notice, the grace we receive at God's throne is designed
to help us "in time of need." Think about that. Grace is given
based on the need of the moment. God will not give you tomorrow's grace until tomorrow, so don't bother asking for it. But
don't worry, the provision of grace we have in Christ will not
run out tomorrow, or ever. So, you can't go to God too often!

WINNING THE BIGGEST BATTLE OF ALL

Christ…is your example. Follow in his steps.
1 Peter 2:21 TLB

*R*ichard Halverson writes: "Do you want to be a winner? Compete against yourself, not somebody else. Outrunning your rival doesn't mean you ran your best race. You can win over another and still not fulfill your potential. To be your best you must compete with yourself. It's life's biggest contest. A loser is a winner—however many his losses, if he conquers himself. And a winner is a loser—however many his victories, if he loses in the battle with himself. Alexander the Great conquered the world, yet cursed his own lack of self-control. Victory over others may in fact be the very thing that contributes to the winner's failure to conquer self. Winning makes him arrogant, independent, thoughtless—and sometimes cruel. To put it another way, it isn't what happens to you that makes the difference, but how you handle it. The one who stops maturing spiritually because he thinks he knows more scripture than others, or has more success in ministry, is still far from being what Christ has planned for him."

If you must compare yourself with another, compare yourself with Christ. "Christ…is your example. Follow in his steps: he never sinned, never told a lie, never answered back when insulted; when he suffered he did not threaten to get even; he left his case in the hands of God who always judges fairly" (1Pe 2:21-23 TLB). Go ahead, measure yourself by that standard! And when you see how far short you fall, get down on your knees and ask God to mold and fashion your life into the full potential, the divine original He intended. Do that, and you can win the biggest battle of all!

FOR WORKING PARENTS

Her children arise up, and call her blessed.
Proverbs 31:28

*T*he story is told of a mother who came home from work after a long hard day. Her little girl ran out to greet her. "Mommy, wait until I tell you what happened today." After listening to a few sentences her mother responded by indicating that the rest could wait as she needed to get dinner started. During the meal the phone rang, then other family members' stories were longer and louder than the little girl's. Once again she tried after the kitchen was cleaned and her brother's homework questions were answered. But by then it was time for bed. When her mom came to tuck her in, the child looked up and asked, "Mommy, do you really love me, even when you don't have time to listen to me?"

Are you a working parent coming home every night to a pile of household chores? Are your weekends hectic playing catch-up? Do you feel guilty about disciplining your children because your time with them is so limited? Do you fear they're growing up without you? That soon the tables will be turned, and maybe one day they won't have time for you?

Every working parent faces it, and it's tough. But it's not impossible. Talk about it to your child! You'd be amazed how much they understand. And make time to listen! Let your child know that they can talk to you any time, about any thing, without having to be afraid, ashamed, or put off till later. And be sure to ask for God's help. He's "a very present help in trouble" (Ps 46:1).

If you practice these principles, one day your children may "Rise up and call you blessed."

GODLINESS

Remember from where you have fallen,
and repent and do the deeds you did at first.
Revelation 2:5 NAS

*H*ow do busy people living fast-paced and complicated lives develop the quality of godliness? By going to church? Billy Sunday said "Going to church will no more make you a Christian than going to a garage will make you an automobile." Your environment—even a spiritual one—won't necessarily make you godly.

Christ speaks to all of us: "Remember from where you have fallen, and repent and do the deeds you did at first." Go back in your mind to your first days as a believer. Do you remember when (a) you talked about the Lord and it would fill your heart with delight; (b) prayer was exciting and you felt empowered as you spent time with Him; (c) the Bible was filled with soul-thrilling insights you'd never seen before; (d) sharing your faith with someone represented the highlight of your week; (e) your devotion to Christ was consistent, fulfilling, enriching, deep? What happened? Do you feel like one of the Ephesian Christians Christ was speaking to?

Distance from God is a frightening thing—because you don't even know it's happening! Understand this: God will not accelerate His pace to catch up with ours; we need to slow down in order to get back into step with Him. God won't speak to us during a commercial break on our favorite TV show. No, we must seek quietness so we can hear His still, small voice. God can't be fitted into the framework of our complicated lives; we must put Him first and keep Him there, if our lives are to be characterized by that all-encompassing word—Godliness.

MANIPULATIVE RELATIONSHIPS

Fear of man is a dangerous trap.
Proverbs 29:25 TLB

*W*hen you enter any relationship, romantic, social, business or otherwise, be careful what you permit in the beginning because it'll come to be expected. For example, if you have to *buy* someone's friendship by letting them manipulate you, be prepared to keep paying. And don't plan on changing them. Just think how difficult it is to change yourself —so what are your chances of changing somebody else? Decide now what you can live with later. And stop living like there's no tomorrow—because tomorrow always comes! Solomon said, "Fear of man is a dangerous trap." Relationships can't thrive with one person calling all the shots while the other struggles for approval.

Paul said he had no interest in "trying to make people accept him." His only interest was pleasing God. (See Gal 1:10 NCV). God will never ask you to violate your values or disobey His will just to be in the good graces of another person. In fact, it's better to be alone than to allow anyone other than God to control you. Let people know up front that while you'd like their approval you can live without it if you have to. Respect others, and make it clear you expect the same in return.

Above all, never let emotion win out over wisdom, or drown out the voice of God in your life. When you're insecure you can be drawn into wrong relationships. Security is a fundamental part of your identity as God's child. Paul says you "are God's masterpiece…created…anew in Christ" (Eph 2:10 NLT). God wants you free to be who you are. That's why when you ask Him to guide your relationships, He'll help you to form the right ones.

BATTLING THE "WHAT IFS?"

Days…are made evil
by anxious thoughts and forebodings.
Proverbs 15:15 AMP

*A*n old sea captain once asked a naval student how he'd handle a sudden storm. "I'd throw out an anchor, sir," he replied. "But what if another storm approached?" asked the captain. "Then I'd throw out another anchor," he said. "And what if storms just kept coming?" the old man asked. "I'd keep throwing out anchors," said the student. "Hold on, son," said the captain, "where are you getting all those anchors?" "From the same place you keep getting all those storms, sir," came the reply!

When you're in the thick of things, it's easy to get overwhelmed by the storm that's raging inside you and start listening to the "what ifs." *What if* the check doesn't come on time… or the stock loses value…or your mate walks out…or the test results are bad. The list is endless. And because Satan knows that "fear involves torment" (1Jn 4:18 NKJV), he'll keep pouring it on. If he can't get you puffed up through pride he'll try to bring you down through fear. It's his best tool. But you don't have to take it! Paul says, "Leave no room…for the devil [give no opportunity to him]" (Eph 4:27 AMP). Jesus told us not to be "fearful…intimidated…and unsettled" (Jn 14:27 AMP). Remember, "The days of the…afflicted are made evil [by anxious thoughts and forebodings], but he who has a glad heart has a continual feast [regardless of circumstances]."

Here's the bottom line: God is "utterly trustworthy…He will…[fulfill His call by hallowing and keeping you]" (1Th 5:24 AMP). So, no matter how big your problem is today, keep trusting God—and He *will* bring you through!

WHAT ARE YOU DEPENDING ON?

There is a way that seems right to a man,
but…it leads to death.
Proverbs 14:12 NIV

There's a broken rope on display at the Alpine Museum in Bern, Switzerland. It's associated with a tragic story. Some climbers who scaled the Matterhorn roped themselves together for the return descent, but one slipped and dragged 3 others with him into an abyss. The other climbers braced for the shock on the rope that linked them together, expecting it to halt their companions' fall. The tug came, but then to everyone's horror the rope snapped, plunging their 4 friends to their death. Nobody knows why an inferior rope was used for such a hazardous venture, but they do know it wasn't genuine Alpine Club rope which was guaranteed and distinguished by a red strand running through it.

Just as reliable equipment is crucial in preparing for the life-and-death adventure of mountain climbing, it's even *more* essential in preparing for the most important journey you'll ever make; the one from here to eternity. And an "anything-goes" attitude…loose connections to the church…casual claims that you're doing your best…and fuzzy notions about God's indulgence, won't cut it. Solomon said, "There is a way that seems right to a man, but…it leads to death."

Peter says: "Jesus is the only One who can save" (Ac 4:12 NCV). Assurance of a place in heaven comes *only* through accepting Jesus as your personal Savior, believing that He died for your sins and rose again to give you everlasting life. No more will be asked; no less will get you in. Today Jesus is waiting to save you—will you let Him?

"STAYING THE COURSE"

The testing of your faith produces endurance.
James 1:3 NAS

*E*ndurance means "staying the course." But endurance is only a word until you have to deal with a strife-torn marriage, the long road back from bankruptcy, divorce or illness, the rebuilding of your life, or the required preparation for success in any field. It takes commitment to keep going when friends fail you, discouragement whispers "give up," and doubt says "it can't be done." That's when *endurance* takes on new meaning. It becomes your anchor in the storm, your compass in times of confusion, and the head of steam that gets you up the next hill.

Remember, God knows when to discontinue a trial because its purpose has been fulfilled. And He gives us 2 great promises: (1) His comforting presence (See Isa 43:2-5). (2) The assurance that He won't permit more pressure than we can handle (See 1Co 10:13).

But there's another reason—others are watching! Paul writes, "People are watching us as we stay at our post... working hard, working late, working without eating; with pure heart, clear head, steady hand; in gentleness, holiness and honest love; when we're telling the truth...when God's showing His power; when we're doing our best setting things right; when we're praised, and when we're blamed; slandered, and honored; true to our word, though distrusted; ignored by the world, but recognized by God...immersed in tears yet always filled with deep joy; living on handouts, yet enriching many; having nothing, having it all" (1Co 6:1-10 TM). That's called "staying the course."

GOD'S FAVOR

When God approves of your life, even your enemies
will end up shaking your hand.
Proverbs 16:7 TM

*Y*ou can't please everybody all the time. And it's a big mistake to try. Your constant need for approval can end up costing you God's best. When you're doing anything worthwhile, *expect* opposition from those who aren't privy to God's plan for your life. That goes with the turf. Notice, Jesus "made himself of no reputation" (Php 2:7). He wasn't always well thought of by others, but He knew He had *God's* approval—and that's what mattered to Him!

In Proverbs 21:1 Solomon says that just like changing the direction of a moving river, God can change hearts and give you favor with those who'd otherwise reject you. He also said, "When God approves of your life, even your enemies will end up shaking your hand." Does that mean you won't encounter opposition or people who disagree with you? No, but when you do, just concentrate on pleasing God and let *Him* deal with the fallout.

Remember, God takes up where you leave off. When you've exhausted all your efforts He can step in and open doors with the right people at just the right time. The truth is, He can get you a better job than you could get on your own, and give you blessings that, humanly speaking, you don't deserve or qualify for. Just like the Holy Spirit enabled Jesus to fulfill His life's mission (See Lk 4:18-19), God will call, equip and enable you to fulfill His plan for your life. So stop trying so hard to make things happen on *your* terms, and begin praying for God's favor!

INFLUENCING THE NEXT GENERATION

You have stayed long enough at this mountain.
Deuteronomy 1:6 NIV

A teenager was telling a senior citizen why the older generation doesn't understand the younger. "You grew up in a primitive world," he said. "We've got space travel, nuclear energy and computers." Smiling, the old man replied, "You're right, we didn't have those things—that's why we invented them!" So, what are you doing to bless future generations? God said, "I will pour my Spirit into your descendants and my blessing on your children" (Isa 44:3 TM). God wants the next generation not just to follow, but to overtake this one! And He wants *you* to be one of those who raise the bar. Don't use the comfort of the status quo as an excuse for not challenging old thinking. To get beyond your mental barriers you must stop saying things like, "That's just the way I am," or, "My family never amounted to much, so I won't either." No, you're contradicting God!

When God delivered Israel and they headed for the Promised Land, a journey that should have taken 11 days, took 40 years. They ended up circling the same mountain repeatedly because they'd been oppressed so long that mentally they couldn't grasp what God had prepared for them. Finally He told them, "You have stayed long enough at this mountain...take possession of the land...the Lord swore he would give to your...descendants." If your history is one of failure and despair, rise up and say, "Enough's enough! I'm going to trust God for bigger and better things!" It's in such moments that your destiny is shaped. Think: the decisions you make today will affect not only you, but future generations—so make sure they're the right ones!

THE WAY OF ESCAPE

God…will provide the way of escape also,
so that you will be able to endure it.
1 Corinthians 10:13 NAS

*I*n the wilderness temptation Satan offered Jesus 3 things. He also offers them to you:

(1) Satisfaction! Jesus was hungry and Satan tempted Him to turn stones into bread. But this was satisfaction without God, because God's plan was to feed His Son supernaturally through angels. Jesus refused to settle for less—and so should you! *(2) Success!* But it was success without God. Taking Jesus to the top of the temple, Satan said "Jump off, God will protect You and everyone will believe in You." Success without the cross. Take the easy way out! And hasn't Satan made you that same offer: "You don't have to take up your cross. You don't have to practice self-denial." Satan lied then, and he's lying to you now. *(3) Significance!* Satan offered Jesus the kingdoms of this world and their glory if He'd just bow down to him. What an offer. Significance without God! But Jesus rebuked him with a reminder from Scripture that God alone is worthy of being glorified.

Satan will take every legitimate desire you have and try to get you to fulfill it in an illegitimate way. But God "will provide the way of escape." You say "I don't see the way of escape." That's because you're focused on the temptation instead of the way out. God's promise of escape doesn't mean you won't have to persevere and be faithful to Him. And, as in the case of Christ, it involves knowing and being able to use the Scriptures. But it does mean that when God's purpose of victory over temptation has been served, you'll come out victorious!

THE TUG OF GOD'S LOVE

*The Spirit Himself bears witness
with our spirit that we are children of God.*
Romans 8:16 NKJV

The story is told of an atheist spending a quiet day fishing when his boat is attacked by the Loch Ness monster. The beast tosses him and his boat high into the air, then it opens its mouth to swallow them both. The man cries out "Oh my God, help me!" Suddenly the attack scene freezes in place. As the atheist hangs in mid air a voice from heaven says, "I thought you didn't believe in Me!" "Come on God, give me a break!" the man pleads. "Two minutes ago I didn't believe in the Loch Ness monster either!"

Billy Graham says, "Whenever anyone asks me how I can be so certain about who and what God really is, I'm reminded of the story of the little boy who was out flying a kite. The wind was brisk and large billowing clouds were blowing across the sky. The kite went up and up until it was entirely hidden by the clouds. 'What are you doing?' a man asked the little boy. 'I'm flying my kite,' he replied. 'Flying your kite?' the man said. 'How can you be sure? You can't see the kite.' 'No,' said the little boy, 'I can't see it, but every little while I feel a tug, so I know for sure it's there!'"

Don't take anyone else's word for it. Find God for yourself by inviting Jesus Christ into your life. Then you too will know by the warm, wonderful tug on your heartstrings that He's there *for sure,* and that He lives in you.

STRIVE TO BE SEXUALLY PURE

Avoid sexual immorality.
1 Thessalonians 4:3-4 NIV

$\mathcal{B}$e grateful that God made you a sexual being. Sex wasn't a mistake He made when He ran out of ideas. When Adam first saw Eve he didn't say "I'll bet she's got a wonderful personality!" No, he said, "This is…flesh of my flesh" (Ge 2:23). But when we don't understand God's original intent for sex, bad stuff happens. God doesn't want to destroy our ability to experience our sexuality. No, He wants to teach us how to enjoy it.

Saying "I'm reserving sex for marriage" tends to raise eyebrows and get you excluded from the guest list of a lot of parties. So be it! When there's physical intimacy without true commitment, count on it; somebody's going to get hurt. You need to resolve in your heart to read God's Word and follow His directives on the subject. And you need to do it *now,* before you get into situations where you're tempted to compromise your character, because then you've waited too late.

We all struggle at times with our sexuality, particularly in today's culture. Sex is such a deep part of us. And guilt about sex has a way of making us feel separated from God like nothing else. So in order to determine your values and set some ground rules, you need to vow before God, "I'm not going to allow my impulses to dictate to me, or sin to separate me from You. I choose to keep Your standards, to rely on Your Spirit to give me strength day by day. And if I do sin to seek Your forgiveness, get back up and move closer to You." Count on it—that's a prayer God will answer!

OVERCOMING THROUGH FAITH!

The Spirit in you is…stronger than anything in the world.
1 John 4:4 TM

*W*hen a diving injury turned Joni Eareckson into a quadriplegic, her world changed radically. Faced with an unknown future her first response was to look for a quick way out. Her second was to live. She learned to paint holding a brush in her mouth, and later took classes at a university. A public-speaking course inspired her to talk about what she knew best: relating to physically challenged people, life in a wheelchair, and her experience as a follower of Christ. When a businessman sponsored an exhibition of her art it launched her successful career as an artist. Each piece included a testimony about her relationship with Jesus. When she made a list of her heart's desires she wrote: "It's time to step out…into a new dream. To be a 'doer' of God's Word…and help other disabled people with dreams of their own."

From that desire was born "Joni and Friends," a ministry that brings together people of faith and disabled persons, sponsors workshops and offers financial aid. Joni's also on the National Council on Disability and has her own radio program on 900-plus stations. She's also married and is a popular speaker who's authored 18 books. She says: "I don't know what lies ahead. But I do know who I am. I have a dream, and I know where I'm going."

John writes, "The Spirit in you is…stronger than anything in the world." And Jesus said, "He who overcomes…I will …acknowledge…before my Father" (Rev 3:5 NIV). Joni Eareckson Tada surely qualifies! The question is, what are *you* doing with the lemons life hands you? Have you developed a woe-is-me attitude, or are you busy making lemonade?

MIND CLUTTER!

One thing I ask of the Lord, this is what I seek.
Psalm 27:4 NIV

If you are really serious about developing your spiritual life, begin by assessing what stands in your way. That requires honesty. The first challenge is how to deal with the stress in our lives and the resulting clutter it produces in our minds. Dr. Howard Hendricks gives us 4 sources of mind clutter. Let's examine them carefully: *(1) Saying yes to far too many things!* Dr. Lewis Sperry Chafer once said, "Much of our activity is little more than a cheap anesthetic to deaden the pain of an empty life." All our "going and doing" fails to address our core of emptiness. *(2) Not stopping to recharge our batteries!* We dutifully pull out our day-planner and fill in the spaces between activities. But let's not fool ourselves; avoiding over-lapping activities isn't planning. As a result we're a stressed-out, short-tempered, horn-blowing crowd, commuting between poorly planned activities that add little to our spiritual well being. *(3) Failure to enjoy what we accomplish!* Solomon wrote, "A desire accomplished is sweet to the soul" (Pr 13:19 NKJV). With always too much to do, we dash off to the next obligation, often without finishing the previous one, or taking time to stand back and savor a job well done. No wonder we worry that our existence seems meaningless. *(4) Owing more than we can repay.* Next time you're faced with a credit purchase, wait! Don't necessarily say no. Just present your so-called "need" to God before presenting it to the bank and see what He says about it. If you're really serious about developing your spiritual life, deal with your mind clutter!

BIGGER ISN'T ALWAYS BETTER

Who…despises the day of small things?
Zechariah 4:10 AMP

*W*hile the world trades in the sensational and stunning, God loves to work through the ordinary and insignificant. In *His* Kingdom, bigger isn't always better. When He gave Gideon victory over the Midianites He used an army of just 300 to defeat an enemy hundreds of thousands strong. That wasn't because there weren't more soldiers available; God just wanted to demonstrate His power in "the day of small things." Jesus could have chosen any number of followers, but He hand-picked 12 to reach the world with the Gospel. On a mountain He fed 5,000 people with 5 rolls and 2 fish from a child's lunch box. He compared God's Kingdom to a mustard seed, the smallest there is, yet it grows into a massive tree. He also likened it to yeast that's barely discernible, yet it can raise an entire batch of dough.

Jesus said, "Whoever can be trusted with very little can also be trusted with much" (Lk 16:10 NIV). So if you're asking God to make you *bigger* instead of *better,* you may be disappointed. All the prayers in the world won't pressure Him into giving you what you're not ready to handle. Henry Wadsworth Longfellow said "Most of us would succeed in small things if we weren't so troubled with blind ambition." The drive to be *bigger* can give you ulcers, keep you awake at night, and stop you from enjoying the blessings God has already given you. *Better* may be harder to measure and not as glamorous, but the inner stability that comes from gradual success is more valuable and lasting.

RIVERS AND RESERVOIRS (1)

Be stingy and lose everything.
The generous…prosper.
Proverbs 11:24-25 NLT

*O*ne reason the Dead Sea is a big tourist attraction is because it's got such high mineral concentrations that even nonswimmers can stay afloat in its waters. The only problem is the smell; because it has no outlets, any fresh water that comes in quickly becomes contaminated. Solomon said, "Be stingy and lose everything. The generous…prosper." God never intended us to be reservoirs that just take in; He called us to be rivers that flow out to bless others. Something interesting happens when you stop focusing on yourself and get concerned with other people's needs. Paul says, "A person who gives cheerfully…will…have…plenty left…to share" (2Co 9:7-8 NLT). If you want to grow you've got to sow! When the Macedonian church was "tested by great troubles, and…very poor…they gave…much…more than they could afford" (2Co 8:2-3 NCV). These folks understood that when you invest in the lives of others, God promises to meet *your* needs too.

So if you need a job today, volunteer at a soup kitchen while you're looking for work. If you're praying for an increase in your business, pour yourself into somebody else's business and ask God to prosper them. The Bible says when you "Give generously…your gifts will return to you later," plus, "In the days ahead you yourself may need…help" (Ecc 11:1-2 TLB). Even if you don't have a specific need right now, sow a seed of kindness anyway. Only God knows what the future holds, and one day when you need it the most it'll come back to bless you with a harvest.

RIVERS AND RESERVOIRS (2)

Your prayers and gifts to the poor have come up
as a [constant reminder] before God.
Acts 10:4 NIV

$\mathscr{T}$he things you do for others don't go unnoticed.
God is keeping track of every single one. He "doesn't miss
anything. He knows…the love you've shown…by helping"
(Heb 6:10 TM). God heard the kind words you spoke to that
person who was hurting. He saw your sacrificial giving when
you could least afford it. By doing what you did you paved the
way for God to help you. He's storing it all up so that in your
time of need you'll have a rich account to draw on.

The Bible speaks about a Roman soldier named Cornelius,
a "good man…always helping people in need" (Ac 10:2 TM).
And what happened to Cornelius? His family became the first
Gentile household to hear and receive the gospel. What a
payoff! Why did God pick Cornelius? Because of his generous
spirit, "An angel…came to him and said…'Your…gifts…have
come up as a [constant reminder] before God.'"

A lady was praying about starting a pet grooming
business but couldn't afford to advertise. So she went to her
local animal shelter and volunteered to groom the pets in order
to help increase their chances for adoption. Interestingly, the
harder she worked the more her own business grew by word of
mouth. Finally she ended up with more clients than she could
handle! Does that mean if you don't help others God won't help
you? No, thankfully His love is unconditional. But a missed
opportunity to *give* is a missed opportunity to *receive,* because
when you are generous with others God promises to be generous with you.

USING YOUR GIFT
FOR THE RIGHT PURPOSES (1)

You are a chosen people...to tell...
the wonderful acts of God.
Peter 2:9 CEV

*R*aised amidst arguments and money problems, Rich Stearns decided that education was his ticket out. Scholarships and hard work got him into Cornell University, then earned him an MBA from Wharton. Business came easy to Rich and he eventually became the CEO for Parker Brothers and Lenox China. He had it all: big house, nice family and secure job. So why did he still feel unfulfilled? He knew *what* his skill was: management. He knew *where* to use it: big organizations. But *why?* He considered becoming a missionary but didn't see how God could use someone whose strengths were budgets and flow charts. In 1998 when World Vision invited him to be their CEO, he declined. It would be career suicide to move his family across the country, take a 75% pay cut and assume the reins of a ministry! But they persisted. When board member Bill Hybels told Rich, "This is a chance to marry your gifts with God's call...to enter the zone in which you were made to live," Rich prayed, weighed his options, and accepted.

Looking back Rich Stearns says, "This is the fulfillment of who I was created to be...I've found my stride...I wonder why I waited 23 years." And World Vision has no regrets either. During his first 6 years their annual budget doubled, making it the largest relief organization in the world. It's amazing what happens when you use your gifts "to tell...the wonderful acts of God." So, what are you doing with *your* gifts?

USING YOUR GIFT
FOR THE RIGHT PURPOSES (2)

Your young men shall see visions.
Acts 2:17

Andrés Segovia was born in Southern Spain and began playing guitar as a small child. In those days the guitar was little more than a folk instrument. Serious composers and musicians didn't respect it. But Segovia saw potential in the guitar for classical music. He began studying the techniques of classical musicians who played the violin and cello. Then he applied those techniques to his playing and developed other methods on his own. He adapted the compositions of masters such as Bach, and learned to play them on his instrument. In 1909, Segovia made his debut—at the age of 16. In 1919, he toured the world and won over the classical establishment. Soon, for the first time, composers were writing classical music for the guitar and a whole new kind of music was born. Over the course of nearly 80 years, Segovia completely changed people's perception of his instrument. But like many big dreams that become realized, his dream made an impact far beyond what he imagined. It could be argued that his efforts opened the door for the guitar, not only to the concert hall but also to the jazz band. That in turn led to the electrically amplified guitar. If you've enjoyed the music of the Beatles or Eric Clapton, then thank Andrés Segovia. If it wasn't for his dream the music of the 20th century may have gone in an entirely different direction.

Big oaks grow from little acorns. When you discover your God-given gift and commit to it, there's no telling how far you'll go or what kind of impact you'll make.

THE "200-UNIT LIMIT"

In quietness and in confidence shall be your strength.
Isaiah 30:15

*W*hen the stock market plunged an investor asked his broker if he was worried. "Nope, I sleep like a baby!" he replied. Amazed, the client said, "Really, even with all these fluctuations?" The broker said, "Yup, just like a baby! I sleep for an hour, then I wake up and cry all night!"

Our capacity for handling stress is limited. Researcher Dr. Thomas Holmes concludes that experiencing 200+ "life change units" in a year can put you over the edge. For example, losing a spouse equals 100 units, divorce 60, illness 45, unemployment 45; even Christmas gets 12! Maybe you're reading this and you've already exceeded your "200-unit limit." Emotionally and physically you're stretched to the breaking point and there's no relief in sight. Be careful; living in an emotional danger zone makes you a target for the devil who has you in his cross hairs! Under pressure you succumb to temptation much more easily than when you're rested. That's why *preventing* stress is always better than trying to deal with it when it's full blown.

Isaiah says: "In quietness and in confidence shall be your strength." And Paul adds: "Don't worry…pray about everything …If you do…you will experience God's peace, which is…more wonderful than the human mind can understand. His peace will keep…your hearts as you trust in…Jesus" (Php 4:6-7 TLB). Nobody understands your stress like Jesus. That's why He says, "Come to me, all of you who are weary and carry heavy burdens, and…you will find rest for your souls" (Mt 11:28-29 NLT). So stop pushing so hard. Give your concerns to God. Then allow yourself the same kind of consideration you'd give to a friend who's on overload.

DEVELOPING FRIENDSHIPS

A friend loves at all times.
Proverbs 17:17 NKJV

*D*r. John Maxwell writes: "If you want deep, lasting friendship, you cannot always be the strong one. And that can be frightening; especially if you've had someone hurt or manipulate you. But you must let a friend see you in your weakness. Some of us have never done this, and we wonder why we're lonely. We're going to have to get vulnerable to have a true friend.

"Friends serve each other. When's the last time you performed an act of servant-hood for a friend to whom you're devoted? If you can't remember, you're probably living with a core of loneliness. A friend is someone you commit to not because of what they can do for you, but just because they're your friend. And friends listen, even though they're busy. Listening is an act of love. It says 'I'm going to put my own agenda on hold and devote myself to knowing and caring for you.' Friends are not generally looking for someone who can talk very impressively or cleverly or with great wit. Mostly what they're looking for is a world-class listener. Furthermore, when something goes right, friends celebrate. Do you do that? When's the last time one of your friends had God bless them— and you threw a party?

"If you're not in this kind of friendship right now, you can't make it happen, but you can open yourself up to it. You can start pursuing it. You can ask God to guide you. You can take little relational risks. And if you already have friends like this, prize them, protect them, enrich them in every way, and take that friendship as deep as you can."

GOD'S PROTECTIVE HAND IS UPON YOU!

Lord...My life is in your hands.
Psalm 31:14-15 CEV

*T*erry Schafer knew what she wanted to buy her husband for Christmas, but it was more than she could afford. So a generous storeowner agreed to gift-wrap it and let her take it, with the agreement that she make weekly payments. When she thanked him and he replied, "Oh, it's nothing," that storekeeper didn't realize the significance of his kind gesture. On October 4th, patrolman David Schafer was pursuing an armed robber when he was shot in the stomach. When an officer went to tell his wife Terry, she was glad she hadn't waited for Christmas to give her husband his gift. And she was doubly grateful for the storekeeper who'd agreed to come to terms, otherwise David would be dead. Instead he was hospitalized, not with a gunshot wound but a bruise—because he'd been wearing the new bulletproof vest she'd given him earlier that week.

When the timing of an event is more remarkable than the event itself, some people attribute it to luck, fate, coincidence, or karma. (They're usually the ones who think birth, death, interruptions and delays are matters of chance, not divine design!). But not David; he wrote: "I come to you, Lord, for protection... Do as you...promised...Protect me from hidden traps and keep me safe. You are faithful...I trust you...and claim you as my God. My life is in your hands...you store up blessings for all who honor and trust you. You are their shelter from harmful plots...The Lord protects the faithful" (Ps 31:1-23 CEV). Wherever you go today, remember that God's protective hand is upon you!

GOD AND YOUR JOB

Humble yourselves in the sight of the Lord.
James 4:10 NKJV

*W*hat does God value in our job performance?
(1) He values humility and servant-hood, not pride and a sense of entitlement that thinks, "You owe me." "Humble yourselves in the sight of the Lord, and He will lift you up." If we are secure in our identity as God's child we can relax and know that, like the loving parent He is, our Heavenly Father will recognize and reward us fairly and generously. Knowing this frees us from having to be recognized by others. Indeed, if being appreciated is your sole reason for working, God will have people overlook you until you get the order of work straight in your mind. You can be appreciated at home, by your friends and your family, but work is just what it sounds like: work!

(2) He values courage and risk-taking. Consider the faith it took for David to leave his home, the humble shepherd's pallet on the hillsides, and travel to King Saul's palace. He must have felt just a little out of place, knowing he was underdressed and uninformed about the culture of the royal court. Like a boy from the slums suddenly finding himself in Buckingham Palace, David was instantly out of his comfort zone. Then later, after it's clear that his new boss is afflicted by an evil spirit and intends to kill him, David coolly maintains his mission because he knows God wants him there. "He will lift you up." One day David would have his boss's position, palace and perks, but he had to leave the *"how"* and the *"when"* up to God and serve faithfully. The same goes for you.

STAND UP TO IT!

There came a lion.
1 Samuel 17:34

*O*ne day a woman was waiting for a bus in a danger-ous neighborhood when a rookie cop asked, "Do you want me to wait with you, Miss?" "No thanks, I'm not afraid," she replied. "Then," he grinned, "Would *you* mind waiting with me?" We all have things that make our palms sweat and our hearts race; God never said we *wouldn't* experience the all-too-real emotion of fear. But He keeps saying: "Fear not." Why? Because He wants you to confront your fear. So while you're asking God to remove your mountain, He wants to give you the courage to conquer it! Michel de Montaigne said, "He who fears he shall suffer, already suffers what he fears." You move from being a victim to a victor by facing your fears head on, not fleeing from them. The Bible says "Fear involves torment" (1Jn 4:18 NKJV). Your fears can actually immobilize you. And they're going to *keep* attacking you, so you must continually face them down. The other option is to bury your fears alive, allow them to erode your mental, emotional and physical health and destroy your relationships. Paul says: "God did not give us a spirit of…[fear] …but…of power…and self-control" (See 2 Tim 1:7 AMP).

Remember in the Old Testament that while David was guarding his sheep "there came a lion?" In God's strength he defeated it, plus a bear, and later he overthrew the giant Goliath. Now that lion was just opportunity in disguise. If David had wavered or run, he'd have missed his chance to become king of Israel. So when a lion comes into your life recognize it for what it is: an opportunity from God—and stand up to it!

SPIRITUAL DEPTH

*That I may...become more deeply
and intimately acquainted with Him.*
Philippians 3:10 AMP

*S*torms reveal the depth and resilience of a tree's root system. When hard times come we need more than just intelligence; we need spiritual depth, the kind Job the patriarch had. When the bottom dropped out of his world, Job said: "When He has tried me, I shall come forth as gold. My foot has held fast to His path; I have kept His way and not turned aside. I have not departed from the command of His lips; I have treasured the words of His mouth more than my necessary food" (Job 23:10-12 NAS). We need the spiritual depth of Paul, who, after praying 3 times for the horrible stake in his flesh to leave (the word translated "thorn" sometimes referred to a pointed instrument, like a spear), and 3 times the Lord said "no." In response, Paul said, "Most gladly I will rather boast in my infirmities, that the power of Christ may rest upon me" (2Co 12:9 NJKV). Instead of looking for a way out, or throwing a pity party, Paul declared, "I chose to go through this so that I can have the privilege of experiencing more of Christ's power working in my life." What spiritual depth!

Don't you want what these people had, so that your spiritual life is such that you walk in step with God whether you feel good or not; whether you get a "yes," "no," or "wait," in answer to your prayers; even when you don't get your own way? Spiritual depth cannot be caught by osmosis, or merely be something on your wish list. It must become your all-consuming goal, and the highest priority of your life. Is it?

STAGES OF SPIRITUAL GROWTH (1)

I am writing to you, little children,
because your sins have been forgiven.
1 John 2:12 NAS

*T*here are 3 stages to spiritual growth. The first is *childhood*. The Greek term "little children" refers to toddlers. And if there's one thing toddlers are good at—it's tripping and falling. Until they learn to walk they need someone to pick them up, dry their tears, bandage their skinned knees, and re-assure them that falling down doesn't mean they'll never walk or that they're not part of the family.

There are 2 things a spiritual toddler needs to understand: first, the difference between their *stage* of growth, and their *standing* before God. Don't get these 2 things mixed up! Trusting in the finished work of Christ is the only thing that gives you right standing with God. From that moment on you are a fully accepted and redeemed child of His. That's how He sees you. If you forget that you'll be in trouble, because every time you fall the Devil will make you doubt your salvation.

The forgiveness you receive at the new birth is a *judicial* act by God, making you a member of His family in good standing. But the forgiveness you receive on a daily basis is a *relational* act. Suppose you enter some wrong numbers into your calculator. What do you do? You have a little button called "clear entry" which allows you to erase your error and start over. That's what the blood of Christ does for you. Repentance allows you to override sin by triggering God's forgiveness so that the flow of His grace continues. And when grace flows, growth follows. The important thing to remember about sin is, "always keep short accounts with God."

STAGES OF SPIRITUAL GROWTH (2)

I am writing to you, young men,
because you have overcome the evil one.
1 John 2:13 NAS

*T*he second stage in spiritual growth is *adolescence.*
John writes, "Young men...you are strong, and the word
of God abides in you, and you have overcome the evil one"
(1Jn 2:14 NAS). But if you've ever had teenagers, you know
that the transition from adolescence into adulthood can be a
bumpy ride. Teenagers clash with their parents and other
authority figures because they're moving from dependence to
independence. They wrestle with conflicting feelings of
wanting their freedom, yet not really wanting it—especially if
mom and dad are still paying the bills. They chafe at observing
curfews, particularly when their friends don't have to. They
don't like getting approval for movies, dates, parties, dress
codes, or using the family car. They especially hate hearing,
"As long as you're under my roof you'll live by my rules. When
you get your own family you can make up your own rules."

The truth is, a spiritual adolescent doesn't know as much
as he or she *thinks* they know. They need guidance, support,
and correction from more mature Christians so they can learn
how to avoid falling into the enemy's trap. They need instruction and training in God's Word to make them strong and keep
them battle-ready at all times. And they need opportunities to
serve, discover and develop their gifts, and gain experience. So,
how can you tell when you've outgrown your spiritual adolescence and begun moving into adulthood? John answers, "You
are strong...the Word of God abides in you, and you have
overcome the evil one."

STAGES OF SPIRITUAL GROWTH (3)

I am writing to you, fathers, because you know Him
who has been from the beginning.
1 John 2:13 NAS

*W*hat makes you a spiritual *adult?* Knowing God; it's that simple! But this raises a question. How can you know —that you know God intimately? It's like a good marriage: two people fall in love and become so close that each one knows what the other is thinking and feeling without a word being spoken.

But such intimacy is not developed overnight. It's the product of time spent together—and commitment! Paul speaks about, "Things which eye has not seen and ear has not heard, and which have not entered the heart of man, all that God has prepared for those who love Him. For to us God revealed them through the Spirit" (1Co 2:9-10 NAS). The mature follower of Christ sees things the human eye can't see and hears things the most acute ear can't hear. And they have thoughts they didn't originate on their own. That's because God's indwelling Spirit is helping them to think God's thoughts. What an advantage!

You'll know you are spiritually mature when God lets you pick up on thoughts and insights from His Word that go far beyond what someone told you, or what you heard in a sermon. That's because the Holy Spirit is now free to send His message clearly and directly to you. In other words we will "know the things freely given to us by God" (1Co 2:12 NAS). But that means we have to be close enough to hear God speaking to us. Such intimacy doesn't just happen. It's not an afterthought. It must be your number one priority and the consuming passion of your life. Is it?

MIND PRAYERS

Through faith in him we may
approach God with…confidence.
Ephesians 3:12 NIV

*D*id you know that you can pray in your *mind* without having to speak a word out loud? All of us know the power of unspoken communication. Many of us grew up with parents who didn't have to say a thing to make their will known. It may have been the way they cocked their heads, a certain look in their eyes or some other signal. But whatever it was, we knew exactly what was being communicated and how we were expected to respond.

Our goal in prayer should be to maintain such a close relationship with God that we can communicate back and forth no matter what the situation, the time of day, or anything else. And we don't have to shout, or use the right words in the right order, because our hearts are in tune with God's heart.

It's like the story of the little boy who wanted a bicycle for Christmas. He was praying one night at the top of his voice, telling God the kind and color of bike he wanted. His mother said, "Son, you don't need to shout for God to hear you." He replied, "I know, momma, but I need to shout if grandpa's going to hear me and buy me that bike!" The truth is, we don't need to shout for God to hear us—and we don't need to try and make our own answers to prayer happen either. Jesus said our Heavenly Father knows what we need before we ask. He gives to us because of our *relationship* with Him, not just because we say it at a decibel level loud enough to be heard!

THE BENEFITS OF HUMILITY

*All of you, clothe yourselves
with humility toward one another.*
1 Peter 5:5 NAS

*P*eter writes "all of you, clothe yourselves with humility…for God is opposed to the proud, but gives grace to the humble. Therefore humble yourselves under the mighty hand of God, that He may exalt you at the proper time, casting all your anxiety on Him, because He cares for you" (1Pe 5:5-7 NAS). Peter expressed 4 very important thoughts. And he combined them for a reason. Let's look at each:

(1) "All of you, clothe yourselves with humility toward one another." Peter's expression "*clothe* yourselves with humility" referred to a white scarf or apron typically worn by servants. Did you get that? We're called to be servants, not celebrities! "All" lets us know we all stand on an equal footing before the cross. *(2) "God is opposed to the proud, but gives grace to the humble."* Those who are self-centered find themselves at odds with God, while the humble enjoy His blessings. *(3) "Humble yourselves under the mighty hand of God, that He may exalt you at the proper time."* The phrase "The mighty hand of God" is used in Scripture to symbolize 2 things: God's hand of discipline, and His hand of deliverance. And you need both. So submit to His discipline today and you'll experience His deliverance. *(4) "Casting all your anxiety on Him, because He cares for you."* Peter addresses the core issue—worry that if we don't look out for ourselves nobody else will. But if we really believe that God "cares for us," we needn't worry about serving our own interests. We can focus on the needs of others, confident that God will spare nothing when it comes to meeting *our* needs.

DIRECT ACCESS

*We have a great high priest
who has passed through the heavens.*
Hebrews 4:14 NAS

*O*nce a year Israel's High Priest would walk through the 2 outer areas of the temple and go into the "Holy of Holies" to obtain pardon for the people's sins. There were many priests, but only the High Priest could do this. The Bible says that Jesus, our High Priest, passed through the Heavens and entered the Holy Place in the heavenly temple to offer a "once-for-all-time" sacrifice for our sins (See Heb 9:24-26).

Jesus passed through the first Heaven, which we call the atmosphere; then the second Heaven, which we refer to as outer space; then into the presence of God, or the third Heaven. Now, if you're living on earth, what you want to do in prayer is get into the third Heaven where God's throne is. The problem is, we can't get there unless someone takes us.

One day during the Civil War a soldier sat on a bench outside the White House looking distressed. A little boy came by and asked him what was wrong. The soldier said he needed to see President Lincoln but the guards wouldn't let him in. Hearing this, the boy took him by the hand and led him directly into the President's office. "Father," he said, "this soldier really needs to speak with you." That boy was the President's son, who had direct and continuous access to his father.

Because Jesus, the Son of God, is related to the Father, He can bypass all the stuff that blocks us. That's why when we pray in Jesus' name, we have direct access to God, are automatically welcome in His presence, and get our needs met.

FAMILY MATTERS (1)

Keep the unity of the Spirit.
Ephesians 4:2-3 NKJV

*W*hen it's easier to talk to outsiders than it is to your own family, something's wrong. Your family should be a support system—a safety net to catch you when you fall. We like to envision "family" as a hard-working dad, a stay-at-home mom, 2 children, a dog, and a house with a white picket fence. But for many people family means money problems, troubled kids and warring spouses. That's why Paul writes: "Walk… with…longsuffering, bearing with one another in love…keep the unity of the Spirit in the bond of peace." It takes a big dose of *grace* to make it all work! So start praying for your kids, instead of just setting boundaries that create distance between you when you don't see eye to eye. You won't always agree, but you must learn to respect each other. When God said, "Train a child in the way he should go, and when he is old he will not turn from it" (Pr 22:6 NIV), He didn't say what qualifies as "old," or when your investment would start paying off. Every family has its ups and downs. And every family tree produces a few nuts! In fact, sometimes the best part is underground! But if you bail out when things get tough you'll miss the rewards you'd have gotten by hanging on. Often the child that blesses you most is the one who *didn't* reflect your views, married someone you don't like, and doesn't invite you over to dinner! In the long run none of that matters because your family is a life-long investment. What's important is to love and support one another unconditionally right *now*.

FAMILY MATTERS (2)

Bearing with one another in love…
Ephesians 4:2-3 NKJV

*N*earing the end of his life when he should have been preparing to bless his sons, Simeon and Levi, Jacob told them: "I…curse…you because of your…anger" (Gen 49:7 CEV). But their behavior should have been no surprise; after all, the apple never falls far from the tree! The fact is, Jacob had already shaped them by his own example when he deceived his father (See Gen 27) and his father-in-law (See Gen 30), and his mother facilitated the deception. Behavioral patterns are passed from generation to generation, and "a house divided against itself will fall" (Lk 11:17 NIV). Mom, Dad, your actions and attitudes will either bless or blight your children. So "Teach [them]…the right path" (Pr 22:6 TLB). Otherwise they'll inherit more than just your eye color, they'll end up with your emotional disposition and volatility!

Don't involve your children in your marital disputes. Solomon warned, "Anger rests in the bosom of fools" (Ecc 7:9 NKJV). Your kids are an easy target for your misdirected rage. Even when your emotional outbursts aren't aimed toward them, they still suffer the effects. For example, your boss reprimands you at work, and because you can't retaliate you come home like a bear with a headache and make everybody walk on eggshells. Even if that's what *you* experienced growing up—you're not a child any more. Lower the decibel level! Don't let your anger run amok. David prayed, "Watch over…my lips. Let not my heart be drawn to…evil" (Ps 141:3-4 NIV). And James says, "Submit…to God. Resist the devil, and he will flee from you" (Jas 4:7). That's the only way you'll ever change the steps in your family dance.

FAMILY MATTERS (3)

Don't sin by letting anger control you.
Ephesians 4:26 NLT

$\mathcal{G}$od doesn't deny us the right to our emotions, but He does hold us accountable for how we handle them. For example, it's *never* okay to abuse those He's entrusted to your care. Paul said, "Don't sin by letting anger control you…anger gives a foothold to the devil." Satan would like nothing better than to gain an entry point into your home, then turn it into a living hell. And every time you fly into a rage you lose ground to him. Hot words don't result in cool judgment. Solomon said, "A hot temper shows great foolishness" (Pr 14:29 NLT). The key to managing your anger is in finding ways to express it so it doesn't end up in an explosion. It's okay to share your feelings, but you must do it the right way. Ultimately the issue is *not* about who's right or wrong, (or who can yell the loudest), it's about finding the answer that's best for everyone.

Nobody can be *everything* you want them to be, *all* the time. It's impossible to have a long-term, loving relationship without learning to accept human weakness. So instead of dwelling on one another's shortcomings, focus on your collective strength as a family. Clinical psychologist Dr. Paul Pearsall says, "Most of us would give our lives for a family member. Yet too often we live our daily life as if we take our families for granted." Learn to control your temper; your family's worth it. After all, who else loves you regardless of what you do? And where else can you find the comfort that comes from such a support system?

FAMILY MATTERS (4)

No one can come to me, unless the Father...
makes them want to.
John 6:44 CEV

*C*oming home from a bar late one night a young man got on a bus where he encountered his very self-righteous aunt. Caustically she said, "Do you know you're headed straight to hell?" "Oh dear," he said, "Don't tell me I'm on the wrong bus tonight again!" Seriously, we all want our families to share our faith, but it can't be forced. Jesus said, "You're not in charge ...The Father...draws people...that's the only way [they'll] ever come" (Jn 6:44 TM). Does that mean you should stop praying for them? Of course not! But despite your prayers and best efforts there may still be family members who decide not to follow Jesus, and some of those who do may join other denominations. Throughout history countless wars have been fought over religion; don't turn your home into a combat zone as well. As former French First Lady Yvonne de Gaulle once said, "Even the presidency is temporary, but family is permanent!"

You don't have to condone somebody's lifestyle in order to let them know you love them and are committed to them. But don't withhold acceptance from those who've been good to you just because they don't worship God the way you do. Maybe they haven't always made the wisest choices, but when the chips are down, chances are, *they* are the ones who'll be there for you. Don't beat them over the head with the Bible; just live it by setting an example they'll want to follow. Jesus said, "If I am lifted up...I will draw all people" (Jn 12:32 NCV). Instead of tearing your family apart, make your faith the glue that holds it together.

WINNING THE BATTLE

For the sinful nature desires what is contrary to the Spirit.
Galatians 5:17 NIV

*H*ow can you win in the unrelenting battle between your flesh and your spirit?

(1) By acknowledging that there is a battle! Your flesh will always crave satisfaction in the very things God hates. This age-old civil war rages on. Your flesh never takes a holiday. *(2) By admitting that you are powerless to win without God's help!* By consciously submitting to God you draw on His strength in the first moments of each test. And your ability to do that will grow as you keep practicing this spiritual discipline. The closer you draw to God, the stronger you become when faced with temptation. *(3) By deciding that self-discipline is a personal matter!* You can depend on no one else to develop it for you. Paul writes, "I run…I box…I discipline my body" (1Co 9:26-27 NAS). This is something only you can do. If someone else has to restrain you, it doesn't work! *(4) By understanding that ignoring the consequences invites disaster!* Lack of self-discipline will inevitably lead to embarrassment for you, and those you love. So before you indulge, consider the fallout! In 1Co 9:27 Paul speaks about being "disqualified." What does that mean? It means losing respect in the eyes of others. It means limiting God's ability to use you for His purposes. It means hurting the cause of Christ in the eyes of a world that's always watching. When David committed adultery with Bathsheba, Nathan the prophet said to him, "By doing this you have made the enemies of the Lord show utter contempt" (2Sa 12:14 NIV). Want to win the battle? Keep these things in mind!

MAKE YOUR LIFE COUNT!

This one thing I do.
Philippians 3:13

*E*dgar W. Work said, "The real tragedy is not in being limited to one talent, but in the failure to use that one talent." To make the most of your life:

(1) Maximize what God's given you. Edison set himself an ambitious goal: to come up with a major new invention every six months and a minor one every ten days. When he died he had 1093 patents. Edison made his dreams a reality by sticking to what he did best. Are you doing that? *(2) Start where God put you.* After losing a baseball game, cartoon character Charlie Brown pours out his heart to his friend Lucy: "All my life I've dreamed of pitching in the big leagues, but I'll never make it!" Lucy replies: "You're thinking too far ahead, Charlie Brown. Set yourself more immediate goals. Start with the next inning, for example. When you go out to pitch, see if you can walk to the mound...without falling down." Success starts with one step. Exercise your faith and take it. *(3) Focus on what God called you to do.* Music was everything to Brahms. He collected music and studied compositions going back to the 15th century. He worked day and night to perfect his craft, refusing to publish anything that didn't meet his exacting standards. That's why he didn't publish his first symphony until he was 40. And he never married, saying it would distract him: "I am in love with music, I think of nothing but, and of other things only when they make music more beautiful." Is that fanaticism? No, it's focus; it's what makes your life count! It's why Paul said, "This one thing I do."

CHANGE YOUR WORLD

Do not love the world.
1 John 2:15 NAS

ohn writes, "Do not love the world." But what does that mean? First, let's look at what it *doesn't* mean. It doesn't mean being so heavenly minded that you're no earthly use. Loving the Lord more doesn't mean loving those around you less; or feeling awkward around them; or losing touch with them; or not knowing how to communicate with them; or alienating them by giving off signals that you are somehow spiritually superior to them. If "we have the mind of Christ" (1 Co 2:16) shouldn't we be as attractive to a lost world as Jesus was?

As the world of finance, politics, education and entertainment, etc. gets more off track, we have 2 choices: condemn it or influence it! Become what we're supposed to be—light! It's the end of the game and Jesus, the head coach, is calling His best players onto the field. Isaiah the prophet spoke into the lives of kings. The 3 Hebrew children changed the politics of Babylon. Joseph the economist saved Egypt from famine. Yes, Satan is at work taking Christ out of Christmas, prayer out of schools, and God out of government. But he won't win, and he knows it. His strategy, however, is to convince you that he *can* win. He doesn't want you to see the real battle between light and darkness. He doesn't want you to feel a sense of urgency and personal responsibility. But the God who promised to "crush Satan under your feet" is raising up an army of spirit-empowered believers who will demonstrate what it's like to live in a *different* kingdom. Will you be part of His army?

DISCOVER YOUR LIFE'S ASSIGNMENT

If anyone serves he should do it
with the strength god provides.
1 Peter 4:11 NIV

*I*f you watch people who are fulfilling their life's assignment, their motivation is high. They have amazing endurance to overcome obstacles. They are growing and learning. There's real joy in what they do. To miss out on your life's assignment is to miss out on why God made you. Whether your job is in a church or a business, you were gifted and called by God—and you'd better take it seriously! Here are some questions to help you find your life's assignment:

What's my raw material? God has given you a certain temperament and talents, and you have to honor your raw material. What unlocks your compassion? (Sometimes the problem that infuriates you most is the problem you were born to solve.) *Why do I do this?* There's a big difference between doing something because you believe God's called you to it, and doing what your parents, your friends or your ego wants you to do. *What are my limitations?* Knowing what you're called to do often starts with discovering what you're not called to do. When you can accept your limitations, you're on the road to understanding your life's assignment.

So let's be clear: you have an assignment. It has to do with what God hard-wired into you. You must seek it with an open mind. When people pretend to be something they're not, they live with a chronic sense of inadequacy and set themselves up for a lifetime of frustration. Don't do that. Be ruthlessly open to the truth about yourself. Your life's assignment is something you discover, not something you choose.

THE NEED FOR HUMILITY (1)

If anyone wants to be first,
he shall be last of all and servant of all.
Mark 9:35 NAS

*H*umility is a quality of character, but it's much more. Notice 2 things:

(1) Although it's a Christ-like virtue, humility is seldom understood or admired. Today many models of leadership consider it strange for the person at the top to show humility too often. Bending the knee to help others, or to admit weakness, is considered making yourself vulnerable to those who might take advantage of you. Too many leaders view themselves as being there to be served, except for short periods when it's advantageous to be seen serving others—but not for too long. We must be careful not to associate too closely with those lower on the ladder or we'll compromise our position. We fear we might lose the respect of our subordinates, and our superiors, if we accept too much responsibility for a poor decision. Not so, for the follower of Christ. For them humility is not a religious concept, it's a way of life.

(2) We appreciate humility in others, but rarely want it for ourselves. The price is too high. Humility is not what gets us ahead, and—let's be honest—we like humble people around because they don't threaten us. They're safe people with a quaint little virtue that keeps them on the sidelines during our scramble to the top of the hill. We can afford to be humble after we're king. Even Christ's disciples weren't immune: "They... discussed with one another which of them was the greatest. Sitting down, He...said to them, 'If anyone wants to be first... he shall be servant of all'" (Mk 9:34-35 NAS). Do you want to become more Christ-like? Practice humility!

THE NEED FOR HUMILITY (2)

If anyone wants to be first,
he shall be last of all and servant of all.
Mark 9:35 NAS

*D*r. Paul Brand was one of the 20th century's most respected physicians because of his work amongst lepers. His love for India's "least of the least," led him to pioneer surgical techniques that surgeons still use today in orthopedic reconstruction. He was a brilliant physician, medical teacher, writer, speaker, and champion for the underdog. Philip Yancey writes, "Meeting Dr. Brand, I realized I had misconstrued humility as a negative self-image. Paul Brand obviously knew his gifts: he had finished first throughout his academic career and had attended many awards banquets honoring his accomplishments. Yet he recognized his gifts as just that, 'gifts' from a loving Creator, and used them in a Christ-like way of service. When I first met him, Brand was still adjusting to life in the United States. Everyday luxuries made him nervous and he longed for a simple life close to the soil. He knew presidents, kings and celebrities, yet he rarely mentioned them. He talked openly about his failures and always deflected credit for his successes to his associates. Most impressive to me, the wisest and most brilliant man I have ever met devoted much of his life to some of the lowliest people on the planet."

Genuinely humble people seek the well-being of others. And they are very secure. They're aware of the attributes that make them successful at whatever they do. And that security—that honest, healthy self-assessment—results in a more humble attitude; one that translates into actions which can be observed, actions which make a difference, and a lifestyle we should want to follow.

BE PASSIONATE ABOUT IT!

So we continued the work...
from the first light of dawn till the stars came out.
Nehemiah 4:21 NIV

*I*n the face of overwhelming odds, Nehemiah rebuilt the walls of Jerusalem in just 52 days. How? Because of a single-minded passion to do so. Some of us are afraid to pray "Lord, I'll do what you want me to do," in case He sends us somewhere we don't want to go or asks us to do something we don't feel ready or qualified to do. You've got it wrong! The Bible says God's will is "good, and acceptable, and perfect" (Ro 12:2). What is there to be afraid of in *that* formula?

Now, while God's will for us is "good" it's not necessarily easy. But He gives us a passion for it. Jeremiah said that when he tried to quit speaking about the Lord, God's Word became "like a burning fire shut up in my bones" (Jer 20:9 NAS). You can't contain a fire that God lights. When He sets your heart ablaze you begin to see things you never saw before and get excited about them. He can even take your chapters of regret and write a story of grace.

But it's not likely you'll experience much of a passion for anything if you're just sitting on the sidelines waiting for something to happen. James says "Don't just be a hearer of God's word, be a doer" (See Jas 1:22). You'll get a passion for God's will once you begin *doing* it! You'll think "this is what I was made for." And when you have a compelling reason for doing something and know that God is watching and smiling on you, it makes all the difference.

CUT YOURSELF SOME SLACK!

No…I have not achieved it…
but I focus on…forgetting the past and looking forward.
Philippians 3:12-14 NLT

A little boy came home one day with his clothes all muddy so his Mom sent him to the basement to drop them into the washing machine. Later, thinking things were a bit too quiet, she shouted, "Young man, I hope you're not down there running around in your underwear." Imagine her embarrassment when a strange voice replied: "No ma'am, I'm down here servicing your furnace."

James says, "We all make…mistakes" (Jas 3:2 NLT). The trick is learning to forgive yourself. Much of the time we're guilty of doing the wrong thing with the right motive. For example, in 1957 Ford Motors described the Edsel as "the car of the decade." But try telling that to all the drivers whose doors wouldn't close, whose horns stuck, and whose transmissions failed! And remember the famous "leaning tower of Pisa" in Italy, where the architect designed a 10-foot deep foundation for a 179-foot tall building? How would you like *that* on your resumé?

The Apostle Paul said, "No…I have not achieved it…but I focus on…forgetting the past and looking forward" (Php 3:12-14 NLT). Chuck Swindoll writes: "Show me the guy who wrote the rules for perfectionism, and I'll guarantee he's a nail biter with a face full of tics…whose wife dreads to see him come home." God said, "I…am he who blots away your sins …and will never think of them again" (Isa 43:25 TLB). Now, if *God* is willing to pardon your mistakes and even bury them, isn't it time you stopped beating yourself up, received His grace and moved on?

THERE'S HOPE FOR YOU!

I have…plans to give you the future you hope for.
Jeremiah 29:11 TM

In Jeremiah 29:11 we have a great promise in a not-so-great chapter. So if things aren't going too well in your life at the moment, this verse is for you!

God's people were living as slaves in Babylon. Why? Because of disobedience to God. And worse, Babylon was about as pagan as you could get. It wasn't the kind of place Christians hung out; it was a moral and spiritual wasteland. And on top of that, the Israelites' own preachers were leading them astray. So God told them, "Don't let all those so-called preachers and know-it-alls…take you in with their lies" (Jer 29:8-9 TM). Yet in the midst of all this, along comes the God of hope saying, "I still have a plan for you. It's not over till I say so. I'm going to turn things around for you. Your best days are ahead."

You say "How do you know that God still has a plan for me?" Because you're still breathing! He has a plan for every single person He ever created, and it never goes out of date. Unlike the milk in your supermarket that has an expiration date on it after which it can't be used, God's plans don't have expiration dates. Even if you've missed His plan entirely for years, that plan can still swing into operation the moment you turn your life over to Him and fall in line with His will. Now, your plan might be somewhat modified from what it would have been 20 years ago if you'd paid attention, but that doesn't stop God. He can adapt to fit anything that comes up, in any life that's ever lived—including yours. So, there's hope for you!

GET RID OF THOSE OLD CLOTHES!

Put off your old self...put on the new self.
Ephesians 4:22-24 NIV

*W*hen you entertain certain thoughts in the privacy of your own mind you may be tempted to excuse yourself by saying, "What harm will it do?" What harm? More than you know! Ultimately you *become* whatever you dwell on. Paul writes, "Take captive every thought and make it obedient to Christ" (2Co 10:5). Take control of your thoughts or they'll take you places you don't want to go!

Again Paul writes, "Put off your old self...put on the new self." Now you may not want to admit that you're still wearing some of those old clothes. But the truth is, you can't put on the new man till you first take off the old one. Furthermore, you can't hang those old clothes in the closet for a rainy day, or leave them on the floor to be tripped over. You've got to get rid of them!

Read these words carefully: "Stop telling lies...tell [your] neighbors the truth...Don't let the sun go down while you are still angry, for anger gives a foothold to the devil. If you are a thief, quit stealing...use your hands for good hard work... give generously to others in need. Don't use foul or abusive language. Let everything you say be...helpful, so that your words will be an encouragement to those who hear them" (Eph 4:25-29 NLT). Because God's Spirit lives within you, you don't have to: (a) lie in order to advance your position; (b) cheat to be prosperous; (c) deceive to achieve; (d) use your anger and your moods to control others; (e) engage in foul talk. Those are old clothes—get rid of them!

EXEMPLARY LEADERSHIP (1)

He gave constant encouragement.
Acts 20:2 TM

A good leader has 2 important characteristics: he or she knows where they're going, and can show others the value of going with them. There are talented people who'll never be effective leaders because they're more interested in themselves than in those they lead. However, once they've gone through the school of hard knocks they become sensitive to other people's needs. But effective leaders don't wait for that to happen. They realize that ideas are a dime a dozen, while the people who implement them are priceless. Legendary football coach Bear Bryant used to say, "I'm just a plow-hand...but I've learned how to hold a team together; how to lift some men up, how to calm others down, until...they've got one heartbeat. There are just 3 things I say: if something goes bad, *I* did it; if it goes semi-good, *we* did it; if it goes really good, *you* did it!"

If you aspire to lead others, consider this: exemplary leaders are approachable; they don't get touchy and fly off the handle; they never let minor problems poison their outlook; they sandwich every slice of criticism between two layers of praise. Robert Louis Stevenson said, "Keep your fears to yourself but share your courage with others." There are people who knock the heart out of you and others who put it back in. Encouraging others simply means giving them "a courage transfusion." "Paul called the disciples together and...gave constant encouragement, lifting their spirits...charging them with fresh hope." That's exemplary leadership! So, do *you* have what it takes to lead?

EXEMPLARY LEADERSHIP (2)

I'm with you all the way.
2 Corinthians 7:4 TM

*F*or leadership at its finest, consider the Apostle Paul. He told the fledgling, often-troubled Christians at Corinth: "I'm with you all the way, no matter what. I have…the greatest confidence in you. If only you knew how proud I am of you…despite all our troubles." Goethe said, "Correction does much, but encouragement does more." In spite of their immaturity, and "fights in the church" (2Co 7:5 TM), Paul was their biggest cheerleader. He knew how to comfort and correct, encourage and sharpen—hallmarks of exemplary leadership.

So, what does it mean to be a good leader? Good leaders: (a) are consistent; they set an example by "walking the walk," so everyone knows that what's heard at the bottom is first practiced at the top; (b) constantly express their appreciation, realizing people need to know they're an important part of the team; (c) always listen to suggestions, opinions, fears and ideas without pre-judging or being dismissive. Author Betty Bender said, "It's a mistake to surround yourself only with people just like you. Throw off that worn comforter—replace it with a crazy quilt of different and imaginative people. Then watch the ideas erupt!"; (d) don't see people as statistics; Mary Kay Ash said, "P & L doesn't just mean 'profit and loss'—it means 'people and love'"; (e) explain *why* they like things done a certain way, because it lessens mistakes and the resentment that can stem from feeling "ordered around." Clarence Francis said, "You can buy a man's time, his physical presence at a given place, and even his skill. But you can't buy enthusiasm… loyalty…and devotion…you have to earn these."

EXEMPLARY LEADERSHIP (3)

Encourage your people…
correcting them when necessary.
Titus 2:15 TLB

*I*t's hard to lead others further than you've gone yourself, especially when you're more concerned about their reaction than keeping the team on course. Does that mean setting yourself up as "the be-all and end-all?" No, but as a leader it's impossible to please everybody. If you constantly need approval you'll end up being controlled by those you're supposed to lead. Paul recognized this, that's why he told Timothy: "Teach…and encourage your people…correcting them when necessary. You have the authority to do this, so don't let anyone…disregard what you say" (Titus 2:15 NLT).

Insecure, inexperienced leaders agonize over decisions they suspect will cause unhappiness in the ranks. They feel responsible for other people's emotional reaction. They fail to realize that when you're doing what you should be doing and others don't agree, that's *their* problem, unless you allow it to become *yours*. A mature leader deals with disappointment and keeps a good attitude; he faces the music even when he doesn't like the tune. Think, as a parent when you warn your children about putting their hand on a hot stove, it's not your responsibility to make them enjoy hearing it, right? Hopefully, as they mature they'll understand. But the truth is, some people won't like hearing "no" regardless of how old they get! However, we all need to hear it from time to time, otherwise we'll never be happy with anything other than getting our own way. Which means—getting nowhere, or getting into trouble!

EXEMPLARY LEADERSHIP (4)

This job is too heavy...to...handle...by yourself.
Exodus 18:18 TLB

*T*he Israelites looked to Moses for everything, and he was wearing himself out trying to meet their expectations. When his "father-in-law saw how much time this was taking he said, 'Why are you trying to do all this alone...You're going to wear yourself out...this job is too heavy...to handle... by yourself...Find some capable, godly, honest men...and appoint them...That way...you will share the burden...be able to endure the pressures, and there will be peace and harmony'...Moses listened...and followed this suggestion" (Ex 18:14-24 TLB).

Asking for help is a sign of strength, not weakness. Some of us are proud of our superhuman ability to do it all. But Moses' father-in-law told him that what he was doing wasn't good for him, or those under his leadership. How so? When God calls and equips someone to do a job that you keep doing for them, they end up frustrated and undeveloped. God created us to be interdependent, not independent. Delegating authority to the right people strengthened Moses for the task of leading Israel the way God intended. You can't be all things to all people. Unless you learn to delegate, you'll disintegrate. Remember, you yourself have legitimate needs, and it's wrong to be too proud to ask for help!

As a leader it's easy to overestimate your own importance. Paul says: "Don't think you are better than you really are. Use good sense" (Ro 12:3 CEV). Theodore Roosevelt put it like this: "The best executive is the one who has sense enough to pick people to do what he wants done, and self-restraint enough to keep from meddling with them while they do it." And that's still good advice!

WISDOM FOR YOUR TRIALS

If any of you lacks wisdom, let him ask of God.
James 1:5 NAS

*Y*ou say "OK, tell me exactly what I need to do to grow in my trials." First, you must realize that the wisdom needed to handle your trials the right way, comes from God. That's why, after spending 4 verses speaking about "fiery trials," James writes, "But if any of you lacks wisdom, let him ask of God, who gives to all generously and without reproach, and it will be given to him." Now this is not an invitation to quiz God about the "why" of your trials. That's information you may never know this side of Heaven. If God didn't tell Job the patriarch the reason for his trials, chances are He won't tell you either. Asking why is a very human response, but it's usually not very productive. Instead of asking why, you need to pray: "Heavenly Father, how do You want to use this trial to develop me spiritually? How can I cooperate with You to reap the maximum benefit? What changes do You desire to bring about in me?" Those are questions God *will* answer.

But it's not enough to ask the right questions, you also need to ask with a willing heart. It's possible to ask God for wisdom, then debate, stall, or mess around trying to decide whether or not to obey Him. James calls this "double-minded." And the result? "That man ought not to expect that he will receive anything from the Lord, being a double-minded man, unstable in all his ways" (Jas 1:7-8 NAS). When you ask God for wisdom your only response should be, "Speak Lord, for I am listening."

ARE YOU THERE YET?

Put up with each other,
and forgive anyone who does you wrong.
Col 3:13 CEV

*T*his light-hearted but revealing commentary appeared in a newspaper: "A lady took my seat in church… She's very nice…a good friend, in fact. I can sit any place…no big deal. My seat is on the right as you enter the sanctuary. I can rest my arm on the end. It's a good seat, but I wouldn't raise a fuss about a seat…never hold a grudge. Actually, it was 3 months ago she took it and I really don't know why. I've never done anything to her…never taken *her* seat. I suppose I'll have to come an hour early now to get my seat. She took it because it's one of the best seats in the house. She'd no business taking it…and I'm *not* going to church 2 hours early to get what's rightfully mine! This is the way great social injustices begin: abusive people taking other people's seats! It's the way seeds of revolution are sown. A person can only stand so much. Where's it all going to end? If somebody doesn't stand up and be counted, nobody's seat will be safe. People will sit where they please, and next they'll take my parking place. World order will be in shambles!"

We smile, but it's amazing how quickly we get bent out of shape when our little routine is disrupted. Paul writes, "Put up with each other, and forgive anyone who does you wrong…as Christ has forgiven you. Love is more important than anything …It…ties everything…together." Plus, when you truly love God and know He loves you, "nothing shall offend…[you]." Are you there yet? Are you even close?

LIVING IN GOD'S APPROVAL

We have been approved by God.
1 Thessalonians 2:4 NRS

*L*iving in the approval of God is so liberating! It frees you from "approval addiction"—worrying about what other people think. When you are addicted, no matter how much of your drug of choice you get it's never enough. And like all junkies, you go crazy when your drug is withheld. Approval addicts are always at the mercy of other people's opinions. As a result their lives become an emotional roller coaster of highs and lows.

Paul was free to speak the truth in love: to confront people, or be gentle with them. When someone told Paul they didn't like him, he didn't lose sleep over it. That's because his life wasn't built upon their approval. "We have been approved by God." Paul didn't go around needing to (a) compare himself with others; (b) demonstrate his superiority; (c) impress or compete with others; (d) be the top dog or the one who's always in charge. Living in God's approval set him free from such ulcer-inducing anxiety, and meant he could enjoy the life God called him to live.

When we're young and insecure we tend to worry about what others think of us. But as we become more mature, we realize that most of the time they weren't thinking about us at all. They were too busy worrying about what we thought of them! Living in God's approval frees us from all that stress. It gives us the strength to deal with criticism and conflict, because we know our identity. And our identity is this: we are God's redeemed children. And since we are accepted and approved by Him, what else matters?

THE LAW OF EXPOSURE!

If anything is excellent or praiseworthy
—think about such things.
Philippians 4:8 NIV

*I*magine that you were really serious about running in the New York marathon. How likely is it that you'd go on an all-candy diet before the big race? The fuel you put into something determines its performance. Which is why it's so ironic that in one of the most important areas of life, we disregard this basic piece of wisdom. That area involves your mind. What you feed everything else is *nothing* compared to what you feed your mind.

Here's a truth that will transform you—think excellent thoughts! What enters your mind repeatedly, occupies it, shapes it, controls it, and in the end expresses itself in what you do and who you become. That's the law of exposure. And it's as sure as the law of gravity. Your mind will *absorb* and *reflect* whatever it's exposed to. The events you attend, the materials you read or don't read, the music you listen to, the images you expose yourself to, the conversations you hold, the thoughts you entertain, are all shaping your mind, and eventually your character and your destiny.

"So what should I do?" you ask. Do a check up from the neck up! Begin to pray: "Lord, what I want is a new mind because I'm tired of this old one. It keeps leading me down the wrong paths. In a world where the messages are so often twisted or trivial or foolish or self-absorbed or downright evil, I want the kind of mind Your Word describes: one that's filled with excellent, admirable, honorable, praiseworthy thoughts." Can you imagine what your life would be like if you constantly prayed that way?

A MOTHER'S MARK!

What a rich faith…handed down from your
grandmother Lois to your mother Eunice…to you!
2 Timothy 1:5 TM

*T*he Bible paints various portraits of mothers, and while they weren't perfect, each one tells a story. Moses' mother broke the law to ensure his safety and teach him the faith of his people. Then there's the mom who came before Solomon, prepared to forfeit her child rather than see him harmed. James and John's mother loved them so much, she wanted them to sit on either side of Christ in His future kingdom. And Paul saw in Timothy a young man of sterling character because of the faith "handed down from [his] grandmother Lois to [his] mother Eunice…to [him]." The most significant thing we know about Timothy's mother is that *her* mom was a believer, because while faith can't be "inherited" it can be passed on through the influence of godly parents.

A little boy forgot his lines in the Sunday School play so his mother leaned over and whispered, "I am the light of the world." The kid beamed, then with great feeling announced, "My mother is the light of the world!" We smile, but the truth is, mothers write on the hearts of their children what the hand of time can't erase. E.W. Caswell said, "It's only in [later] life that men gaze backward and behold how a mother's hand and heart …shaped their destiny." Chuck Swindoll adds: "If you were blessed with a good mother, you reap the benefits the rest of your life. If your mother neglected your needs…much of what you suffered can't be erased. For good or ill, a mother's mark is permanent." So, Mom, what kind of mark are you leaving on the lives of *your* kids?

ARE YOU WILLING TO DO IT GOD'S WAY?

Naaman…was a great man…but he was a leper.
2 Kings 5:1 NAS

*N*aaman the leper made 3 common mistakes. *(1) He tried to buy his healing* (See 2Ki 5:5). Even though God says, "Come…you who have no money…buy…without cost" (Isa 55:1 NAS), most of us would rather buy our way, than believe our way into heaven. But it doesn't work! "By grace are you saved through faith" (See Eph 2:8). *(2) He turned to a non-believer for answers* (See 2Ki 5:6 NAS). The Bible says, "Seek the Lord…call upon Him" (Isa 55:6 NAS). Christ is the answer; through Him alone we have access to God's saving grace. *(3) He had preconceived expectations.* Naaman, "was a great man" used to commanding armies. So when he got to the prophet's house, instead of Elisha observing protocol and coming out personally, he sent a servant to say, "Go…wash in Jordan seven times, and…you will be clean" (2Ki 5-10 NAS). That's when Naaman exploded and "stalked away" (2Ki 5:11 TLB).

Here's what we can learn: (a) Until you're willing to acknowledge your need, God can't meet it. (b) God used a servant girl in his own house to tell Naaman the truth. So be open to whomever God sends you. (See Jn 8:31-32 NIV). (c) You've got to exhaust your own resources before you're ready to tap into God's. (d) God said, "My thoughts are not your thoughts, nor are your ways My ways" (Isa 55:8 NAS), which means doing what *He* (and nobody else) says, if you want the answer. Only when Naaman was willing to do it God's way, was he healed of his leprosy. So, are *you* willing to do it God's way?

JESUS UNDERSTANDS

[Jesus] has been tempted in all things as we are.
Hebrews 4:15 NAS

*W*ell-intentioned friends sometimes say, "I know how you feel." But deep down we think, "No, you really don't." But Jesus does! He was "tempted in all things as we are," so He can interpret and present our feelings to God. And He does. When you pray in Jesus' name, pouring out your heart to God, Jesus acts as your attorney and says, "Father, I know what this person is feeling. I know what it's like to be under pressure to sin. I stand with this child of Yours who needs Your help."

You say, "But Jesus was without sin, so can He really feel my sin the way I feel it?" Yes, He can. In fact, because of His purity He actually feels the pain of sin even *more*. Perhaps an illustration will help. In our everyday world we live with germs all around us, and even on us. Because we aren't in a sterile environment we don't notice these germs and we learn to live with them. But it's an entirely different story in a hospital operating room. There, any contamination from germs is a real threat that demands the attention of the entire staff. So they sterilize everything because bacteria can kill the patient. The purity of the room demands close attention to the presence of even the slightest impurity that could lead to a life-threatening infection.

So Jesus' separateness from, and sensitivity to sin, actually *increases* His ability to sympathize with us. Bottom line: Jesus understands what you're struggling with!

LET GOD DECIDE WHO MINISTERS TO YOU

Angels ministered to Him.
Mark 1:13 NKJV

*E*ver notice how the devil attacks you when you're most vulnerable? After fasting for 40 days in the wilderness Jesus was in "a state of extreme hunger, which the Devil took advantage of" (Mt 4:2 TM). Though hunger is a legitimate need Satan will offer to satisfy it in illegitimate ways. But after Jesus rebuked him, "The Devil left…And…angels…came and took care of [Him]." At that point Jesus was willing to allow the lesser (the beings He had created and commanded in heaven) to minister to the greater. And by doing so He set an example for each of us to follow.

Perhaps you're struggling today with issues that should be history. Maybe you were "wounded in the house of [your] friends" (Zec 13:6). As a result you no longer trust anybody. Now God can't minister to you through His chosen channels. You *want* to be healed as long as it's on *your* terms. Understand this: when you're in enough pain you won't care who God uses; you'll do whatever it takes! Think, if you were hurt in an accident would you *really* care who the doctors were that helped save your life? Would you question their financial status, church affiliation or cultural background? Frequently it's not the *plan* of God we struggle with so much as the *people* He chooses to accomplish it through. James says, "God sets Himself against the proud…but…gives grace to the lowly" (Jas 4:6 AMP). That means when you really want God's help and are ready to accept it, you'll set aside your pride and open yourself up to those He sends your way to minister to you!

IN THE MELTING POT!

He will sit as a refiner…of silver.
Malachi 3:3 NKJV

*R*ick Warren says: "God has a purpose behind every problem. He uses circumstances to develop our character. In fact, He often depends more on circumstances to make us like Jesus than He does on our reading the Bible. And the reason is obvious: we face circumstances 24-hours-a-day."

We learn things about God when we're in trouble that we can't learn any other way. Adversity draws us closer to Him! "The Lord is close to the brokenhearted" (Ps 34:18 NLT). Problems force us to look to God and depend on Him instead of ourselves. Paul writes, "We…saw how powerless we were to help ourselves; but that was good, for then we put everything into the hands of God" (2Co 1:9 TLB). Submitting the situation to God and trusting Him with the ways, means, and timing, is hard for most of us to do. Why? Because it means giving up control!

If you feel like you're in the melting pot today, maybe God put you there. Have you thought of that? The refiner is burning away the impurities and removing the obstacles in your life: "He will sit as a refiner…of silver; he will purify…them like gold…Then the Lord will have men who will…be acceptable." Since God's plan is to make us more like Jesus, He'll take us through the experiences Jesus went through. What are they? The wilderness of temptation; rejection by your family; the strain of caring for others; criticism from religious folks; and betrayal by those you love and have invested your life in. So, are you in the melting pot?

LOVE YOURSELF—GOD DOES!

*Because of what Christ has done
we have become gifts…God…delights in.*
Ephesians 1:11 TLB

$\mathcal{D}$ennis Waitley said, "It's not what you are that holds you back, it's what you think you aren't." Sadly, some of us think so little of ourselves that we'd rather be in a wrong relationship than none at all. But being around others doesn't guarantee you won't be lonely; you can be around people 24/7, and still feel empty and used.

Until you overcome your fear of being alone and are willing to wait for God to give you the right relationships, you'll *keep* feeling lonely! Loneliness is more about not liking yourself, than about not having people around who like you. Otherwise why would we spend so much time avoiding rejection instead of taking the time to build healthy relationships? We're afraid of being hurt so we keep up our defenses. We think if we don't get involved we can't get hurt, and as a result we end up lonely. We're afraid to be vulnerable in case people criticize us for sharing anything personal. Such anxieties just contribute to our sense of isolation.

Instead of wishing things were different—begin to make them different! The Apostle Paul says, "Because of what Christ has done we have become gifts…God…delights in." When you start to see yourself as God sees you, you'll start liking yourself! A famous actress once said, "Cherish and celebrate what makes you unique, because you're only a yawn once that goes!" Does that mean strutting around thinking you're better than others? No, it means humbly, but confidently, accepting yourself because you know that God "take[s] great delight in you" (Zep 3:17 NIV). So the word for you today is, love yourself—God does!

ARE YOU HOOKED ON LOGIC?

Don't assume that you know it all.
Proverbs 3:7 TM

*O*ne day a scientist asked an old preacher how come the Bible version of creation defied logic. Smiling, he replied, "The reason God came from nowhere is because there wasn't anywhere for Him to come from. And coming from nowhere He stood on nothing, for there was nowhere for Him to stand. And standing on nothing He reached out where there was nowhere to reach, and caught something when there was nothing to catch. Then He hung that something on nothing and told it to stay there, and nobody said a word, because there wasn't anybody around to say anything. Then God said to Himself, 'That's good!'"

As humans we tend to try and figure things out in advance. But we're not nearly as smart as we think. Solomon said "Don't assume that you know it all," or you'll find out the hard way that you don't! One Christian author writes: "I...couldn't feel at peace. Unless I'd everything figured out...I became anxious, restless, nervous, worried and grouchy... similar to...a drug addict who needs a 'fix'; the...severity wasn't the same but the symptoms were. I was a Christian and supposedly walked by faith...I trusted Jesus for salvation, but in other areas I trusted myself." Sound familiar? Chronic worry proves you're trusting in yourself more than God. And worry, like any other sin, needs to be dealt with.

Jeremiah said, "Mere mortals can't run their own lives... men and women don't have what it takes" (Jer 10:23 TM). So stop trying to control every possible outcome! Life is much more peaceful when you decide to stand on God's Word and trust Him, regardless of circumstances!

PERSISTENCE

The people had a mind to work.
Nehemiah 4:6

*I*n 1947 Lester Wunderman was arbitrarily fired from his advertising job in New York. But he felt he still had a lot to learn from the head of the agency, Max Sackheim. So the next morning Wunderman went back to his office and began working as he had before. He talked to co-workers and clients; he sat in on meetings—all without pay. Sackheim ignored him for a month. Finally he walked up to Wunderman: "Okay, you win," he said, shaking his head. "I never saw a man who wanted a job more than he wanted money." Well, guess what? Wunderman went on to be one of the most successful advertising men of the century. He's credited with having invented preprinted newspaper inserts, plus subscription cards such as those used by Time-Life Books and the Columbia Record Club; ideas that have produced billions of dollars in profit. Now, advertising may not be your thing—but action must be. What are you willing to do to achieve your dream? Work without pay? Refuse to quit? Success begins at the beginning, and it continues with consistent action.

Now, ponder these thoughts: (1) You don't have to be great to start, but you have to start to be great. (2) The first 2 letters in the word goal, are GO. (3) Some people dream of worthy accomplishments, others wake up and do them. (4) Anybody who brags about what they're going to do tomorrow probably did the same thing yesterday. (5) You will never be what you ought to be, until you're doing what you ought to be doing. (6) If you're having trouble thinking outside the box, you're probably in the wrong box. Get out of there!

IDENTITY CRISIS!

I know where I came from and where I am going.
John 8:14 AMP

A national news network recently reported on a man who was released from prison after serving time for a crime he didn't commit. A case of mistaken identity had stolen many of his best years. And unless *you* understand who you are before God, Satan will sentence you to a life of worthlessness, fear and manipulation. *Identifying* somebody means having the ability to recognize and say exactly who they are; so when you identify with what *people* say you are versus what *God* says, you're setting yourself up for problems. Jesus identified only with God's opinion. "I know where I came from and where I am going." People said terrible things about Jesus, yet the Bible says, "The stone...the builders rejected has become the... cornerstone" (Ps 118:22 NKJV). Sometimes we're so busy telling people what to *do,* that we neglect to tell them who they *are*. Knowing who you are in Christ gives you the confidence to hold your head high! Paul says, "In [Christ] you have been made complete" (Col 2:10 NAS). "Complete!" That means you lack nothing! Once you accept that, you stop feeling like you constantly fall short. When you've money in the bank and you need to withdraw it, you don't feel pressured to. That's because you know it's there with your name on it, right? You don't have to struggle to be right with people when you know you're right with God. He loves you and has a plan for you; never lose sight of that! Instead of focusing on people, begin looking to "Jesus the author and finisher of our faith" (Heb 12:2), because you already *have* His approval!

WHEN THE GRACE LIFTS

My grace is sufficient for thee.
2 Corinthians 12:9

*W*hen God has "graced" you, you can handle just about any situation! Listen to Paul: "Three times I called upon the Lord...begged that it might depart from me; but He said to me, My grace (My favor and loving-kindness and mercy) is enough for you [sufficient against any danger and enables you to bear the trouble manfully]; for My strength and power... *show themselves most effective in [your] weakness*...So for the sake of Christ, I am well pleased and take pleasure in infirmities, insults, hardships, persecutions, perplexities and distresses; for when I am weak [in human strength], then am I [truly] strong (able, powerful in divine strength)" (2Co 12:8-10 AMP). But there's something you should understand: when the grace lifts, it's God's way of getting you to recognize that things are changing, that it's time to consult Him as to your next move. Pay attention! Why? Because when the grace *lifts*—we tend to become "ungracious" toward others, and risk tearing down valuable relationships we've spent our lives building. Don't let that happen to you. We're not talking about having a bad day in which you're irritable and impatient. We all have those. No, we're talking about reaching the place where your *attitudes* and *actions* consistently hurt others; it's not an occasional thing, it's a pattern.

So, has the grace you've experienced lifted? Has an old season or relationship ended? Are you now hurting the situation more than helping? Ask God for fresh direction. Search His Word for wisdom as to your future. When the grace lifts—it's time to say, "Lord, what do You have in mind for me now?"

BE YOURSELF

He chose us…before the foundation of the world.
Ephesians 1:4 NAS

The following is reprinted by request:

Ruth Lee writes: "It was the last day of a writers' conference and we gathered in one of the dormitories. In our pajamas we all looked alike. One by one we shared. After the introduction of two authors with published books, and others with claim to fame, it was my turn. 'My name is Ruth,' I said, 'and I feel so inferior, I think I'll just go back to my room.' Everybody laughed, so I ploughed ahead. 'I guess you could call me a producer. In the last 30 years I've produced a well-adjusted respiratory therapist, a machinist and another happy homemaker. I'm also involved in the co-production of seven grandchildren.' I told them how full my life was. Full of checking on cows, helping to fix fences and praying it would stop raining. I told them of busy hours spent babysitting and contending with my household. Then I told them how hungry I was. Hungry for the type of spiritual and emotional food I received at this conference. From the far corner of the room a quiet girl spoke up. 'Would you please turn so that I can look at you?' she asked. I did, and she continued. 'I want to remember your face when I write,' she said, 'I want to write for people just like you.' Suddenly I had no need of title or degree. I served a purpose. With her words she helped me realize what I should have known all along: God doesn't make nobodies— everybody is somebody important to Him!" So, dare to be yourself. After all, who's better qualified?

THINKING ABOUT HEAVEN

We…would prefer to be…at home with the Lord.
2 Corinthians 5:8 NIV

*T*he sense that we will live forever somewhere, has shaped every civilization in history. In the pyramids of Egypt, the embalmed bodies had maps placed beside them as guides to the future world. In A.D. 125, a Greek named Aristides wrote, "When a Christian passes from this world, they rejoice…and escort his body with songs of thanksgiving as if he were setting out from one place to another nearby." In 1952 young Florence Chadwick stepped into the Pacific, just off Catalina Island, determined to swim to the mainland of California. She'd already been the first woman to swim the English Channel— both ways. The weather was foggy and chilly; she could hardly see the boats accompanying her. Still, she swam for 15 hours. When she begged to be taken out of the water, her mother, who was in a boat alongside, told her she was close and that she could make it. Finally, physically and emotionally exhausted, she stopped swimming and was pulled out. It wasn't until she was on the boat that she discovered that the shore was less than half a mile away. At a news conference the next day she said, "All I could see was the fog…I think if I could have seen the shore I would have made it."

Heaven is not a myth; it's a magnet that pulls us in the direction of home. A home, which Paul describes as "better by far" (Php 1:23 NIV). Child of God, no matter how tough life gets, keep your eyes on the heavenly shore; draw strength each day from God, and you'll make it!

FINISHING STRONG

I have finished the race.
2 Timothy 4:7 NIV

*B*en Johnson of Canada won the 100-meter dash, setting a new Olympic record and a new world record. The American contender, Carl Lewis, came in second. Most were shocked that he hadn't won the Gold. After the race the judges learned that Johnson had an illegal substance in his body, so they took away his medal. Though he ran faster and made an unforgettable impression, he forfeited the prize.

When Dawson Trotman, founder of *The Navigators,* drowned in Schroon Lake while saving someone's life, *Time* magazine reported: "Dawson Trotman was always holding somebody up." Ben Johnson lived for himself—Dawson Trotman lived for others. One finished strong, the other didn't. There are 3 kinds of people who arrive at the finish line of life: *(1) Those who start wrong but finish right.* Like Paul: "I persecuted the church...and tried to destroy it" (Gal 1:13 NIV). But after he met Christ on the Damascus Road, Paul's life was captioned in one phrase, "For me, to live is Christ" (Php 1:21). *(2) Those who start right but finish wrong.* King Saul was one. He strayed from God's will and lost his crown at Mount Gilboa (the word Gilboa means pride). His life is summed up in these his final words, "I have acted like a fool" (1Sa 26:21 NIV). *(3) Those who are afraid to run.* The following poem describes them: "There was a very cautious man who never laughed or played; he never risked, he never tried, he never sang or prayed. And when one day he passed away, his insurance was denied; for since he never really lived, they claimed he never died." Which of the 3 are you?

DON'T JUST STUDY—SERVE!

Remember today what you have learned about the Lord through your experiences with him.
Deuteronomy 11:2 TEV

$\mathcal{G}$ene Getz says, "Bible study by itself will not produce spirituality. In fact, it will produce carnality if it isn't applied and practiced. The truth is, study without service produces people with judgmental attitudes and spiritual pride. And the more they think they know, the prouder they become." So, "Remember today what you have learned about the Lord *through your experiences with him.*" There are some lessons you can learn only by experience. Solomon writes, "Sometimes it takes a painful experience to make us change our ways" (Pr 20:30 TEV). If Christianity was just a philosophy then our primary activity might be studying. But since it's about walking in relationship with Christ, the last thing many of us need is another Bible study. We already *know* far more than we're putting into practice. We need experiences where we can apply what we know. James says, "Do not deceive yourselves by just listening to his word; instead, put it into practice" (Jas 1:22 TEV). The reason nothing lives in the Dead Sea is because it takes in water but doesn't give any out. If you have biblical input but no outflow of service, you stagnate spiritually. And churches actually do a disservice by keeping people so busy going to the next Bible study, without showing them practical ways to apply what they learned at the last one. They file away and forget the truth before it can be internalized and put into practice, thinking they're growing because their notebooks are getting thicker. So, "don't just study—serve!"

WHAT ARE YOUR CONVICTIONS?

Don't let the world…squeeze you into its…mould.
Romans 12:2 Phps

*H*oward Hendricks says, "A belief is something you'll argue about. But a conviction is something you'll die for." Knowing *what* to do (knowledge), *when* to do it (wisdom), *how* to do it (ability), is worthless without the conviction to actually *do* it (obedience). People without conviction follow the crowd, which is why Paul wrote, "Don't let the world… squeeze you into its…mould." If we don't take a stand for something, we'll fall for everything! Ironically, a lot of us have strong convictions about weak issues such as football, fashion, etc., while having weak convictions about major issues such as what's right and what's wrong before God. Conviction helps us grow spiritually. But growth requires *time* and *effort*. Without a deep conviction of our need to grow spiritually, we become discouraged and give up. No one stays with a task that's difficult unless they're convinced there's a good reason for doing so. Jesus' life was dominated by the conviction that He came to do His Father's will—nothing else! This conviction kept Him from being distracted by the agenda of others. Check the number of times Jesus used the phrase "I must."

Why do cults attract so many people? Because we all want something to believe in, something to give our lives for. Without clear, strong convictions we'll never attract the level of commitment that Christ deserves. We must *burn* with a conviction that advancing the Kingdom of God is our calling and reason to live. Vance Havner said, "Jesus demands greater allegiance than any dictator that ever lived. The difference is, Jesus has a right to it!"

OVERCOMING LIFE-LIMITING THOUGHTS

I will strengthen you and help you;
I will uphold you with my righteous right hand.
Isaiah 41:10 NIV

*L*abels tend to stick. When we're young and our parents say things like "Oh, she's just a plain Jane," or, "He'll never be as smart as his brother," we drag those life-limiting thoughts around like a ball and chain for the rest of our lives. Fortunately, God sees your potential differently. Listen: "God can pour on the blessings in astonishing ways so that you're... more than...ready to do what needs to be done" (2Co 9:8 TM).

Thirty years ago Johnnie Weissmuller, also known as *Tarzan* to movie-goers, was called the greatest swimmer in the world. Doctors and coaches said, "Nobody will ever break Johnnie's records." He held more than 50 of them. Today 13-year-old girls break them on a regular basis! For decades experts declared nobody would break the 4-minute mile. But Roger Bannister refused to believe it. As a result, he broke the "impossible" 4-minute mile. Today hundreds of runners do it every year. Understand this: others can stop you *temporarily,* but you are the only one that can do it *permanently.* If God says you can—you can! And His opinion is the only one that counts. Edgar Guest wrote, "There are thousands to tell you it cannot be done, there are thousands to prophesy failure; there are thousands to point out, one by one, the dangers that wait to assail you. So buckle right in with a bit of a grin, take off your coat and go to it; just start to sing as you tackle the thing that 'cannot be done,' and you'll do it."

PRAYING, FOR THE RIGHT REASONS

To you, O Lord, I lift up my soul.
Psalm 25:1 NAS

*P*salm 25 describes a person who's chosen the right road, yet not found it easy to walk. In the first 10 verses we learn 5 important things about the person who prays: *(1) They know where to go for help.* "To you, O Lord, I lift up my soul" (v.1). Others may assist us, but only God can sustain us. *(2) They know who to trust.* "In thee I trust…do not let my enemies exult over me" (v.2). Love your enemies, because God does. Pray for them, turn them over to Him, then move on. *(3) They know the purpose of prayer.* "Lead me in Your truth and teach me" (v.4). Richard Foster writes, "To pray is to change. Prayer is the central avenue God uses to transform us. If we are unwilling to change, we will abandon prayer. The more we pray the more we come to the heartbeat of God. Prayer starts the communication process between ourselves and God. All the options of life fall before us. At that point we will either forsake our prayer life and cease to grow, or we will pursue our prayer life and let Him change us." *(4) They know the basis of their acceptance.* "According to Your lovingkindness remember me" (v.7). We cannot approach God on the basis of our own goodness, only on the merits of His saving grace. *(5) They know prayer works.* "He teaches the humble His way" (v.9). When you can't see your way forward, pray. God will reveal it to you one step at a time— all you have to do is follow.

IS GOD CALLING YOU?

A woman who fears the Lord is to be praised.
Proverbs 31:30 NIV

*A*my Carmichael was born in Ireland in 1867. From the get-go she didn't fit the mold. Her unconventional outlook made problems for those who were more dedicated to maintaining tradition than to reaching a lost world. During her early missionary years, a "Get-Amy Carmichael-out-of-India" movement was started by those who didn't understand her unwavering obedience to what she believed to be God's will for her life. In her book, *Roots,* she writes: "It's not that we think… ours is the only way of living, but we are sure…it's the way meant for us." Amy ministered in Japan, China and Ceylon before being called to India where she spent her time working with children, especially young girls forced into temple prosti-tution. Tenderness marked her life, but not the kind associated with weakness and fragility. Hers was more of an "iron fist in a velvet glove" approach. Burning with moral indignation she'd plow through a mob to rescue a little girl, then weep openly about the child's situation. When she died in 1951 she was buried under a tamarind tree in a grave marked by the Indian word for mother: AMMAI.

Ever notice how often single women are called to do some of the toughest jobs? Or that many (though certainly not all) missionaries are women? The Bible says, "Charm is deceptive, and beauty…fleeting but a woman who fears the Lord is to be praised." Today if God's calling *you* to be another Amy Carmichael, don't be afraid to say yes, because the safest place in the world—is in the center of His will.

HEALED FROM PERFECTIONISM!

Instead of worrying, pray.
Philippians 4:6 TM

*S*triving to do better is a good thing, but *perfectionism* guarantees misery, for in life "it's always something!" The mother of 3 children complained to her doctor, "I just can't get the house cleaned the way I like it before everyone leaves in the morning." She was so stressed out, he put her on antidepressants. It was like she'd a gun at her head and a voice inside saying, "Every dish must be put away and every towel folded—or else!" Life had become one big emergency and she could never "catch up." Yet no one but herself had created the stress she was experiencing—and distributing to others! Answer these questions: (1) Have my goals and responsibilities become so all consuming that I've forgotten how to rejoice along the way, or to cut myself some slack? (2) Have I made my preferences a condition for my happiness? (3) Do I beat myself up when I can't meet my self-created deadlines?"

The first step toward recovering your peace of mind is to admit that *you* are creating most of your stress. Life will go on wonderfully even if it doesn't go according to your plan. Don't wait until you lose your family or have a heart attack before you discover that. Whether it's obsessing over your looks, or your performance at home or on the job, the roots of perfectionism grow in the soil of insecurity. It whispers, "You'll never measure up!" That's a lie; don't believe it. You are loved, approved and accepted—by God! Your worth comes from *Him*, and His opinion of you never changes!

GUARDING, GIRDING, GUIDING

If anyone does not provide for…his…family,
he…is worse than an unbeliever.
1 Timothy 5:8 NIV

*P*arent, you've got 3 major responsibilities: *(1) Guarding them:* apart from safeguarding your kids spiritually (television, the Internet, pedophiles, and peer groups), you need to look out for their total well-being. If they're struggling in school, *you* go and talk to their teachers. If a stranger comes to the door, *you* answer it. If you hear a noise during the night, *you* get up. This calls for being sensitive to their needs, sacrificing yourself for them. *(2) Girding (surrounding/strengthening) them:* Paul says if you don't provide for your family you're "worse than an unbeliever." You need to provide them with food, shelter and clothing, as well as making sure your spouse has what he/she needs to do the job. Make your family feel secure by letting them know you're there for them. *(3) Guiding them:* Solomon writes, "Train up a child in the way he should go" (Pr 22:6). Lead your kids into a greater understanding of God. Equip them for the future by teaching them to honor and love Him, His Word and His church. And involve them in your long-term planning. They won't have hope if you don't have a plan for something *better* in the future. For example, if you're struggling financially, tell them where you plan to be in 12 months, in 5 years, and by the time they reach college age.

Guarding…girding…guiding…make that your motto. And one more thing, ask God to do the same for *you,* as you work to honor Him in the life of your family. Come on, parent, get serious about it!

YOU'LL GET THROUGH IT!

In all these things we are more than conquerors.
Romans 8:37

*H*ave you heard the story of the old farmer whose mule fell into a well? Since there was no way to get him out the farmer decided to bury him there. But the mule had a different idea. Initially when the shovels of dirt began landing on him he became hysterical. Then this thought struck him; "Just shake it off and step on it." So he did. Hour after hour as the dirt fell on him he kept telling himself, "Just shake it off and step on it." No matter how much dirt they threw on him, he just kept shaking it off and stepping on it—until finally he stepped triumphantly out of the well.

Life will either bless you or bury you; the difference lies in having the right attitude. When they throw dirt on you, and they will, just shake it off and step on it. Use it as fertilizer and grow stronger. No one can make you feel inferior without your consent. What's important is not what others say about you— it's what you say to yourself after they get through talking! Jesus said, "Offenses will come" (Lk 17:1), so expect them. People will take from you without giving back. They'll criticize you for simply rising above your beginnings. When you decide to seize the moment and move ahead, you'll leave others behind and some of them won't be too happy about it. The only way to avoid that, is to do nothing and stay where you are. And that's simply not acceptable—is it?

HANDLING DIFFICULTIES

Consider him who has endured such hostility.
Hebrews 12:3 NAS

*M*ake sure the issue you're dealing with is worth your time and energy. Often it isn't. Ask yourself, "Have I allowed myself to get distracted by something insignificant instead of keeping my eye on the ball?" The Bible says, "Consider him who has endured such hostility by sinners against himself, so that you may not grow weary and lose heart." Check and see how Jesus handled the circumstances you're facing today. You'll learn a lot if you do!

Don't destroy the other person's self-confidence. Stay away from all-inclusive statements like "you always" or "you never." They're not true! Assure them that you have confidence in them and their ability to recover and handle things better next time. After all, that's what God does with you. Correction will do much; encouragement will do much more. Deal with people on an individual basis. Comparisons always cause resentment. Why make the problem bigger? It's easier to be critical than creative, but unless you're willing to *help* you're not qualified to get involved. Straighten out the problem, not the person. When confrontation becomes a personal attack you destroy your own credibility and end up in a "no-win" situation. Your goal should be to leave them with 3 things: (1) a clear understanding of the problem; (2) the assurance of your love; (3) encouragement and confidence that they can turn it around, and that you'll help them to. Are these 3 things easy to do? No. They call for love, patience and Christ-like character. But when you practice them they produce a joy that transcends problems and is never subject to the actions of others.

DO YOU WANT TO CHANGE?

As the spirit of the Lord works within us,
we become more and more like him.
2 Corinthians 3:18 TLB

$\mathcal{D}$id you hear about the frog that fell into a big hole and couldn't get out? Several of his friends tried to help but finally gave up. "Since you're going to be in there for a while," they said, "we'll go and get some food." But no sooner had they left than the frog came hopping up behind them. "We thought you couldn't get out" they exclaimed. "Oh, I couldn't," he replied, "but suddenly there was a big truck coming right at me —and I discovered I could." Usually it's only when we're *forced* to change that we discover we can. That's because we're more comfortable with old problems than new and untried solutions. If you believe nothing can ever be done for the first time, you'll never see anything done—and nothing will change.

There are 3 times in our lives when we're most receptive to change: (1) When our pain levels get so high we're forced to. (2) When we accept the fact that what we're doing no longer works. (3) When we realize that by God's grace we *can* change. Nothing sparks the fires of faith more than the sudden realization that "I don't have to stay this way anymore." And you don't! Stand on these 2 Scriptures: "God'[s]…gracious word can make you into what he wants you to be and give you everything you could possibly need" (Ac 20:32 TM). "As the spirit of the Lord works within us, we become more and more like him" (2Co 3:18 TLB). So, do you want to change?

GROWING THROUGH TRIALS (1)

Every detail works to your advantage and to God's glory.
2 Corinthians 4:15 TM

*W*hen you were a child, do you remember being irritated whenever your favorite television program was interrupted for 30 seconds by a test of the Emergency Broadcast System?

Those emergency system tests are a lot like the trials that come into our lives. They're unscheduled, usually unwelcome interruptions, and they always seem to come at the worst possible time. But unlike the test patterns on television, life's trials don't last for 30 seconds and then disappear. No, they can last for days, weeks, even years. And the exact reason for them may never be completely clear to us. Trials can make us feel helpless, but we do have control over one vital element of a trial —how we respond to it. Understand this: trials are indispensable to our spiritual growth. In fact, we cannot grow as we should without them, as much as we might wish we could. It's your test that leads to your testimony!

Paul writes, "Every detail works to your advantage and to God's glory: more and more grace…more and more praise! So we're not giving up. How could we! Even though on the outside it often looks like things are falling apart on us, on the inside, where God is making new life, not a day goes by without his unfolding grace" (2Co 4:15-18 TM). And Job adds "But he knows the way that I take; when he has tested me, I will come forth as gold" (Job 23:10 NIV). It takes a lot more heat to produce gold than it does tin. So which do you want to be?

GROWING THROUGH TRIALS (2)

Consider it all joy, my brethren,
when you encounter various trials.
James 1:2 NAS

*N*ow, be honest. You've probably read today's verse and wondered if James was living on the same planet you live on. This may be one of the hardest commands to obey in all of Scripture. James said we are to respond to our trials with "joy." That leaves no room for complaining. Start praising God when your life is interrupted by a problem or circumstance you didn't plan on or see coming. Why? Because the truth is, we are either in a trial right now, coming out of a trial, or heading towards the next one.

James speaks of "various trials." You won't get bored by the trials you face because they'll come in every variety you can imagine. They're like some of the mail we receive, simply addressed to "occupant." All you have to do to undergo trials is occupy space on the planet. Notice, James didn't say "if" they come, but "when." Will Rogers once read a newspaper headline "Innocent Bystander Shot In New York." "How about that?" he said. "All you have to do to get shot in New York is be innocent and stand by." That's how it is with trials. Just stand by and you'll get hit. But why? James answers: "Under pressure, your faith-life is forced into the open and shows its true colors. So don't try to get out of anything prematurely. Let it do its work so you become mature and well-developed, not deficient in any way" (Jas 1:2-4 TM). Adversity produces maturity. The truth is, it can't come any other way!

ESTABLISHING PRIORITIES (1)

Make every minute count.
Ephesians 5:16 CEV

*P*astor Adrian Rogers says: "The misuse of anything as precious as time should be a crime. If somebody steals
your car…you can acquire another. If they snatch your wallet…
a few phone calls would salvage the majority of your concerns.
But who can you call when you lose your time?" Solomon
reminds us we "must give an account to God for everything
[we] do" (Ecc 11:9 NLT), because for most of us, "one of these
days" generally means "none of these days."

How you spend your days is how you spend your life, so
Paul writes: "Make every minute count." To do that success-
fully you must: *(a) learn to say no:* stress is what happens when
your gut says no but your mouth says yes! Jesus said, "I have
finished the work…You have given Me to do" (Jn 17:4 NKJV),
because there's always time to do what God wants done.
Notice, Paul said, *"One* thing I do" (Php 3:13), not "50
different things I'm caught up with!" Don't let the good steal
the best; back off on some activities so you can embrace others;
(b) walk in the power of the Spirit: Jesus said, "You cannot be
fruitful unless you remain in me" (Jn 15:4 NLT), because by
walking in the flesh you burn the wick and not the oil. Paul says
when you're "guided by the Spirit, you won't obey…selfish
desires" (Gal 5:16 CEV); *(c) avoid procrastination:* we joke
about it, but there's nothing funny about delayed obedience.
James says, "If you don't do what you know is right, you have
sinned" (Jas 4:17 CEV). A real mark of maturity is doing what
you *don't* feel like doing, when you *don't* feel like doing it!

ESTABLISHING PRIORITIES (2)

Teach us to use wisely all the time we have.
Psalm 90:12 CEV

$\mathcal{G}$rowing up, Dr. Tony Campolo says he spent many Saturdays at The Franklin Institute in Philadelphia visiting Ed Bailey, the guy who ran it. Campolo writes: "His encyclopedic mind fascinated me. He knew something about everything…I was friends with Ed until he died. After a serious stroke I went to visit him…I told him all the places I'd been to speak and how I'd come right from the airport to see him. He heard me out, then said, *'You go all over the world to people who 10 years from now won't remember your name. But you haven't time for those who really care about you.'*" Campolo continues, "That …hit me hard and changed my life. I decided not to let all my time be used by people for whom I make little difference, while I neglect those for whom I'm irreplaceable. One day a friend of mine got a call from The White House asking him to consult with the President. He said no, because it was a day he'd promised to spend with his granddaughter. The nation survived …the President didn't miss him, and his granddaughter had precious time with her Pop-Pop."

Somebody said, "the main thing is to keep the main thing the main thing!" Let that be your motto. David put it like this: "Teach us to realize the brevity of life, so that we may grow in wisdom" (Ps 90:12 NLT). Time is an equal-opportunity employer. We all get 24 hours, 1,440 minutes, 86,400 seconds daily, and we must account for how we use them. So ask yourself how you would spend the next 24 hours if you knew that you'd stand before God tomorrow—then get busy!

THE BLAME GAME (1)

'The woman you put…with me…
gave me…the fruit, and I ate it.'
Genesis 3:12-13 CEV

A man smokes 3 packs of cigarettes a day for 40 years, dies of lung cancer and his family sues the tobacco company. A woman crashes while driving drunk then blames the bartender. Your kids are out of control so you blame violence on TV, lack of discipline in school or the influence of their friends. Excuses—we've got hundreds of them! Our parents failed us… our friends let us down…somebody gave us bad advice…our mate doesn't understand us. The blame game isn't new; we've been playing it since the dawn of creation. In Genesis the first couple offered God every excuse in the book to avoid responsibility for their actions. Adam actually blamed God by saying, "It was the woman you put…with me." And Eve was no better; she said, "The snake tricked me."

Solomon says, "The wise are glad to be instructed…fools fall flat on their faces" (Pr 10:8 NLT), because the ability to accept responsibility is the measure of your character and maturity. But more importantly, God can't forgive and restore you till you acknowledge and turn away from your sin. Nowhere in Scripture does He ever excuse your sin because of somebody else's behavior. In fact, when you make a habit of blaming the other guy you'll never reach the place of honest repentance. The Bible says we'll all "appear before Christ and take what's coming to us as a result of our actions" (2Co 5:10 TM). Acknowledging your sins and shortcomings here and now frees you to receive God's forgiveness and move on to maturity.

THE BLAME GAME (2)

Don't…disclaim responsibility
by saying you didn't know.
Proverbs 24:12 TLB

*B*laming others for our shortcomings and mistakes is usually the way we avoid facing the truth about ourselves. Dr. Wayne Dyer says, "All blame is a waste of time. Regardless of how much fault you find, it will not change you. The only thing blame does is keep the focus off you when you're looking for external reasons to explain your unhappiness or frustration. You may succeed in making another feel guilty but you won't succeed in changing whatever's making you unhappy."

The Israelites spent 40 years in the wilderness, making a journey that should have taken 11 days (See Dt 1:2). That's because they blamed God, and Moses, and whatever, for all their problems; everything that happened was somebody else's fault. Sound familiar? Solomon says, "Don't try to disclaim responsibility by saying you didn't know…God…knows all hearts… and he will reward everyone according to his deeds." The truth may be hard to face, but hiding from it doesn't make it go away. In fact, until you're willing to admit your mistakes you'll keep having problems and fixing blame. Remember, Satan will never stop trying to engage you in the blame game through your thoughts and emotions. And when you go there he wins and you lose! Paul said, "Do not let yourself be overcome by evil…overcome…evil with good" (Ro 12:21 AMP). Did you get that? *You* get to decide how much ground you'll give to "the accuser" (Rev 12:10). Winston Churchill once said, "The price of greatness is responsibility." So stop passing the buck, get honest with God and begin to correct the things in your life that are out of order.

YOU'RE NOT ALONE

He will be called Immanuel...God is with us.
Matthew 1:23 NLT

*S*chool was out and 10-year-old Charlie was thrilled to be out of London celebrating Christmas in the country. Driving along the winding roads with his Mom he was captivated by the snowy winter landscape. But suddenly the snow got heavy, the visibility turned bad and the car slid out of control ending up in a ditch. Charlie tried to push while his mother pressed the accelerator, but it was no use. They left the car and walked down the road where they knocked on the door of a little house and asked for help. Flustered, the lady invited them in to use the phone and warm up while she made them tea and cookies.

"What's so special about that?" you're asking. "Just another everyday event, right?" No. At least not to the woman who opened the door that day; she's already told the story hundreds of times. And can you blame her? It's not every day the Queen of England and Charles, Prince of Wales, turn up on your doorstep!

On a winter's night over 2,000 years ago the Prince of Peace knocked on our door—and it was no accident. The Bible says it "happened to fulfill the Lord's message...he will be called Immanuel...God is with us." Christmas can be a lonely time if you've lost your job or your family or your sense of hope. And the joy of others can be a painful reminder of what you've lost. But you're not alone. You may feel lonely, but you're not alone—God is with you. He really is! Believe that, open your heart to Him, and have a blessed Christmas!

FOR THE ONE WHO HAS EVERYTHING

They…presented him with…
gold…incense and…myrrh.
Matthew 2:11 NIV

*I*t's Christmas. Jesus' birthday. But what can you possibly give to the One Who not only has everything, but created it all? The wise men probably asked the same question. As scholars they were astute enough to navigate thousands of miles guided by a star, influential enough to warrant an audience with King Herod, and rich enough to undertake such a long journey carrying expensive presents. But in addition to "gold…incense and…myrrh," they gave Jesus some gifts that are priceless—note what they gave:

(1) Their time. Long before His birth they'd invested years researching and preparing for it—not counting the 2 years it took them to travel to where He was born. Do you know what? You are as close to God today as you want to be, planned to be, took time to be. Want to get closer? Spend more time with Him.

(2) Their worship. Once they found Him, "They fell down and worshiped Him" (Mt 2:11 AMP). Worship changes us profoundly because when we stand in God's presence with an open heart and let His Spirit work in us, "We are…changed to be like him" (2 Co 3:18 NCV).

(3) Their hope. While those around saw only darkness these men recognized, "The Light shines in the darkness" (Jn 1:5 NCV). And that hasn't changed. God's healing love shines brightest in the darkness of our dashed dreams and broken hearts. So in the midst of your family celebrations, take time out to be with Jesus: and how about a special gift to His Work? After all, it's His birthday.

WHEN IT'S HARD TO BELIEVE

How can this be?
Luke 1:34 NASB

*W*hen the angel told Mary God had chosen her to be the mother of His Son, her response was understandable: "How can this be, since I am a virgin?" Imagine how she must have felt. What would people think? How could she care for a baby? What would Joseph say? Would he abandon her? No wonder she "was greatly troubled" (Lk 1:29 NIV); if ever something was impossible this was it. *But that's what makes a miracle miraculous!*

Maybe you're out of work and trusting God to provide for your family, nevertheless you're asking, "How can this be when I'm unemployed?" Or perhaps you're sick and although you know that He's the Lord who "healeth all thy diseases" (Ps 103:3), you're wondering, "How can this be when I still have my symptoms?" We all have times when our faith goes through the wringer and comes out dry.

But what's even more challenging is that Mary's situation was caused by God. He's not supposed to do that. He's supposed to bless and rescue you, right? But God had a plan. Mary was about to do something nobody would ever do again. And with that plan came a promise that can sustain you during your greatest tests of faith: "The Lord is with you" (Lk 1:28-30 NKJV). Once you understand that "The One who called you is completely dependable. If he said it, he'll do it" (1Th 5:24 TM), your outlook changes radically. So if you're struggling, remember what the angel said to Mary, "Nothing is impossible with God" (Lk 1:37 NIV), because He's saying the *same* to you!

THE COST OF BEING BLESSED (1)

Run to win.
1 Corinthians 9:24 TM

*S*easoned long-distance runners have learned to focus on endurance, not just speed. They pace themselves so that as they approach the finish line they can pull out all the stops. Paul says, "I'm running hard for the finish line…giving it everything I've got…I'm not going to get caught…telling everyone else…then missing out myself" (1Co 9:26-27 TM). For *spiritual* long-distance runners, quitting isn't an option. Despite some delays and disappointments along the way, they know they'd never be satisfied just sitting on the sidelines cheering for those who have paid the price to run the race. So if you're that kind of person—one who *needs* to attain the hope of your calling and fulfill your God-ordained purpose—go for it! And don't forget, Jesus said, "Great gifts mean great responsibilities" (Lk 12:48 TM). Winning will cost you in terms of pressure, criticism, loneliness and sacrifice.

So, what's the secret to staying power? Paul said, "Jesus …finished this race…Because he never lost sight of where he was headed…he could put up with anything" (Heb 12:2 TM). You'll only endure the pain when you've something to look forward to. God exposes us to opposition and criticism to strengthen our character. That way when greater blessings (and responsibilities) come, we won't crack. Success comes only when you're committed and have the passion to cross the finish line. So the question is: can you stand to be blessed? When the pressure is on will you say like Nehemiah, "My work is too important to stop" (Ne 6:3 CEV)? If your answer is yes, get your eye on the goal, "run to win," and you're sure to cross the finish line!

THE COST OF BEING BLESSED (2)

Sit down and figure the cost.
Luke 14:28 TM

*H*ow many times have you prayed for a particular thing without realizing how much it would ultimately cost you? Success always comes with a price tag. Being blessed can be hard work. Everything God gives us requires maintenance. When He placed Adam and Eve in the Garden, they still had to tend it. Jesus said when you're "planning to build...sit down and figure the cost." For example, when God blesses you don't expect everybody around you to rejoice. Some people will figure your blessing came at their expense. That's because they don't want you to move ahead faster than they do. Or they want what God's given you, but they're not prepared to pay the price you've paid.

James says, "Where you have envy and selfish ambition ...you find...every evil practice" (Jas 3:16 NIV). And it's not just your enemies you have to watch out for; betrayal often comes from within your own ranks. Jesus sat at the table with John the beloved on one side and Judas the betrayer on the other. One was close enough to lay his head on Jesus' breast while the other had sufficient access to betray Him with a kiss. You need to know who's sitting at your table!

However, as painful as it is to be criticized by people you respect and trust, it's worse to veer from the course God's charted for you in order to gain their acceptance. As good as it feels to be affirmed and applauded, at some point you need to stop and ask, "How much am I willing to sacrifice to be blessed?" Your answer will determine your destiny!

THE COST OF BEING BLESSED (3)

You were loyal with small things,
I will let you care for…greater things.
Matthew 25:23 NCV

*T*o succeed at any worthwhile venture you need a thick skin when it comes to handling criticism. That's what separates those who say they want something from God, from those who are prepared to pay the price to get it. For example, if you've been praying for a mate, ask yourself are you really ready for the sacrifice and responsibility that comes with marriage? Are you stable, unselfish and mature enough to provide for a family? Or, if you're praying for an increase in your business, are you giving outstanding service to your current clients? Remember, a peacock that rests on its feathers is just another turkey! Sometimes we're in love with the image of success, but we haven't counted the actual cost of succeeding. That's why it's a good thing God doesn't automatically give us everything we ask for! Often we want things because they look good in the lives of others, but God in His wisdom knows it would destroy us to receive what we're not equipped to handle.

God tests you with what you *already* have in order to develop consistency and strength. He wants to see how you handle the pressures that accompany the blessings He's already given you. He wants to get you to the place in Him where you're immune to adversity; where you've learned to appreciate the Giver more than the gift. And when you get there you'll hear Him say, "You are a good…servant…Because you were loyal with small things, I will let you care for much greater things"— and that will make it all worthwhile!

NO EXPERIENCE IS WASTED

God called to him from within the bush, 'Moses, Moses!'
Exodus 3:4 NIV

$\mathcal{G}$od doesn't waste anything: He uses all our experiences to prepare us. Moses grew up in a "foster home." He spent 40 years in Pharaoh's palace learning the language and ways of the Egyptians. That's because God was going to use him to lead Israel out of Egypt. What better preparation for understanding your enemy than to be raised among them. But Moses also needed to learn some personal lessons, so God took him out into the desert for another 40 years to tend sheep. The grandson of Pharaoh is now a lowly shepherd. Nothing will humble you more than having to take a job for which you're overqualified, especially when it's your own failure that put you there. Those years on the poor side of town taught Moses what it's like to identify with the hurting. Finally, at 80, he's ready to fulfill his calling. God spoke to him personally out of a burning bush, "Moses, Moses!" It was at this most unlikely place that God revealed to Moses his calling as Israel's deliverer. And even though he experienced fear, made excuses and raised objections, he ended up doing the job. The point is—Moses' 80 years of training weren't wasted. His 40 years in the palace prepared him to deal with Pharaoh, and his 40 years as a shepherd prepared him to lead God's people through the wilderness and into their destiny. So even though you may be going through a difficult time, rejoice. God never wastes an experience. Never! He'll use it for your good and His glory.

WHAT'S YOUR DREAM?

Look, this dreamer is coming!…let us…kill him.
Genesis 37:19-20 NKJV

*E*verybody has a dream. What's yours? If you could do *anything,* what would it be? Most of us don't achieve great things because we give up, we fall short, we get off track, we settle, or we dream too small. Only two things stand in your way: dreaming it, then doing it. Have you dared to dream, really dream? If something is within your apparent reach, it isn't a dream. If it doesn't stretch you, cost you, or involve risk, it isn't a dream. Dreams change you even as they change the world around you.

Maybe you're listening to critical people. Remember the story of Joseph? He dreamed big dreams. God-given dreams. And what was the response of his brothers? They said, "Look, this dreamer is coming!…let us…kill him." People who aren't pursuing their own dreams are usually the first to criticize people who are. So, who are you listening to?

Maybe you're afraid to dream too big. You don't want to fail. Nobody does. But "safe living" leads to regret. Theodore Roosevelt said, "Far better it is to dare mighty things, to win glorious triumphs, even though checkered by failure, than to rank with those poor souls who neither enjoy much nor suffer much because they live in the gray twilight that knows neither victory nor defeat." What's the worst thing that could happen if you pursue your dream and don't achieve it? You could end up where you are now. And what's the best thing that could happen? You could find yourself in new territory, enjoying new blessings, living the life God meant for you to live!

Therefore
we ought to give
the more earnest heed
to the things
which we have heard,
lest at any time
we should let
them slip.

HEBREWS 2:1 KJV

3 Reasons

Why You Need Jesus...

Jesus loves you! He desires to have a relationship with you, and to give you a life full of joy and purpose. Why do you need Him in your life?

1. Because you have a past. You can't go back, but He can. The Bible says, "Jesus Christ the same yesterday, and today, and for ever" (Hebrews 13:8). He can walk into those places of sin and failure, wipe the slate clean, and give you a new beginning.

2. Because you need a friend. Jesus knows the worst about you, yet He believes the best. Why? Because He sees you not as you are, but as you will be when He gets through with you. What a friend!

3. Because He holds the futere. Who else are you going to trust? In His hands you are safe and secure—today, tomorrow, and for all eternity. His Word says, "For I know the plans I have for you... plans for good and not for evil, to give you a future and a hope. In those days when you pray, I will listen" (Jeremiah 29:11-13 TLB).

If you'd like to begin a personal relationship with Jesus today, please pray this prayer:

Lord Jesus, I invite You into my life. I believe You died for me and that Your blood pays for my sins and provides me with the gift of eternal life. By faith I receive that gift, and I acknowledge You as my Lord and Savior. Amen.

NOTES
My Personal Reflections

_____
_____
_____
_____
_____
_____
_____
_____
_____
_____
_____
_____
_____
_____
_____
_____
_____
_____
_____
_____

JOURNAL
My Personal Prayer Notes

Prayer Needs   Answered Prayer   Favorite Prayer

NOTES

My Personal Reflections

JOURNAL

My Personal Prayer Notes

Prayer Needs   Answered Prayer   Favorite Prayer

Acknowledgments

How to Live Through a Bad Day
Jack Hayford/Thomas Nelson

Heaven
Randy Alcorn/Tyndale

The Purpose Driven Life
Rick Warren/Zondervan

It's Not About Me
Max Lucado/Integrity Publishers

Life Essentials
Tony Evans/Moody Publishers

A Resilient Life
Gordon McDonald/Nelson

The Top Ten Mistakes Leaders Make
Hans Finzel/NeXgen Cook Communications Ministries

Habitudes
Dr. Tim Elmore/Growing Leaders, Inc.

Today Matters
John Maxwell/Warner Faith

The 10 Commandments of Working in a Hostile Environment
T.D. Jakes/Berkley

Now What?
John Ortberg/Inspirio/Zondervan

Come Before Winter and Share My Hope
Charles Swindoll/Living Books

Cure for the Common Life: Living in Your Sweet Spot
Max Lucado/W. Publishing

Stories for the Heart
Alice Gray/Multnomah